The Essential Guide to
Business Etiquette

Library of Congress Cataloging-in-Publication Data

Chaney, Lillian H.
   The essential guide to business etiquette / Lillian Hunt Chaney and
Jeanette St. Clair Martin.
      p. cm.
   Includes bibliographical references and index.
   ISBN 978–0–275–99714–4 (alk. paper)
1. Business etiquette. 2. Interpersonal relations. 3. Business communication.
4. Self-presentation. I. Martin, Jeanette S. II. Title.
HF5389.C468 2007
395.5′2—dc22   2007022771

British Library Cataloguing in Publication Data is available.

Library of Congress Catalog Card Number: 2007022771
ISBN: 978–0–275–99714–4

First published in 2007

Praeger Publishers, 88 Post Road West, Westport, CT 06881
An imprint of Greenwood Publishing Group, Inc.
www.praeger.com

Printed in the United States of America

The paper used in this book complies with the
Permanent Paper Standard issued by the National
Information Standards Organization (Z39.48-1984).

10 9 8 7 6 5 4 3 2 1

The Essential Guide to Business Etiquette

LILLIAN HUNT CHANEY

AND

JEANETTE ST. CLAIR MARTIN

PRAEGER

Westport, Connecticut
London

Contents

Introduction xi

1. *Job Interview Etiquette* 1

 Applicant Etiquette 2

 Interviewer Etiquette 8

2. *Business Dress and Grooming* 13

 Dress Considerations 14

 Attributes of Dress 17

 Research Findings Related to Business Dress 18

 Business Professional Attire 18

 Business Casual Attire 21

 Dress for Special Events and Occasions 22

3. *Office Politics* 25

 Self-Promotion 26

 Honesty and Truth-Telling 28

 Compliments and Flattery 29

 Gossip 30

Favors and Hidden Motives   32

Dress and Grooming   32

Business Socializing and Etiquette   33

4. *Social Sensitivity*   37

Office Courtesies   38

Disabled Persons   42

Office Conflict   43

Sexual Harassment   44

Office Romance   46

5. *Electronic Communication Etiquette*   49

Telephones   49

Speakerphones   52

Cellular Telephones and Pagers   52

Answering Machines and Voice Mail   54

Electronic Mail (E-Mail)   55

BlackBerry Devices   57

Facsimile (Fax) Transmissions   58

6. *Manners for Special Occasions and Events*   61

Births and Birthdays   61

Illnesses and Injuries   63

Hospital Etiquette   63

Holiday and Office Parties   64

Weddings and Wedding Anniversaries   66

Business Receptions, Conventions, and Trade Shows   67

Promotions and Retirements   68

Funerals   69

7. *Written Communication Manners*   73

Letter and Memorandum Formats   73

Stationery   75

Writing Guidelines   76

Thank-You Notes   77

Condolence Letters   79

Congratulatory Letters   80

Invitations   80

Acceptance or Regrets   81

Announcements   82

Complaint Letters   83

Cards   84

8. *Dining Etiquette*   85

Styles of Eating and Place Settings   86

Basic Guidelines for Business Dining   86

Problem Dining Situations   89

Manners for Difficult-to-Eat Foods   91

Cultural Variations in Dining Etiquette   92

9. *Business Entertaining*   97

Restaurant Entertaining   97

Wine and Toasting Etiquette   99

Entertaining at Private Clubs, Sporting Events, and the Theater   101

Cocktail Parties and Receptions   102

Home Entertaining   103

Entertaining International Visitors   104

10. *Meeting Etiquette*   107

Meeting Planning and Preparation   108

Introductions and Seating Arrangements   109

Chairing Responsibilities   110

Participant Responsibilities   112

Refreshments   113

Follow-Up Activities   113

Business Meal Meetings   114

Conventions   115

Virtual Meetings 116

Multicultural Meetings 116

11. *Presentations* 119

Eye Contact, Posture, and Gestures 119

Presentation Attire 120

Vocal Characteristics 121

Presentation Organization 122

Humor 123

Visual Aids 124

Presenter Etiquette 125

Distracting or Annoying Presenter Behaviors 126

Presenter Introductions 127

Audience Etiquette 128

12. *Sports Etiquette* 131

Rules of Etiquette for All Sports 131

Handball and Racquet Sports Etiquette 133

Golf Etiquette 134

Water Sports Etiquette 136

Gym or Health Club Etiquette 136

Hunting and Fishing Etiquette 138

Running, Biking, and Rollerblading Etiquette 138

Spectator Etiquette 138

13. *Travel Etiquette* 143

Suggestions for Business Travel 143

Air Travel Etiquette 144

Bus, Train, and Mass Transit Etiquette 147

Automobile Etiquette 148

Taxicab and Limousine Etiquette 149

Cruise Ship Etiquette 150

Hotel Manners 151

14. *Global Manners*   155

   Travel Preparation   155

   Guidelines for Global Interactions   157

   Tips for Women Business Travelers   158

   Manners for Selected Regions of the World   160

Notes   167

Index   185

Introduction

> Etiquette alone will not enable you to reach your targeted goal. It will give you the extra edge that will make the difference between you and the competition.[1]

Business etiquette is the behavior and manners considered appropriate in the business and professional world. Business etiquette involves rules of conduct that allow us to communicate with people in business and to interact with them in a civilized manner. Most people who are successful in the business and professional world conform to these guidelines of expected behavior.[2]

Research findings indicate that etiquette is important to business success. Results of a survey of 200 members of the American Marketing Association revealed that a majority of respondents (91.1%) rated etiquette as either very important or important to business success, regardless of age, gender, educational level, income, or marital status.[3] Despite the acknowledged importance of business etiquette, research has shown that a lack of courtesy and respect for others is currently a serious problem in the United States. In fact, a study by a nonprofit organization revealed that 79% of U.S. persons surveyed expressed the belief that a lack of respect and courtesy was a serious problem in U.S. businesses. In addition, 73% felt that U.S. Americans treated each other with more respect in years gone by than they treat each other today.[4]

According to corporate trainers who conduct sessions on civility, as well as professors at well-known universities who study workplace behavior, people are becoming increasingly rude to their office colleagues. They seem oblivious to the fact that a standard of behavior exists.[5] Top executives in major corporations agree; many feel that some of the problems their companies are experiencing are directly related to a lack of knowledge about proper business etiquette.[6] According to Leonard, "Like it or not, management equates good manners with competence in business and poor manners with incompetence."[7] Thus, employees will want to invest the necessary time to become knowledgeable about the rules of polite behavior and to practice their etiquette skills in the office environment so that they will not only be perceived as competent but will also be considered as assets to the firm. Confidence comes with knowledge; nothing else quite compares to knowing that you know—how to dress, how to eat, and how to behave in various situations. Knowing that you will make a positive initial impression is a great confidence booster. Keep in mind that when you make a negative initial impression, about eight subsequent encounters that are positive are needed to reverse an initial bad impression.[8]

The Essential Guide to Business Etiquette features fourteen chapters on the most critical areas that can help you succeed in your career. It is a practical guide for interacting effectively with colleagues, supervisors, and customers. The book begins with information essential to getting off to a good start during the job interview by preparing an effective résumé and dressing appropriately; correct behavior during the interview and suggestions for follow-up procedures are also included. In addition to job interview attire, dress appropriate for the work environment, including both professional dress and business casual attire, are discussed.

The chapters on office politics and social sensitivity provide strategies for dealing with situations that go beyond hard work and good performance; they involve becoming adept at political maneuvering and being sensitive to appropriate behavior in certain situations. The chapters on electronic communication etiquette, manners for special occasions and events, and written communication manners provide guidelines for communicating electronically and in writing, in addition to the nuances of proper behavior at such special events as birthdays, office parties, weddings, business receptions, promotions and retirements, and funerals. Information in the chapters on dining etiquette and business entertaining includes U.S. styles of eating and business entertaining as well as cultural variations in dining and entertaining. The chapters on meeting etiquette and presentations include chair and participant meeting responsibilities and suggestions for making effective presentations, including attire and other nonverbal behavior, use of humor and visual aids, and audience etiquette. The chapter on sports etiquette addresses the importance of correct behavior as a player and as a spectator. Business executives often find that observing the behavior of potential clients or business partners during these sporting events provides useful information upon which to base business decisions.

The growth in international trade, as well as increased numbers of minorities in the U.S. workplace, has led to more interactions with people from other cultures. Thus, knowledge of the rules of etiquette must be expanded to include manners of other countries. If your job involves travel abroad, you will benefit from information in the final two chapters on travel etiquette, global manners, and tips for women business travelers. Air travel guidelines, as well as rules when using other modes of transportation, are addressed; appropriate behavior when staying in hotels is discussed as well. In addition, special tips for behaving appropriately in selected regions of the world—Asia, Africa, Europe, Latin America, and the Middle East—are provided.

Since many companies are expressing concern over the lack of social skills in the workplace, resolve to set an example of exemplary manners in your office. The chances are excellent that your *savoir faire* will be rewarded when salary and promotion decisions are made.

1

Job Interview Etiquette

You may have an impressive résumé, but if you have an unimpressive interview, chances are you won't get the job. The first few moments of an interview often provide enough information for an experienced hiring manager to make a decision.[1]

Smart job seekers know that securing employment often depends upon their social skills as much as on their job skills and educational credentials. Applicants who demonstrate knowledge of etiquette have a competitive edge in the job search. The place to showcase these social skills is during the job interview.

Getting an invitation to interview for a job can sometimes be challenging. Job seekers are currently finding that networking—using relationships to gain entrance to companies—is successful. The well-known adage, "It's not what you know, but who you know that counts," often applies when it comes to gaining access to jobs. Estimates are that from 65 to 85 percent of jobs are now found as a result of networking. Many jobs are not advertised; these unadvertised positions are known as the hidden job market. Gaining access to the hidden job market is often accomplished by networking. Joining professional and social organizations, participating in local fund-raisers, and becoming active in church activities and community service organizations are excellent ways of making contacts with people who may be able to connect you with representatives of companies who have job openings. Once you make connections with other business professionals, it is important to make frequent contact via e-mail or telephone to keep in touch. When attending network events, dress appropriately and have plenty of business cards. If nametags are provided, place them on the right shoulder. Women should not wear a

Sometimes all people need is a little polish to make a positive initial impression. Like diamonds, people "have a basic market value, but it is only after they have been polished that the world will pay their real value."[6]

heavy shoulder bag at these events—the strap will also be on the right shoulder and may obstruct the view of the nametag. When drinks and appetizers are provided, eat very little and limit alcohol to one drink. The purpose is circulating, not eating and drinking. Good networking involves good manners. Make introductions, shake hands, and exchange business cards when appropriate. After you leave the event, make notes on the backs of business cards to help you remember details of the people you met.[2]

Online networking is also becoming popular. The top job boards, in order of average number of job listings, are CareerBuilder (www.career builder.com), Monster (www.monster.com), and CollegeRecruiter (www.collegerecruiter.com). Job seekers should be aware, however, that the personal and professional information they provide online may result in unwanted nonprofessional contacts.[3] Some job seekers feel that company Web sites are the best way to find a job online; they feel that information they provide is more confidential than when they use big board sites.

Since the job interview is often critical to obtaining a position, making a positive first impression is important. Interviewers admit that 75 percent of the time a hiring decision is made during the first few minutes of the interview; the decision is based on first impressions.[4] First impressions are made on the candidate's verbal and nonverbal communication. Verbal impressions are conveyed by tone of voice, choice of words, rate of speech, and pronunciation and enunciation. Nonverbal impressions are made by observing the applicant's posture, gestures, and facial expressions, as well as clothing, hair, and overall appearance. People are in control of these verbal and nonverbal ingredients of impressions.[5]

APPLICANT ETIQUETTE

Your success in the employment interview includes following certain guidelines in preparing for the interview, in participating in the interview, in terminating the interview, and in following up after the interview.

Preparation for the Interview

To prepare for the interview, you should develop an impressive résumé, research the organization, plan what to wear, and prepare questions to ask as well as possible responses to typically asked questions.

The résumé is another opportunity you have to make a positive initial impression. To project a favorable image on paper, prepare a résumé that:

- is perfect in appearance and accuracy, is one to two pages in length, and is presented on good quality paper (such as linen finish) in an appropriate color (such as white or ivory);
- uses mechanical means of emphasis, such as bullets and bolding, as well as varied font sizes to emphasize key points; and
- contains a job objective, uses an attractive, logical format (such as a two-column arrangement with education and experience in reverse chronological order), and includes names of three to five people, with complete job title, addresses, and telephone numbers, who are willing to give an accurate evaluation of the applicant.[7]

In addition to a traditional résumé, you should prepare an electronic version, which can then be included in an e-mail message or posted to job banks or company databases. Many companies are now requesting résumés that can be electronically scanned; they then use key words to scan résumés submitted to search for applicants with the desired qualifications. After making the necessary changes in typeface, font, and format, the résumé is saved as an ASCII or Text Only file to be retrieved by the prospective employer. Specific guidelines for preparing electronic résumés include the following:

- Use standard typefaces, such as Times New Roman or Courier (no script), and a font size of 10–14 points.
- Place your name at the top of each page.
- Avoid use of graphics, italics, or underlines—use plus (+) signs or asterisks (*) rather than bullets; bold-faced type and all capital letters are acceptable.
- Avoid use of tabs; use the space bar where spaces are desired.
- Shorten the line length to five inches; insert hard returns after each line.
- In addition to the usual headings of Job Objective, Education, Work Experience, Honors and Awards, and References, include an additional heading called Keyword Summary of about 25 words; use nouns or noun phrases instead of verbs. For example, use "project coordinator" rather than "coordinated project."[8]

People often make mistakes on the job application form. In the section requesting a description of job duties, one applicant who had been a carpenter wrote that he was a "crapender"; another person who was a sales clerk wrote that she had been a "sales cluck"; still another person who had been a forklift operator in a warehouse wrote that he "Ran a frocklift in the whorehouse."[10]

The importance of having both traditional and electronic résumés cannot be overemphasized; they often get you the interview. However, completion of an application form for the company records is also a significant aspect of the job search. When you sign the completed application (fill in all spaces provided), you are legally responsible for the truthfulness and accuracy of the information. Candidates who are less than truthful concerning their degrees, grade point averages, and dates of employment should be aware that if the information provided is later found to be incorrect, this may be grounds for termination.[9]

Researching the prospective organization is another important step in preparing for the interview. Current and former employees can be excellent sources of information since they can provide facts about the company that might not be available from printed sources. Annual reports are another source worth investigating. The Internet and company web site are also good sources of information. In addition, local libraries can provide many helpful publications.

Deciding what to wear to the interview deserves careful consideration as apparel gets scrutinized closely. In fact, results of one survey revealed just how important appearance is to getting the job. "When one college's career planning and placement center surveyed 150 employers, they discovered that the number one reason for rejecting an applicant after the first interview was poor personal appearance."[11]

Personal appearance includes not only being immaculately dressed but also making sure that hands are clean and nails are manicured. When in doubt about what to wear, dress conservatively. Even if you know that employees in this firm typically dress casually, wearing a business suit to the interview is still recommended by most hiring officials and impression management experts. Perhaps the dot-com crash is causing job seekers to return to more traditional ways of dressing. After all, "Who wants to aspire to T-shirts, jeans, and pink slips?"[12]

Select a dark basic suit with appropriate accessories, including well-shined shoes in good repair that are the same color as the hem of the garment or darker. Avoid clothing and accessories that send a negative message. Specifically, men should not wear short-sleeved dress shirts or shirts that have a home-laundered look; women should avoid clothing that is too tight, skirts with high slits, strapped shoes, and excessive makeup, perfume, or jewelry. Tattoos should not be visible. Tongue piercing, nose rings, or eyebrow rings are not considered acceptable by most employers. Removing them before the interview is advised, especially when the job is with a conservative company.[13] Grooming should be impeccable; an expensive suit and shoes will not overcome the negative impression conveyed by unkempt nails and an outdated hairstyle. Take a leather notepad with a pocket for extra copies of your résumé.[14] Additional information on business professional dress is included in Chapter 2, "Business Dress and Grooming."

Your preparation involves making a list of questions to be asked when the interviewer invites questions. Most applicants would be interested in knowing what some of the early duties would be, whether the company has codes of dress and ethics, if travel is part of the job, and what opportunities exist for professional growth and promotions. Avoid asking about vacations, salary, and other fringe benefits; it is best to wait for the interviewer to bring up these subjects. You do not want to give the interviewer the impression that you are primarily interested in what the company can do for you. Think carefully about answers you will give to such expected questions as:

- Why should we hire you?
- What are your strengths? Weaknesses?
- How do you spend your spare time?
- What computer skills do you have?
- Do you work well as a member of a team?
- How would you rate your dependability and attitude?

In addition, review questions that are illegal to ask in the interview and decide how to answer them should the situation arise. According to the EEOC (Equal Employment Opportunity Commission), applicants cannot be discriminated against on the basis of age (40–70), race, color, gender, religion, national origin, or disability. EEOC guidelines require that all questions and qualifications for candidates be job related. Asking about marital status or child care is inappropriate. Further, candidates should not be asked if they have any disabilities or whether or not they have ever been arrested. While interviewers may ask about professional memberships and military service, they cannot ask about memberships in social clubs or the type of discharge from the military. In addition, you may not be asked about your national origin. While it is acceptable to ask you if you speak a foreign language, you may not be asked how you acquired the ability to read, speak, or write a foreign language. If you are asked questions that are illegal or inappropriate, you may just decide to answer them anyway or may ask how the information is related to the position, since seemingly illegal questions may be legitimate if related to the requirements of the job. You could always refuse to answer the questions and remind the interviewer that they are inappropriate. However, this response may not be viewed in a positive way by the interviewer.[15]

Participation in the Interview

Successful candidate participation in the employment interview involves making a favorable initial impression by using positive nonverbal communication, using proper social skills, and avoiding inappropriate behaviors.

Arrive for the interview about 10 minutes early, unaccompanied by a friend or family member. While punctuality is highly valued in the United States, arriving too early is not advised as it may be perceived as being overanxious. After checking in with the receptionist, take a seat and wait for the interviewer's arrival. While you wait, peruse company publications usually provided in waiting areas or engage in some other positive activity; be polite and considerate to everyone. The interviewer sometimes asks the receptionist what the applicant did while waiting. If the candidate is snobbish or rudely uses the cell phone while waiting, the receptionist is even more likely to report that behavior than when the candidate is friendly and polite.[16]

Positive nonverbal communication is indicative of a person with good social skills. Upon meeting the interviewer, make eye contact and offer a firm handshake. Etiquette mavens and those with interviewing and hiring responsibilities recommend that you take the initiative in shaking hands as this shows leadership and assertiveness. Wait for the interviewer to indicate where you are to sit and to take charge of the questioning; the actual interview is usually preceded by a short period of small talk. Listen attentively and respond to questions in an organized manner. Listening behaviors include eye contact, nodding periodically, and smiling when appropriate. If an associate comes into the office to converse briefly with the interviewer, give no indication that you were listening to the conversation.[17]

The questioning part of the interview often begins with, "Tell me about yourself." If you are goal oriented, you would say so and identify some specific goals you have set and attained. You may also mention hobbies, especially if they relate to the prospective job. Should you possess qualities universally admired by employers, such as punctuality, dependability, accuracy, or perseverance, you would certainly mention them. Talking about your personal life, however, is not recommended. When questioned about weaknesses, acknowledge weaknesses that are least related to job performance and that may not be viewed as a weakness by everyone. For example, you may acknowledge that you are a perfectionist and are very detail-oriented. Some employers would view this as a positive characteristic. However, if you fear flying, you should be candid, especially if the job involves travel. Speaking negatively about former employers is not a good idea as this suggests problems getting along with people.[18]

Behaviors you should avoid are interrupting the interviewer, smoking, chewing gum, or accepting candy if offered. Do not place personal belongings, such as a leather notepad, on the interviewer's desk. However, when you are invited to show samples of your work, you may place them on the interviewer's desk. Even then, polite behavior dictates that you ask, "May I?" before placing anything on the person's desk.[19]

Termination of the Interview and Follow-up Activities

While you should not look at your watch repeatedly, it is advisable to be aware of the time allocated for the interview and watch for indications that the interview is nearing an end. When the interviewer summarizes what was discussed, stands, and says something like, "Thanks for coming in for an interview," you should recognize this as the conclusion of the interview. If the interviewer has not mentioned the company's timetable for making a final hiring decision, ask for this information. You will want to take advantage of this final opportunity to summarize your qualifications for the position. You would then rise, offer a firm handshake, express appreciation for the interviewer's time, and leave in a self-assured manner.

If the interviewer invites you to lunch, always accept the invitation. When a meal is part of the interview, remember to use correct table manners as social skills are being observed and evaluated. In many companies, the meal is considered part of the interview so you must continue to be on guard.[20]

When invited to lunch, order food that is easy to eat and in small portions. Avoid ordering fried chicken, pizza, or spaghetti as these foods are difficult to eat neatly; your attention should be on the conversation rather than on the food. French onion soup is another poor choice—unwinding the stringy cheese topping will require your full attention and leave little time for discussing the job. Abstain from liquor even if others order an alcoholic drink. This may be part of the test to see if you know that drinking and working do not mix.[22] Keep in mind that when you are invited to lunch by a prospective employer, what you order and how you eat may be factors in the hiring decision.

Mario had been interviewed by a number of people in the organization. Since the interviews concluded about noontime, Mario was invited to join two of the interviewers for lunch. On the way to the restaurant, Mario expressed his relief that the interviews were over; he became opinionated about topics that were discussed and did not answer questions with the same care he had shown in the interviews. When the interviewers saw what he was really like, they decided they did not like the real Mario. Mario forgot that "you are on stage until you take your exit."[21]

Hiring officials were favorably impressed by one young applicant who had outstanding qualifications for a managerial position. After lunch, however, they decided against hiring him because of his table manners. One example of the applicant's poor table manners was his removing the aluminum foil from the baked potato on his plate; he then crushed the foil into a small ball and placed it in an ashtray.[23]

After the interview, send letters of appreciation within a few days to all who participated in the interview process. Include specific details about points covered in the interview or say something complimentary about the company or its employees. Send letters of appreciation; this indicates that you have good social skills and leaves a positive impression with the interviewer. Always send thank-you letters even when you did not get the job; you may ask the interviewer to keep you in mind for future openings. While some well-known authorities on etiquette say that these letters of appreciation should not be sent via e-mail, some employers consider e-mail notes of appreciation acceptable provided e-mail exchanges were made with the applicant prior to the interview. However, you should remember that e-mail messages are not acceptable substitutes for regular mail in most situations and should take advantage of this final opportunity to make a favorable impression on the interviewer. You will want to follow up within two weeks, preferably by e-mail or telephone, to express continued interest in the position.[24]

INTERVIEWER ETIQUETTE

Interviewer etiquette is just as important as candidate etiquette. Interviewers want to create a positive impression of the organization they represent since they are trying to attract the most desirable applicants. Most interviewers realize that these impressions should be consistent with the actual work environment as this will eventually lead to increased job satisfaction and employee retention. Impressions candidates form from the employment interview may also carry over to perceptions of the organization in general. When candidates form negative impressions of the interviewer, they may decide that they have no desire to be associated with such an organization, regardless of how good the job offer is.[25]

Interviewers can enhance their hiring effectiveness by avoiding the most common mistakes usually made by those conducting interviews. These mistakes are the interviewer's lack of adequate training in interviewing techniques; failing to determine the

While attending a national business administration conference, a Mid-South instructor interviewed for a faculty position at a university on the West Coast. The candidate, who was dressed professionally in a business suit, was surprised when the two professors who were conducting the interview for the hiring university wore shorts, T-shirts, and sandals. Although she was offered the position at a substantial increase over the salary she was presently receiving, the candidate declined. She later explained that she knew she would be uncomfortable in an environment where the business professors were apparently unconcerned about the image of the university they represented.

critical factors needed for success in the position; failing to make lists of interview questions; inadequate follow-up questions to gain complete information; relinquishing control of the interview to skilled applicants; failing to give sufficient thought to workplace diversity; making comparisons between or among candidates, rather than comparing candidates with the identified success factors; and making hiring decisions on "gut feelings" instead of on candidates' qualifications for the job. Avoiding these mistakes can increase the hiring officials' chances for selecting the most qualified person for the position.[26]

The primary roles of an interviewer are to build a positive relationship with the candidate through small talk at the outset, to give information about the company and the position, and to obtain information about the applicant's qualifications. To be successful in the employment interview, interviewers should make adequate preparation, use good manners during the interview, and follow specific guidelines for terminating the interview and for following up after the interview.

Interviewer Preparation

Before the interview, interviewers should prepare a checklist to assure that everything is in order. The important points include reserving a room, making arrangements for refreshments, having available copies of the job description with qualifications highlighted, the candidate's application and résumé, and a list of questions to ask and those that are illegal and may not be asked. To avoid expensive litigation, interviewers should be sure that questions they ask are related to the job requirements.

People who conduct interviews without knowing the legal aspects involved have been compared with someone who insists upon "navigating a minefield blindfolded when the exact location of each mine has been marked with a big red flag."[27]

Attire should be chosen that is consistent with the company's image. In addition, the interviewer should either have an authorization to offer the position at a certain salary or be prepared to tell the applicant what the procedure will be. If a plant tour, interviews with others in the company, or lunch is part of the interview, times and locations should be confirmed.[28]

Behavior During the Interview

As the interview commences, the interviewer should attempt to create a positive atmosphere that is free from stress. The interviewer greets the applicant, shakes hands, and indicates where the candidate is to sit. The first few minutes are usually spent in small talk: comments about the weather or some other nonsubstantive topic to help put the candidate at ease. Then the interviewer lets the candidate know how the interview will be structured. For example, "Betty, I will first explain the job responsibilities and give a little information about the company; then I will ask you to describe your duties on your last job. After that, you may feel free to ask any questions. We will finish with a brief description of the next step in the interviewing process, including when we plan to make a hiring decision."[29]

Interviewers will want to anticipate questions the candidate may have about the job and the company and start the interview by covering this information. When asking questions of the applicant, the interviewer should listen attentively to the candidate's responses. Talking too much is a major mistake interviewers make, so they should make a real effort to listen without interrupting. Experts in hiring say that the interviewer should talk only 20 percent of the time and permit the applicant to talk 80 percent of the time. Attentive listening will provide the interviewer with valuable information from the candidate's verbal responses; it will also provide an opportunity to observe the applicant's nonverbal communication. In addition, listening attentively will help in determining what follow-up questions to ask. Including some structured questions is recommended; answers to these questions will be helpful in choosing the most qualified person for the job.[30]

When the applicant asks questions about the job and the company, the interviewer should be honest. If the interviewer misrepresents the job or the firm, the applicant who is hired will soon discover the truth, which will result in loss of credibility for the interviewer and the company. When interviewers are guilty of gross exaggerations about the job or the company, the chances are good that the unhappy employee will soon leave, and the interviewing process will have to be repeated.[31]

Termination of the Interview and Follow-up Activities

According to Dr. Martin Luther King, Jr., "the ultimate measure of a man is not where he stands in moments of comfort, but where he stands at times of challenge and controversy." While job interviews are not exactly "moments of comfort" for either the interviewer or the candidate, they can provide opportunities for learning and for making connections that may be useful in the future.[32]

The interviewer has the responsibility of bringing the interview to a close by thanking the candidate for coming in and by explaining what the next step in the process will be, as well as when a final decision will be made. The interviewer then signals the end of the interview using verbal and nonverbal signals. Such verbal signals as asking, "Are there any final questions?" alert the applicant that the interview is nearing an end. Nonverbal signals, such as standing, shaking hands, and walking the candidate to the door, are clear indications that the interview is over.

At the conclusion of the interview, the interviewer takes time to evaluate each applicant; waiting until later to complete the evaluation will result in a loss of some information since forgetting takes place immediately. Interviewers should keep in mind the schedule they gave applicants and should contact them in a timely manner. Even when someone else was given the position, it is important to communicate this information to all candidates who came in for interviews so they can focus on expanding their job search. Making applicants call repeatedly to get a decision is very inconsiderate.

In summary, job seekers and those with interviewing and hiring responsibilities should remember that good social skills can have a powerful effect on the outcome of the interview. In addition, a positive attitude toward the interview process can result in a positive outcome for both the candidate and the hiring organization.

2

Business Dress and Grooming

In social or business settings, clothing acts as a communicator of ourselves, our company, and our position.[1]

First impressions are often lasting impressions; research shows that 55 percent of this first impression is based on appearance. Those who protest the unfairness of evaluating someone based primarily on appearance would be wise to face the reality that people make judgments of others in less than a minute; these assumptions about another person include educational level, occupation, social and economic status, credibility, personality, trustworthiness, and probability of succeeding.[2]

Most of us can cite examples of successful, affluent people who have risen to the top of their profession without observing the recognized guidelines for appropriate professional attire. For example, Microsoft Chairman Bill Gates is well known for his ultracasual attire. However, in his first appearance before Congress a few years ago, Gates' casual attire had been replaced by a conservative suit and tie. When his credibility was at stake, Bill Gates knew the importance of wearing professional business attire. Dressing casually before Congress would have been perceived as a lack of respect. Showing disrespect for such a distinguished group given the responsibility for determining certain facts about Microsoft's operations would not have been in the company's best interest.

Appearance is also a basis for determining a person's starting salary and for career advancement. Research conducted on the relationship between appearance and starting salary found that beginning salaries for people with a polished business appearance were considerably higher than those who presented a mediocre appearance. Promotion decisions

Author John Steinbeck told about asking a local boy he had hired to repaint his house to go to the store to buy additional paint. The boy, whose clothes were spattered with paint, said he would need to go home first to change clothes. When Steinbeck told him to go dressed as he was, the boy replied: "I can't do that; you've got to be awfully rich to dress as bad as you do."[3]

also take into account appearance. Promotions at upper-managerial levels go to employees who, in addition to having records of excellent job performance, convey an image of professionalism through appearance and demeanor.[4]

DRESS CONSIDERATIONS

Considerations in business attire are gender and age, as well as geographic, cultural, and industry variations.

Gender

Gender differences exist in the importance of attire to career advancement. While men can sometimes be promoted to managerial levels despite their attire, women typically cannot. This double standard exists. According to research, women who dress inappropriately are almost always assured of failure; those who dress professionally are the ones most likely to be promoted to managerial positions.[5] Research has also confirmed a link between a woman's appearance and self-esteem. A survey of 21,000 women revealed that satisfaction with one's image is highly correlated with self-esteem. The more satisfied women were with their appearance, the higher their level of self-esteem.[6] In addition to attire, the importance of hair style, jewelry, and makeup has been researched. Hair that is short, styled simply, and worn away from the face is consistent with managerial success. Simple gold jewelry and moderate facial cosmetics complete the look of a serious business professional.[7]

Age

When Bill Clinton entered the presidential race, Hillary Clinton's friends urged her to lose the headband and have her hair styled by a professional so that she would fit the image of a First Lady. They reminded her that the American public would not be comfortable with a First Lady who did not wear a serious hairstyle. Fortunately, she listened to their advice.

Age is another consideration in business dress. Both men and women should dress like adults, rather than trying to reclaim their youth by wearing attire typically worn by the younger generation. Men should wear serious ties, rather than ties featuring cartoon characters. Watches should likewise be consistent with a professional image; Mickey Mouse watches are not recommended business accessories for men. Women seem to be more prone to dressing like the younger generation than men. To be taken seriously in the business world, women should avoid wearing jumpers and any other attire featured in stores catering to teens. Makeup that is typical of teenagers, such as frosted lip gloss or those with fruit scents, is inappropriate for women who wish to advance in their professions. Hairstyles, such as high ponytails and flips, should be avoided, as well as such hair accessories as headbands.[8]

Geography

In addition to gender and age considerations, geographic differences exist in what is considered appropriate professional attire. In Texas and Wyoming, for example, men typically wear cowboy boots with their business suits. Wearing Western boots with a suit in other parts of the country is often viewed as an affectation and could have negative consequences. Dress standards are more casual in California and Florida than in New York. In fact, dress is typically more conservative on the East Coast, especially in Atlanta, Boston, Chicago, and Washington, DC., than on the West Coast. Even within some states, however, variations exist in what is considered appropriate. In Florida, for example, dress is more conservative in Tampa than in Palm Beach. Regional differences are also apparent in what is considered proper footwear. In Boston, the thin-soled leather slip-on shoe popular in Atlanta would be viewed as too informal; Bostonians prefer the wing tip leather shoe.[9]

Culture

When conducting business in other countries, it is important to consider cultural variations in dress. The general rule to follow is to dress more conservatively and more formally than is usually expected when conducting business in the United States. Men should wear good-quality suits in solid, dark colors that are styled conservatively, regardless of the season. In certain situations lighter shades of brown and gray are also considered acceptable; however, pastel-colored suits have no place in a traditional work environment.[10]

With their dark suits, men would be wise to wear white long-sleeved shirts and conservative ties, avoiding striped ties when in England as they symbolize certain schools in that country. Black shoes that lace are considered more appropriate for business in Asia and Europe than loafers.

A columnist for the *New York Times* wore a tan suit to a cocktail party during a business conference in Tokyo in July. He said, "From the looks I got, I might as well have been wearing sandals, white socks, and a T-shirt with a beer company's logo." He added: "I had never been to Tokyo before—who knew men do not wear anything but dark suits in business settings here?"[11]

Women should wear skirted suits or good quality dresses in solid muted colors; pantsuits are inappropriate in many countries. Shoes with very high heels or boots should be avoided; women should wear good jewelry, especially when doing business in Europe. Women who do business in Japan should wear muted colors, few accessories, and conservative makeup. In addition, they should avoid tight, suggestive dresses; full, loose skirts are recommended as sitting on the floor is expected when dining in Japanese restaurants and in other situations. In Arab countries, women should wear long, loose-fitting dresses that cover the arms and legs.[12]

In selecting attire to wear in other countries, color should be a consideration. Wearing white in China is inappropriate as white is worn to funerals and suggests sadness. In fact, in more than three-fourths of the countries of the world, white has a funereal connotation. In addition, wearing red in other countries may not be a good choice. In Ghana, for example, red is associated with sadness, and to many Koreans red is bad luck. Wearing red is associated with witchcraft and death in many African countries, so wearing red in these countries is not recommended. When visiting Brazil, wearing green and yellow is inappropriate as these are the colors of the Brazilian flag. Since Brazilians do not wear them, visitors to that country should do likewise.[13]

Industry

Industry differences in dress are also apparent. Employees in accounting and law firms, banks, government agencies, and financial institutions are expected to dress more conservatively than people who work in travel or advertising agencies. The preferred look for accountants continues to be conservative, especially for women. One research study found that clients of major accounting firms preferred to work with female accountants who dressed in skirted suits of blue, gray, or beige.[14] Bank customers expect employees to dress conservatively. They feel that bank employees who dress casually would be casual in handling their money as well. People who work in creative jobs and who dress to reflect their creativity would be wise to wear more conservative attire when dealing with corporate clients.[15] Over the years, little has changed regarding what is considered appropriate for medical doctors to wear. The white doctor's coat is still considered the most effective attire. Clients of legal firms expect attorneys to look competent and authoritative. When deciding how to dress, attorneys must consider whether they should wear high-authority attire—a business suit—or dress less formally, taking into consideration the judge, jury, and geographic location of the courtroom. Results of one survey found that jury members responded favorably to a look that was businesslike, affluent, and understated.[16] Attorneys should advise their clients concerning appropriate attire during court appearances; most attorneys recommend conservative attire for

Martha Stewart should probably have been advised on what to wear during her insider-trading trial. Her fur wraps and expensive handbags emphasized to jury members their socioeconomic differences. Dressing down might have been good advice to minimize juror resentment.[17]

lower-income juries and more elegant attire when courts are located in affluent suburbs.

ATTRIBUTES OF DRESS

Attributes of dress include color, fabric, and quality. Color is one of the first things people notice about a person's attire; fabric and quality can convey high or low status. These attributes are important considerations when choosing a business wardrobe.

Color

Colors have different meanings and are important attributes of dress. Neutral, basic colors are usually safe for business attire. Generally speaking, people who wear darker colors convey power and authority, while those who wear lighter colors are viewed as more approachable. Blue is associated with dignity and white with cleanliness.[18] Green is an inappropriate color for a man's suit. Since certain shades of green are often associated with hospital and hotel uniforms, green does not convey the status desired by business professionals. Gray conveys success and is a popular color for business attire for both men and women. Black is an effective color for women. A simple black dress of high quality is an important part of a woman's wardrobe; it can be dressed down for the office or dressed up for a party after work. By simply changing jewelry, adding a dressy belt, and taking the small bag she keeps in her attaché case, a woman can easily make the transition from business to evening events. Women can use blouses or scarves in pastels to soften basic colors and jewel tones of emerald, sapphire, and amethyst to brighten a solid-color basic suit.[19]

Fabric and Quality

In addition to color, the fabric from which a garment is made is an important consideration in clothing selection. Pure, natural fibers, such as cotton, linen, silk, and wool, are associated with higher status, whereas synthetic fibers, such as polyester, are associated with attire of the lower middle class. While natural fibers are preferred, blends of good quality that have the look and comfort of pure fibers are becoming more popular since they are usually wrinkle-resistant and are easier to care for than clothing of natural fibers. The preferred fabric for clothing for both men and women is 100 percent wool; wool blends that are at least 50 percent wool are a good second choice. Fabrics traditionally considered inappropriate for business wear include leather, suede, velvet, and satin.[20]

Quality is an additional aspect of business dress. Although quality clothing is usually associated with designer apparel, quality can be found in clothing with less prestigious labels. Inspect the workmanship, including seams, hems, darts, and buttons/buttonholes. Investing in a few pieces of quality clothing is preferable to having a large wardrobe of clothing of lesser quality. To get a good fit, learn which brands seem to fit your particular body type. Since expensive garments seem to be cut more generously, try on a smaller size than you typically wear.[21]

RESEARCH FINDINGS RELATED TO BUSINESS DRESS

A review of literature on the importance of proper attire and grooming to business success has revealed the following facts:

- Dress is a major factor in hiring decisions.
- Employees who disregard the company's dress standards will probably lose out at promotion time.
- Dress fabric is important to conveying status; clothing made of pure fibers is associated with people of high status.
- Good grooming projects a positive image; it conveys respect for self and for others.
- Shoes are highly visible and convey either positive or negative impressions.
- Glasses send positive nonverbal messages; people of both genders who wear glasses are viewed as more intelligent, hardworking, and successful than people who do not wear glasses.[22]

The consensus of the literature on the meaning of appearance in society is that clothing, accessories, grooming, and hairstyles communicate powerful messages. Guidelines for business professional attire and business casual attire, including accessories, hairstyles, and grooming, are detailed in the following sections.

When Matt Lauer, cohost of *The Today Show,* was interviewed on *Larry King Live,* Larry asked Matt whether he had changed his attire since being in his current position. Matt stated that he now wears a suit every day because he never knows when he will be called upon to interview someone of high rank and that a suit gives him the visual credibility he needs.[23]

BUSINESS PROFESSIONAL ATTIRE

Business professionals need to be aware that clothing can project credibility and power. Research has found that people who wear suits, whether male or female, are perceived as more professional than those who wear any other type of attire. The most effective suit colors for both genders are dark blue and gray in a classic style with an appropriate shirt or blouse to complement the suit.

When choosing their clothing and accessories, both men and women should remember that a double-breasted jacket should be worn buttoned when standing or walking. They should also remember that double-breasted jackets are not flattering to all figure types and should consult a professional for advice regarding the suitability of this type of jacket. Another guideline that applies to both genders is that the color of hosiery should match the shoes, which should be the same color as—or darker than—the hem of the garment. Furthermore, jewelry worn in a visible body piercing, such as an eyebrow ring, is inappropriate in most companies. The exception to this rule is earrings women wear in pierced ears.[24]

In addition to the preceding rules that apply to both men and women, the following guidelines for professional business dress apply specifically to men:

- Men should not wear both braces (suspenders) and a belt. Wearing the two together suggests that the man is either exceedingly insecure or lacks knowledge of their proper use.
- Men should not wear short-sleeve dress shirts with suits; they have no authority or power. Further, their use would violate another rule of proper attire: that the shirt sleeves should be long enough so that about a half inch extends below the jacket sleeve.
- Men should always wear an undershirt; choosing a V-neck style when wearing a shirt open at the neck is recommended so that the undershirt does not show. [25]

Guidelines for women include the following:

- Women should limit the number of rings to two; numerous rings are distracting and unprofessional.
- Women should avoid jewelry that is overpowering or noisy; earrings that are long enough to touch the shoulder or bracelets that clank are distracting.
- Women should keep makeup to a minimum and should avoid unusual colors of nail polish.
- Women should not carry both a purse and an attaché case; a small purse may be placed inside the attaché case.
- Women should avoid wearing sleeveless dresses and blouses to the office.
- Women can damage their credibility by wearing skirts that are too short or skirts with slits that extend to the thigh area.[26]

One of the most important accessories for men and women is shoes. Positive impressions are conveyed by shoes that are made of leather, well shined, and well maintained. Inexpensive, unkempt shoes leave a negative impression, regardless of gender, age, or culture. Shoes considered conservative and appropriate for men include wing tips, laced oxfords, and leather loafers, except for penny loafers, which are too casual to be worn with a suit. Hose (thin socks) worn with a business suit should be the same color as the shoe and in a solid color or with a subdued pattern. They should be sufficiently long so that no skin shows when the legs are crossed. Women should wear plain pumps with a closed heel and closed toe in a conservative color to match the suit; mules and sling-back styles are too casual for suits. The shade of hose usually matches the shoes, but a neutral tone is acceptable. The height of the heel depends somewhat on the length of the hemline but typically ranges from one to two inches. The rule for both men and women is that the shoe color should match the hem of the garment or darker. When shoes are lighter than the hem of the garment, attention is focused on the feet rather than on the face.[27]

In addition to shoes, other accessories include ties/scarves, glasses, belts, briefcases, watches, and other jewelry. Men should select a coordinating tie of silk or a silk and polyester blend in a medium width; it should be tied so that the bottom tip of the tie just touches the top of the belt. When a tie and pocket-handkerchief are worn, they should not be identical but should share some colors. Scarves, once a popular accessory for women but not currently viewed as fashionable as they were a few years ago, are still worn by some successful businesswomen. Expensive, designer scarves in colors that complement the outfit and in conservative patterns are good choices. A study conducted by Molloy determined that both men and women can identify an expensive scarf; those surveyed associated expensive scarves with professional women and inexpensive ones with women in administrative support positions, such as secretaries and clerks.[28]

Glasses can either contribute to a credible look or detract from it. Studies have indicated that both men and women are perceived to be richer and smarter when wearing glasses. The proper glasses, with frames of moderate size in plastic or bone (not wire), can make a woman look more authoritative and more intelligent. Men are advised to choose wire, plastic, or frameless glasses that blend with the hair color.[29] Avoid wearing half glasses (reading glasses) when credibility is important, such as when making a presentation; looking down at people over the top of the glasses is viewed as condescending. Glasses are not a hair ornament; wearing them on top of the head damages credibility. Wearing sunglasses indoors, regardless of how bright the lighting, is ludicrous.

A leather belt to match the shoes is recommended for both men and women. Men who prefer braces should buy the ones with leather attachments rather than the clip-on style and should not wear a belt in addition to the braces.[30] Briefcases, a term used to describe leather attaché cases, envelopes, and portfolios, are important accessories for both genders. Research shows that women receive better treatment when carrying briefcases, especially when traveling or when dressed casually; the briefcase signifies that they are business professionals.[31]

Keep jewelry to a minimum; it should not be distracting. Wearing multiple rings destroys credibility. Women should limit the number of rings worn to two; the only jewelry men need is a good watch and their wedding band.[32] Accessories that suggest activities associated with one's personal life, such as class rings and religious symbols, should be avoided.

Attention to grooming and hairstyle can enhance one's appearance or detract from it. Women should avoid long, bright-colored fingernails; they are considered inappropriate for business regardless of age. Hair should be clean and styled conservatively. A woman with long, straight hair gives the impression she is clinging to her youth. Hair below shoulder length makes a woman less effective in business situations. Men appear more credible with a moderate haircut and sideburns. Since facial hair does not work well in some professions, men who choose to wear mustaches and beards should make sure that they are considered acceptable by their professional colleagues; when worn, they should be professionally trimmed.[33]

BUSINESS CASUAL ATTIRE

Business casual dress, which was the norm in many U.S. firms in the 1990s, now appears to be on the wane, especially among companies concerned about their corporate image. During the decade of business casual attire, company executives observed that many employees were unable to distinguish between business casual dress and attire that would be appropriate for a picnic or sporting event. Permitting employees to dress too casually not only conveys a negative image of the company but may even cost the firm business.

Since clothing is linked to credibility, men should realize that their credibility can be seriously questioned when they come to work in torn jeans, sweatshirt, and sneakers. (Jeans are acceptable in some firms provided they are clean, neatly pressed, and contain no holes.) Men should invest in good khakis and gray flannel slacks; both can be worn with a navy blazer. Vests, sport jackets, and cardigan sweaters in such basic colors as black, gray, or navy are also recommended pieces of a man's casual wardrobe.[35] Shirts considered acceptable for casual wear include a button-down shirt without a tie, a long- or short-sleeved polo or sports shirt, or a dress shirt worn open at the neck. In addition to

One company reported losing a large contract to a competitor after representatives from the prospective client made visits to both firms. Later, during an off-the-record conversation, the CEO of the client company admitted that the final decision was based on the fact that the competitor's employees dressed and acted in a more professional, businesslike manner.[34]

When Shelia was passed over for promotion, she asked her boss for an explanation. He replied that although her work was excellent, her professionalism was not consistent with someone in a high-level position. Shelia was not perceived as ambitious or professional, not because of her work record, but because of her overly casual attire.[37]

soiled or torn jeans, casual dress for men does not include sweat suits, shorts, military surplus apparel, "muscle" shirts, and T-shirts with artwork or printed messages in questionable taste. Fabrics of pure fibers, such as wool and cotton, are just as important for casual attire as they are for professional dress. While loafers are appropriate casual footwear, soiled sneakers, athletic shoes, or sandals are not appropriate. Baseball caps, regardless of gender, are never appropriate office wear.[36]

According to research, women may be more negatively affected by casual dress codes than men. They should, therefore, purchase the highest-quality business casual attire they can afford and should make sure it is made of natural fibers or blends that give the appearance of natural fibers. Recommendations for women's casual dress include a denim or chambray skirt, knit top, linen shirt, khaki or navy slacks, blazer, and sweater set. Sleeveless dresses and blouses, halter tops, tight skirts and slacks, and shorts are inappropriate in most offices. Wearing colors and color combinations usually found in traditional men's sportswear, such as khaki, gray, navy, and black, is recommended. Pastels, large floral prints, and bright colors are not viewed as favorably as neutral colors—beige, taupe, and brown. When dressing casually, women may wear stacked-heel loafers; however, sandals and sneakers are not good choices. Jewelry may be more casual than that worn with professional attire; however, it should not be distracting.[38]

Molloy made this observation based on extensive research on business casual attire: "When men dress casually and have to deal with relative strangers, they lose some of their authority; when women do the same, they lose most of theirs." Thus, he recommends that women wear business casual attire that is conservative, upper class, and traditional.[39]

DRESS FOR SPECIAL EVENTS AND OCCASIONS

When invited to special business events, selecting the proper attire for the occasion is important. Propriety and appropriateness should be considered when choosing what to wear. When in doubt, women should dress modestly and avoid calling attention to themselves in a negative way. Being the center of attention because of wearing inappropriate attire is not a favorable way to be remembered.

For black-tie events, women would wear an evening gown (either short, long, or somewhere in between) with an evening bag, evening sandals or other dress shoes, and jewelry that is dressier than that normally worn to the office—pearl earrings and necklace, button earrings and necklace in gold or silver, or earrings that sparkle. Black-tie attire for men is a black dinner jacket with a black tie, worn with either a plain shirt or one with a pleated front. Wearing this attire before 6 P.M. is inappropriate.

For white-tie affairs, which are the most formal occasions and rarely attended by the average person, women would wear a full-length ball gown with long white gloves, more ornate jewelry, and perhaps a fur wrap, depending upon the acceptability of wearing fur where the event is scheduled. In some geographic areas of the United States, wearing fur is politically incorrect. Men would wear a black tailcoat with starched white shirtfront, white vest, and black patent shoes; a black silk top hat is also sometimes worn.[40]

For a cocktail party or other event calling for informal dress, women may choose a dressy pants suit or a short cocktail dress or suit in such fabrics as brocade, chiffon, crepe, or silk. Evening footwear, such as dressy sandals or fabric pumps, and a small bag in some dressy fabric, such as velvet, satin, or *peau de soie,* would complete the outfit. Jewelry worn to black-tie events would also be appropriate for cocktail parties.[41] Men would usually wear a black or other dark suit, which would be given a festive look with a white shirt with French cuffs and cuff links, a dressy tie, and a coordinating pocket square. For black-tie and many informal events, shoes for men would be well-shined leather shoes or black patent leather.[42]

Dress for more casual, informal events, such as company picnics, would depend upon what activities are scheduled and where the event is to be held. Dress for a picnic held at the supervisor's country club would be more formal than attire for an event held at a local park. Company outings are always viewed as informal, so attire should be somewhat casual, such as sports shirts/blouses and khakis. When attire is not specified on the invitation, simply call the host or ask someone who has attended these functions previously. If the event includes swimming, women may choose to sit on the sidelines or to bring along an appropriate tank suit (not a bikini) and cover-up; men who decide to participate would be prepared with swim trunks (not Speedos) and a shirt for modesty between swims. Some employees, especially women, decide against wearing such revealing attire as a swimsuit around their supervisors and colleagues and simply join the others poolside without actually getting in the water.[43]

Office parties, usually during the holidays or to commemorate special occasions, such as an employee's retirement, are often held at a local restaurant or some other location off the company premises and outside of office hours. Employees' families are often invited to these events. Clothing worn to these office parties is usually professional attire, unless the invitation states otherwise. Employees need to be aware that their behavior at office parties may affect their future success with the

When George's name came up as a possible employee to add to the company's development team, the person in charge of the team recalled George's behavior at a recent office party, which included complaining loudly about how hard he was working. This negative behavior, in spite of the good job he had done on previous projects, resulted in his being dropped from further consideration for this important assignment.[45]

company. Dressing inappropriately, drinking too much, speaking too loudly, acting flirtatious, or telling off-color jokes at one of these events may result in irreparable damage to one's career.[44]

Appropriate attire for the job interview is covered in Chapter 1, "Job Interview Etiquette"; presentation dress is detailed in Chapter 11, "Presentations." A reality of life is that people are judged by their appearances just as books are judged by their covers. Dressing appropriately may not guarantee success, but dressing inappropriately often assures failure. Since first impressions are often lasting ones, businesspeople should make sure that the impression they make through their choice of clothing is a positive one. "Successful people generally look successful. They wear clothes that look attractive on them, are well groomed, and hold themselves with confidence. The intended message is that they feel good about themselves and that others will feel good about them as well."[46] This statement summarizes the importance of dress to success in the business world.

3

Office Politics

> Although it is emotionally and intellectually draining at times, there is no way of totally avoiding political environments that exist within organizations. If you choose to be successful in your career then, as someone once said, 'You've got to play to stay.'[1]

Office politics involves the strategies people in various types of organizations use to gain a career advantage. Office politics can affect a person's salary, promotions, and work environment.[2] In a perfect world, employees who deserve raises and promotions would receive them, and people who get the corner office and new furniture and equipment would have earned these perks. Job success would be the result of good performance and hard work, rather than of currying the favor of those in a position to determine employee rewards and advancement.[3]

Some political maneuvering goes on in most work environments, especially in those where influence and monetary gain are important. This political maneuvering, usually referred to as office politics, is actually a game; employees who do not play the game pay the price. The game of office politics has specific rules and boundaries. While these rules will vary with the company, some rules are invariant; they include behaving ethically and treating people fairly rather than behaving in a deceitful, unethical manner. The game of office politics is competitive, but it does not include playing unfairly to assure winning at another person's expense. Office politics and behaving ethically are not mutually exclusive; principled persons can create an office environment that rewards appropriate behavior, not political sneakiness.[5]

An important rule of office politics is that of being loyal to and showing support for the supervisor. Accomplishments are often a team effort so accomplishments should be shared with supervisors. While it is unwise to agree with everything your supervisor says as you may be considered

This statement by one employee expresses the frustration many workers feel when dealing with office politics: "I am completely fed up with this situation. All I want to do is get on with what I'm paid to do—I don't want to be continually bogged down in all of the politics that goes on around this place. It saps up so much of my time and energy; I spend most of my day taking the daggers out of my back."[4]

a "yes-person," offering valid suggestions will give the impression that you have a mind of your own. In addition, remember to avoid correcting or outshining the supervisor, especially when others are present, as this could result in retaliation later on. Making a supervisor look good, on the other hand, could result in a move up the corporate ladder as the supervisor moves up. Employees with strong work skills who do not show support for their supervisors are less likely to succeed than are employees who support their supervisors.[6]

Employees who have issues with some of the concepts of office politics need to understand that favoritism exists in every firm and that their ability or inability to use office politics effectively can advance or impede their careers. In fact, employees who are inept at office politics may be perceived as people who are not team players and not good candidates for promotion; they may also be viewed as persons who are untrustworthy and lack social skills and common sense.[7] Decisions concerning raises and promotions are not, after all, based entirely on merit; they may be a way of paying back favors or rewarding an employee for making a favorable impression on prospective clients when entertaining them.[8]

Since the office politics game is part of the reality of the workplace, it is important to become knowledgeable about it. The following areas of office politics can have a major impact on business success: self-promotion, honesty and truth telling, compliments and flattery, gossip, favors and hidden motives, dress and grooming, and business socializing and etiquette.

SELF-PROMOTION

Office politics involves self-promotion; perceptive employees know that they must make sure that their efforts and accomplishments are recognized. Tooting one's own horn, when done in a low-key manner, is highly recommended especially when trying to convince a supervisor that a raise or promotion is deserved. Tooting one's horn too loudly, however, is not characteristic of a well-mannered person and may result in being called a braggart, which may fail to impress influential people. The best advice for self-promotion is to document all accomplishments by keeping a work journal, by regularly updating your job description to reflect new responsibilities, and by keeping a file of copies of written documents that provide evidence of your contributions. Providing such records will add strength to requests for promotions and salary increases.[9]

Astute employees "have learned the art of self-promotion"; they know that blowing your own horn gets rewarded.[10]

Zsa Zsa Gabor received much publicity when she slapped a police officer. What she really received was notoriety; no positive recognition resulted from the episode. Zsa Zsa herself said, "I am so famous, it's sickening!"[12]

Self-promotion should also include such basic rules of etiquette as keeping commitments, sending letters of appreciation and congratulations, being accessible, and having business cards readily available when meeting others.[11] In your efforts at self-promotion, you should be sure to distinguish between positive recognition for accomplishing something and notoriety. People tend to avoid someone who is a publicity hound.

In addition to personal attributes, office décor, including displays of awards and certificates of achievement, can be used for self-promotion. Displays and office furnishings, however, should be business-related; pictures of a child's artwork or lamps and other accessories that belong in one's home are in poor taste. Office décor should convey a message that is congruent with the person's business image and with the manner in which he or she wishes to be perceived. In some offices, such as those supported by public funds, décor should be practical, inexpensive, and conventional. When an impression of affluence is desired, such as waiting rooms of attorneys who deal with prestigious clients, the office décor would be opulent, including artwork of substantial monetary value.

An executive had on his wall over 100 plaques, certificates, and trophies, some of which related to his children's accomplishments and others that some described as having been bought at a garage sale. Instead of enhancing the executive's credibility, the display revealed his insecurity and actually had a negative impact on his credibility. Visitors, who were always given the Hall of Fame tour, were not impressed.[14]

Aesthetic objects convey favorable impressions of a person's interpersonal skills. Plants, aquariums, and living things seem to make visitors feel more comfortable and give the impression that the person is friendly. Job-related certificates and awards imply that the person is competent; they provide evidence of recognition for exceptional performance. Research related to the appropriateness of framed family photographs suggests that family photographs by medical doctors who specialize in family practice and CEOs of organizations are acceptable. However, such displays are not recommended in other types of offices.[13]

Other aspects of the environment that are related to self-promotion include color, lighting, furniture selection and arrangement, and office cleanliness. The consensus of those who have researched the use of color in offices is that color should be used sparingly. They recommend the use of more subdued colors to convey a friendly, professional environment.

The amount and type of lighting, such as task or overhead lighting, influence visitors' impressions and are also important in self-promotion. More light makes employees seem more energetic; dark offices give the impression of employees who are somewhat sedate and reserved. Rooms with peripheral wall lighting convey friendliness and spaciousness to a greater extent than rooms that use overhead diffused lighting.

In selecting an office desk, it is important to remember that bigger is usually better; desks should be arranged to indicate the person with higher rank. (The person with higher rank is located farthest from the door.) One's chair should be compatible with body size; the chair back should extend no more than an inch or so above a person's shoulders. A padded chair with arms adds to a person's sense of presence and authority.

Office tidiness and cleanliness are also important to employees concerned with self-promotion. A well-organized office suggests that the person has good interpersonal skills and is a high achiever; an office in disarray conveys a negative impression. In fact, research indicates that visitors do not feel as comfortable and welcome in a messy, cluttered office as they do in an office that is tidy and well organized. Unpleasant odors emanating from food, employees' poor personal hygiene, or strong-smelling perfume in some cases negate other positive impressions. Since these sensitive areas are important to personal success and to the company's image, correcting these negative aspects of the office environment is important.[15]

HONESTY AND TRUTH-TELLING

Part of playing the game of office politics is making decisions on the extent to which one feels compelled to be honest and tell the truth in all situations. Honesty and truth-telling should be a way of life in the workplace. A public relations executive was known for telling clients who were unsure about how much information to reveal, "When all else fails, try the truth." Telling the truth in one's business and personal life, regardless of the consequences, is better than being caught in a lie.[16] The chances of being caught in a lie are high; the results are a loss of personal and corporate credibility and integrity. Customers who catch company representatives lying will either proceed cautiously in their future dealings with the company or decide to take their business elsewhere.[17] While honesty is important, being ruthlessly honest to the extent of hurting

Sara had a stressful job that often involved travel; she sometimes took a day off to relieve the stress. She would ask her assistant Larry to cover for her. On one occasion Sara asked Larry to tell the company owner should he call that she was attending a meeting in Reno; actually she was at Pebble Beach. The owner, when he called from Pebble Beach and was told Sara was in Reno, fired Larry over the phone. It seems the owner had just seen Sara on the golf course; he fired her at the third tee.[19]

other people's feelings is inconsiderate. For example, telling an employee in the presence of others that his job will be eliminated by the end of the year is demoralizing and serves no useful purpose.[18]

Supervisors should not ask their subordinates to lie for them, nor should subordinates agree to lie for their supervisors. When Sara asked Larry to lie for her, Larry could have simply replied: "Are you asking me to lie?" If the supervisor cannot read between the lines and understand the subtextual message being conveyed, it may be necessary for the subordinate to state his or her refusal to lie more explicitly. When supervisors choose to engage in personal activities on company time, they should simply tell their subordinates that they are unavailable.[20]

White lies, sometimes referred to as social lies, are intended to spare another person's feelings. When a colleague asks your opinion of a new outfit, you may decide to tell him or her that it looks great on him or her even though you find it unbecoming. A more polite response would be to comment on something that you do like about his or her attire, such as the color, without telling him or her that the outfit is unflattering. People have to decide for themselves whether they should tell a white lie or be brutally honest and hurt a person's feelings.[21]

In some cases, employees may find that total honesty is less important than telling supervisors what they want to hear. For example, when asked how the annual report is progressing, employees may assure the supervisor that everything is on schedule even when that is not totally accurate because a positive report is what the supervisor wants to hear. In short, what a person tells should be truthful; however, gauging how much to tell requires skill, and one's words must be chosen carefully and politically.[22]

COMPLIMENTS AND FLATTERY

Compliments, defined as giving sincere praise to recognize the efforts and accomplishments of others, are always appreciated. Employees react favorably to being complimented for doing a good job. Compliments given to make a person feel good, even when not completely truthful, are usually justified by etiquette mavens. Paying a person a compliment is also a good way of starting a conversation.[23]

Two men who appeared to be from the same company were observed waiting in the airport gate area for a departing flight; they were having a difficult time making conversation. Then one said, "Frank, when you arrived I noticed how great you look in that suit." His colleague smiled and said, "Thanks; I just bought it last week." After that, the two seemed to converse easily about a number of topics.[24]

Some compliments leave the person being complimented with something less than a feeling of appreciation. Here are some examples:

- "You look terrific—did you have a face-lift?"
- "Great earrings—are they real?"
- "Another new outfit! You must really be rolling in money."
- "I see you finally took off all that weight; it certainly is an improvement."[26]

Other occasions that are deserving of a compliment, in addition to when someone has on a new outfit, include when someone makes an effective presentation, receives an award or recognition, does a good job on a project, improves his or her physical appearance, or plays a good game, regardless of whether the game was won or lost. Knowing how to accept a compliment is just as important as knowing how to give one. In no case should a compliment be denied, protested, or corrected. For example, when a person says you look great in your new blue suit, do not reply with, "This old grey suit? It makes me look ill." Accept the compliment graciously by saying something like, "Thank you; I appreciate the compliment."[25]

Flattery, defined as excessive or insincere praise, has not traditionally been viewed in a positive manner. When it comes to the office politics game, however, "flattery will get you everywhere—if it's used properly."[27] Flattery is effective in influencing others and makes the office environment more pleasant. One of the most effective ways of using flattery is perhaps giving a compliment on another person's behalf, which is then passed on. For example, an employee mentions to a colleague that he or she is impressed with the supervisor's business acumen; the colleague then conveys the compliment to the supervisor. Thus, a person's ulterior motive is less obvious; and the compliment is perceived as more genuine. Giving such compliments when they do not reflect one's true feelings, however, is not recommended; false praise can have unpredictable consequences.[28]

GOSSIP

While office gossip in years past has not been considered in a positive light, it is currently being taken more seriously. In fact, gossip improves

Donna, a supervisor in the sales department, would often approach staff members with the question, "What's the scuttlebutt?" Although they regularly shared information with Donna, rarely did she share any inside information with the staff. When one staff member confronted Donna and pointed out that she seldom shared gossip with them even though she was in a better position to provide inside information than they were, she laughed but did not change her behavior. Her sources quickly dried up.[31]

employee morale, builds peer relationships, and makes a dull job more bearable. People who spread gossip must remember, however, that it is unwise to pass along negative information about someone unless it is factual and would soon be public knowledge.[29] For example, when information you have received about an executive guilty of tax evasion will soon be made public, it is acceptable to tell other employees. However, bear in mind that gossip is a two-way street; to get information from others it is necessary to give it. Otherwise, people will stop sharing gossip.[30]

Employees who gossip may have hidden agendas so office colleagues should take such information at face value. The desire to gossip is often fueled by the human need to fit into a group. Rather than fitting in, however, employees may find themselves ostracized when they spread gossip that maligns another person.

Gossip may be personal or professional. Responses to personal gossip and backstabbing should be noncommittal and limited to slow nods or short verbal responses such as, "Oh, really!" Silence is an even better response; such gossip should not, of course, be repeated. Employees who regularly reveal personal information about colleagues, such as details of their sex life, health problems, personal finances, and problems with a spouse or partner, will be seen as busybodies who do not have enough to keep them occupied. In addition, those who share personal and confidential information will question the trustworthiness of the person they confided in; the result will soon be that no one will tell the busybodies anything.[32]

While personal gossip should not be given attention, professional gossip should be given attention since it is a technique for becoming skilled in office politics and is approximately 80 percent accurate. The reason for the high degree of accuracy is that the information is shared by employees who have usually been with the company for some time and have formed information groups with members who trust each other. The most valuable professional gossip includes company reorganization, promotions, terminations, and transfers, while the least valuable gossip is related to office romances or such personal information as extramarital affairs and problems with children. Sharing professional gossip with one's supervisor is simply part of office politics.[33] Keep in mind that information should be shared with your supervisor before your colleagues. The supervisor should never be the second person to know.[34]

FAVORS AND HIDDEN MOTIVES

Doing favors for colleagues and supervisors is central to the concept of office politics. In fact, *quid pro quo* arrangements with coworkers are a common way of accomplishing things. Exchanging favors is especially effective when favors are done with no expectation of receiving anything in return. Examples of such favors are giving a job referral, lending professional materials, and helping colleagues who are trying to meet a deadline. These favors are important to building successful relationships and are usually remembered later when promotion decisions are made. Although people may not be in a position to return the favor immediately, they may be able to repay the favor at a later time. Perhaps the saying, "what goes around, comes around" applies when doing favors for those who are not currently in a position to return the favor.[35]

Requests for favors must be made wisely and should never be used to create win–lose circumstances in which the person requesting the favor wins and the person granting the favor loses. Having a well-developed relationship with the person who is being asked for a favor is important. Be direct when requesting a favor: "I have a favor to ask. Would you mind speaking to my focus group on global etiquette next month?" Further, the person requesting a favor should remember that once another person has done the favor, he or she is owed a favor in return. In addition, it is important to thank the person by writing a note of appreciation or giving a small gift. When the favor is making a presentation to a group without charge, a thank-you note and a gift are expected.[36]

Sometimes when a person does a favor for someone, the recipient of the favor may question the other person's motives. The best advice is to remain friendly toward the person until a determination can be made regarding a hidden agenda. Being open in one's dealings with other people is advised; otherwise, people may sense a lack of complete honesty and may be reluctant to trust others. Regardless of the hidden motives of the person granting the favor, doing favors is implicit in the workplace politics game. When people go out of their way to do favors for other people, they are making a deposit in the "favor bank" that they can cash in later when the need arises. Stated succinctly, asking for favors should be done wisely; and spending one's favor account should also be done wisely.[37]

DRESS AND GROOMING

Clothing is a highly visible source of nonverbal communication and makes a difference in how individuals are perceived. One connection people often make is between a person's manner of dress and performance:

"sloppy dress, sloppy mind, sloppy work."[38] The implication is that someone who is considering doing business with a company would question the advisability of doing so when dealing with someone wearing frayed jeans and sandals, for example.

Dressing appropriately for the job enhances one's corporate image and lends credibility to one's ideas and accomplishments. Select clothing and accessories that reflect the company culture and that is appropriate to one's career stage. Wearing scuffed shoes with run-down heels, using cheap ballpoint pens, and carrying a worn out attaché case are not recommended for those aspiring to supervisory positions.[39] If the corporate culture is casual, employees should remember that it is wise to invest in high-quality casual clothing with high-quality accessories as well. Employees can make themselves more promotable by following the dress standards set by their organizational leaders. While some persons would consider conforming to the company's dress codes as a form of dishonesty, others know that doing so is simply good office politics. Employees who follow the firm's dress standards will send the message that they are aware of the importance of appropriate attire to the company's image and that they wish to conform to the standards of the corporate culture. Employees on the way up should, however, avoid dressing better than their supervisors.[40]

Grooming is an important part of a person's appearance. Employees who are well groomed, in addition to being well dressed, convey the message that they are detail-oriented, confident, and capable. Good grooming supports an expensive outfit; a lack of good grooming destroys the overall image.[41] Successful employees know that looking good when doing a job is equally as important as the job itself.[42] (See also Chapter 2, "Business Dress and Grooming.")

BUSINESS SOCIALIZING AND ETIQUETTE

Business socializing can be important to your career. Networking with people during business meals and social events can cement relationships; deals are often made during business meals. You would probably be wise to accept all invitations from those of higher rank. In addition, reciprocating invitations is important. However, it is considered inappropriate to invite your supervisor to your home before you have been invited to the supervisor's home. Further, do not invite your supervisor to lunch; let the supervisor initiate the invitation. Socializing outside of the office can increase one's power base which often leads to career advancement. Furthermore, befriending colleagues who seem likely to get promoted is good office politics; they may be able to provide exposure to people who can help your career.[43]

Business lunches provide employees with opportunities for showing their good manners and can, therefore, afford some political edge in the future. Selecting the right restaurant and the right table and ordering appropriate food and beverages are all aspects of the power lunch that contribute to making a favorable impression. Suggestions for making a positive impression at business lunches include eating lightly, ordering foods that can be eaten easily and neatly, and waiting until after the meal to order coffee or hot tea. In addition, order foods in the mid-price range; ordering the most expensive item on the menu is not the mark of a well-mannered person. Remember, it is the host's responsibility to pay the bill and leave the tip; gender is not a consideration. Employees should wait to talk business until the host initiates the discussion, which will usually be at the conclusion of the meal.[44] Additional information on business lunches is included in Chapter 9, "Business Entertaining."

Employees should be aware that in some companies, however, going out for lunch regularly is viewed less impressively than eating at one's desk. To serious-minded executives in such companies, the nonverbal message being conveyed by eating in the office rather than joining friends at a restaurant is that the employee is too busy to spend time eating lunch out.[45]

Using good table manners during business meals can send positive nonverbal messages about a person. On the other hand, poor table manners call attention to the person in a negative way and could block career advancement. Poor table manners give the impression of carelessness about details, and employers know that taking care of details is an important part of business. More specific information on table manners is included in Chapter 8, "Dining Etiquette." When in doubt about correct table manners, it is sometimes advisable to follow the lead of the host. This is not always good advice, however, as the boxed story illustrates.

In addition to dining etiquette, displaying good manners in other situations can project a positive personal and professional image. Networking has become an excellent technique to advance one's career. To make the most of networking situations, be prepared to exchange business cards with those you meet and make follow-up calls to people who gave you ideas or advice. In addition, participate in sports and join clubs and professional associations to expand your network base.[47] Remembering names is important when attending mingling events; address people by name in business

When President Calvin Coolidge invited some of his hometown friends to dine at the White House, some of them expressed concern about their table manners. They decided to simply follow the President's lead. The strategy worked well until coffee was served. When President Coolidge poured his coffee into the saucer, the guests did likewise. When the President added cream and sugar, his guests did, too. Then Coolidge leaned over and placed the saucer on the floor for his cat.[46]

conversations. When conversing with business associates, avoid bringing up topics that characterize you as stingy and overly concerned with money. For example, avoid complaining about the cost of gasoline, the increase in property taxes, or high insurance rates.[48] Other indicators of good manners that convey a positive image include standing for visitors who come by infrequently. In addition, making appointments with persons of higher rank, rather than dropping in unannounced, is the mark of a well-mannered person. Being diplomatic, being sensitive to other people's feelings, and using bias-free language are just as important for people with career aspirations as are dressing appropriately and using proper table manners. Additional ideas are given in Chapter 4, "Social Sensitivity."

In summary, while some employees are comfortable with the game of office politics, others are unwilling to participate in it. Individuals who are uncomfortable with office politics must realize that a certain amount of participation in office politics is necessary for them to receive promotions and get along with supervisors, coworkers, and clients. To reap the rewards to which you are entitled, you would be wise to recognize that working hard and performing well on the job may not be enough to advance in your career. Playing the office politics game, especially in some organizations, could mean the difference between career stagnation and advancement.

4

Social Sensitivity

Being nice doesn't mean acting wimpy. In fact, nice may be the toughest four-letter word you'll ever encounter.[1]

Social sensitivity simply means being sensitive to what is the appropriate thing to do or say in a given situation. Proper behavior for dining, entertaining, and travel, which are planned events, will usually be included in books on etiquette. Some events, however, such as the terrorist acts of September 11, 2001, cannot be anticipated, so how people should behave in these situations will depend largely upon common sense and upon being sensitive to the feelings of others and to the gravity of the event. Businesses and educational institutions who simply conducted business as usual on September 11 were criticized by people in the community for their lack of social sensitivity. Many of these same companies and schools dismiss their employees and cancel classes when snow and ice have been predicted, yet they continued to conduct business as usual during and shortly after the worst terrorist act in the country's history.

Social sensitivity in an office is important to getting work accomplished in a pleasant, harmonious manner. People are going to do things incorrectly occasionally and say things that they later regret; how other employees react to these negative situations can mean the difference between a pleasant or an unpleasant work environment. When only one person behaves in an insensitive manner, other workers may dread coming to work. If we think about how we would like to be treated before responding in a negative situation, we would probably be more socially sensitive and have a better work environment. Social sensitivity should be so deeply ingrained in daily behavior that appropriate reactions become automatic. Supervisors should, of course, set an example of a

Being nice pays off, as one employer found out. A former employee gave $40 million of advertising business to his previous employer because the employer had been nice to the employee when he had been a junior executive in the firm 20 years previously.[2]

social sensitivity. Supervisors who possess social sensitivity are polite, courteous, gracious, considerate, and professional.

Areas of social sensitivity that will be examined are office courtesies, including greetings, introductions, and nonverbal courtesies; behavior toward the disabled; and how to handle office conflict, sexual harassment, and office romances.

OFFICE COURTESIES

Courtesy to fellow employees and visitors is instrumental in conducting business successfully. Courtesy is shown by greeting customers and colleagues and by introducing them when appropriate. Other courtesies include refraining from irritating behaviors, being polite when riding elevators or escalators, and showing deference. Courtesy is just being considerate of others.

People remember when others notice them, speak to them, or spend time with them. While you may think some people are not important, only time will tell who is important and who is unimportant to your career. To be on the safe side, be nice to everyone. Share the credit for a project well done, take your share of the blame when something goes wrong, and offer to help the other people with whom you work. Your colleagues will appreciate your generous, caring attitude and will probably return the favor at a later time. Additional suggestions for getting along with others in the office are included in Chapter 3, "Office Politics."

Greetings and Introductions

The customary U.S. greeting of, "Good morning, how are you?" is a ritualistic greeting; it is not an inquiry into the state of your health. The correct response to the greeting is, "Fine thanks, and how are you?" or "Great! And you?" Greeting strangers, such as a taxi driver or the hotel doorman, with "How are you?" and a friendly nod is not uncommon in the United States. When greeting those you know, you may wish to personalize the greeting by including the person's name: "Good morning, John."[3] People who fail to observe this greeting ritual and simply pass by without speaking are viewed as unfriendly. Sometimes people think that those who do not greet others feel that they are superior. Rank is important in determining who is to initiate the greeting; the person of higher rank speaks first. Impressions are made quickly, so it is important to respond quickly to a greeting and to respond in an upbeat fashion.

The ability to introduce people correctly just takes a little knowledge and practice. First determine which person has the higher rank; be sure you know their correct name and title. The name of the person of higher rank, regardless of age or gender, is mentioned first in introductions. Thus, when introducing the president of the organization to your administrative assistant, say, "Mrs. Smith, I would like for you to meet my administrative assistant, Teresa Gaston. Teresa, this is Mrs. Smith." If people are of equal rank, it does not matter whose name is mentioned first. Nicknames, such as "shorty" or "stretch," are inappropriate in introductions. However, shortened versions of names, such as "Ed" for "Edward," are acceptable. When you forget a person's name, simply admit it or say, "Do you two know each other?" Well-mannered persons will understand the situation and will introduce themselves. The correct response to an introduction is "How do you do?"[4]

When introducing yourself, use both your first and last names but no title, such as "Hello; I'm James Dawson." You may wish to give some additional information about yourself, but this is not necessary. During introductions both men and women stand, smile, and shake hands. While women may choose to remain seated when introduced in social situations, they should stand during business introductions. The U.S. handshake is firm with one or two shakes; eye contact is direct for two or three seconds. Shake hands when meeting someone in an office, when running into someone outside of the office, and when saying good-bye. Handshakes should include the whole hand rather than just the finger tips; a proper handshake should not include sandwiching someone's hand between your two hands. This type of handshake is often viewed as condescending, especially if the person initiating the handshake turns the other person's hand to a horizontal position. While the sandwich handshake is used as a sign of affection in some parts of the country, it is not considered appropriate during business interactions. In office settings, the visitor extends the hand first during greetings. If a person appears to be incapacitated in any way, that person should initiate the handshake. When people are missing a right hand, you would shake their left hand. Hugging people, putting your arm around them, or patting them on the back is not considered appropriate during introductions in the United States.[5]

When no one is available to introduce you, introduce yourself. This is easily done by saying, "I don't believe we've met. I'm Barbara Smith from International Paper." Do not include a title before your name. The other person should reciprocate by giving you his or her first and last names. Do not use a person's first name until you are given permission to do so.[6]

Remembering names is difficult. Some techniques to use are concentrating on the other person, listening carefully to the name, and repeating the name immediately. Other suggestions for remembering names include envisioning the person's name on a billboard or associating the name with a visual image, with someone else that you know, or with other words the name sounds like.[7] While remembering names is difficult for most of us, people appreciate having their name remembered; therefore, it is an important skill to develop.

Nonverbal Courtesies

Nonverbal office courtesies include showing consideration in the use of fragrances, avoiding annoying habits, exhibiting polite behavior on elevators, showing deference, and being considerate when using common areas and office equipment.

Fragrances should be used with discretion; they should not linger after you have left an area. If your fragrance lingers, you have applied it too heavily. Some people are allergic to fragrances; others may become nauseated when the fragrance is too strong. Sometimes fragrances appear to be applied to attempt to cover certain body odors; this technique is rarely effective. Diet may be a culprit in some body odors; garlic and onions tend to stay on the breath and seep out through the pores more than many other foods. Some odors are caused by a disease or medical condition that may require a visit to a doctor.[8]

A habit that is annoying to people in an office is chewing gum. When gum is chewed (outside the office, of course), the mouth should be kept closed; there should be no cracking or popping noises and no blowing of bubbles. Further, the gum should be disposed of properly by wrapping it in a piece of paper and discarding it in a waste basket. Chewing gum in an office is inappropriate; it does not convey an image of professionalism in an office.

Another habit that is equally annoying is the use of tobacco. Most corporations now do not allow tobacco use except outdoors; however, it is not appreciated when smokers hover around the door where others are coming and going.[10]

Correct behavior in elevators is sometimes problematic for people of the United States, because they prefer a lot of space and do not like to touch or to be touched by strangers. Therefore, when U.S. people enter elevators, they face the front and only speak to say "please press 7" or "excuse me" if they accidentally touch someone. Carrying on a conversation in an elevator, unless there are only two of you, is rude. If the elevator is crowded, it is considerate of the people in the front to momentarily step off the elevator so those behind can exit when they reach their floor. Generally, the person nearest to

Most supervisors would no doubt agree with Stewart's concise edict on chewing gum etiquette: "Chewing gum is crass; that is the bottom line. If you must chew, try to confine your activity to the privacy of your own home."[9]

Because we now have gender-free chivalry, it is appropriate for persons of either gender to open a door, help someone put on a coat, or pay for meals. The correct response whenever someone performs an act of chivalry or kindness, whether they are male or female, is "Thank you." Comments such as, "I can do that myself," are rude.

the control panel will hold the "open" button while people exit. When you are waiting to enter the elevator, permit those in the elevator who are getting off to exit before you attempt to enter.[11]

If you are waiting for someone, stand away from the elevator doors so that people do not have to walk around you. Always help the elderly or handicapped who may need assistance getting on or off the elevators. Crowding onto an elevator that is full is impolite. If the elevator doors are closing as you approach, wait for the next one. While the people on the elevator may choose to push the "open" button to allow you to enter, it is also permissible for them to continue to their floors.[12]

Deference is a form of respect that is often nonverbal. Deference is shown by rising when someone important enters the room, being seated at the proper time and in the proper location, and going through doorways in a correct order. It is proper to rise when a visitor enters your office, unless the person is a close colleague, and then rise again when the visitor leaves the office. Junior executives should wait to sit until their senior executives have taken seats or the person in charge of the meeting indicates where they should sit. The first person to reach a door would hold the door open for others; however, those of higher rank should be allowed to pass through first. When a door is held for you, the correct response is "Thank you" after going through the door.[13]

Showing consideration for others who use the common areas in a firm, such as the break room and restrooms, and the common equipment, such as printers and copiers, is important. When using common areas, they should be left clean and neat for the next person to use. Break rooms should have no dirty dishes in the sink and no spoiled food left in the refrigerator. In addition, always make a fresh pot of coffee when you take the last cup. Do not "borrow" other people's food items from the pantry or refrigerator. Restrooms should likewise be left clean. Do not leave the sink area wet. Pick up the paper that has dropped to the floor. Use air fresheners when they are provided. When using common equipment, let the designated person in the office know if a copy machine jams or when it is out of paper so that repairs can be made or the machine replenished with paper before the next person needs to use it. Limit your use of the copier to about five minutes; if you have a large job, stop to let others who have smaller jobs use the machine. Also, if you have put special paper in a copier, remember to remove the remainder before you leave so that the people following you will not waste resources.[14]

DISABLED PERSONS

People are often uncomfortable around those with disabilities; they do not know how to act and, although they may want to be helpful, are unsure of proper etiquette when dealing with the disabled.

Most rules of etiquette related to persons with disabilities require little more knowledge than being polite, helpful, and considerate. Some rules, however, apply specifically to persons with certain disabilities, such as not petting a blind person's guide dog. Other rules are somewhat flexible, depending upon the type of disability and the personality of the disabled person. Here are some guidelines to make you feel more comfortable when interacting with someone with a disability:

- Use the correct terminology; avoid using "handicapped," even though people who mark certain parking spaces for the disabled continue to use the words "handicapped parking." (Is the parking handicapped? Those who insist upon using "handicapped" should at least use correct grammar and say "parking for the handicapped.") Rather than saying someone is "wheelchair-bound," simply say that the person uses a wheelchair. (Actually, "wheelchair-bound" is inaccurate, since the wheelchair gives the person mobility and independence.)

- Do not touch a person's wheelchair, crutches, or anything else used to help that person get around.

- Do not assume that disabled persons need help; they are often comfortable doing things for themselves, including crossing streets or entering elevators. Feel free to offer assistance, but be prepared to have the person thank you and decline your offer.

- When conversing with a person in a wheelchair, try to get down to eye level whenever possible, especially when carrying on a lengthy conversation.

- When you encounter someone with a vision impairment, introduce yourself and those with you. Offer help if you think it is needed, especially if the person has no guide dog. If your assistance is accepted, offer your elbow. As you walk, alert the person to obstacles. Announce your departure when you leave.

- People with hearing impairments often read lips; thus, try to place yourself in a position so that the person can watch you speak. Although you will want to speak slowly and clearly, avoid exaggerating lip movements.

- When conversing with people who have speech impairments, listen patiently; do not finish their sentences when they hesitate. In addition, do not pretend to understand when you do not; paraphrase what you thought the person said and request confirmation.[15]

With the passage of the Americans with Disabilities Act, more disabled persons are in the workplace. However, according to a 1998 survey of Americans with disabilities, only 29 percent of adults who are disabled hold part-time or full-time jobs, in contrast to 79 percent of adults with no disability. Most employers welcome people with disabilities; the disabled persons have often overcome numerous obstacles and faced many challenges. They usually value their jobs, work hard, and have excellent attendance records. The disabled make an important contribution in the workplace and deserve to be afforded the same respect as those who are not disabled.[16]

OFFICE CONFLICT

The word "conflict" has a negative connotation to most people. While it is true that conflict can have negative results, including wasted time and resources, reduced cooperation, and increased stress, conflict can have positive results, such as increased productivity, new ideas, and a better understanding of another person's position. Conflict is part of working with others. People disagree; someone wins, and someone loses. Whether you win or lose, handle it will grace. Maintain a calm, unruffled demeanor.[17]

While certain types of conflict can be helpful, such as when a group is brainstorming about a new idea, other types of conflict are very divisive in an office environment. Conflict in an office may occur for several reasons. For example, many of the codes for appropriate office behavior are not written down but have become part of the corporate culture over the years. Some of these codes of behavior may include being to work on time, maintaining confidentiality, behaving ethically, not asking subordinates to run personal errands for you, asking others if they would like a cup of coffee if you are getting one for yourself, and keeping fund-raising activities to a minimum. Employees who violate these rules of conduct cause conflict in the workplace.[18]

Many times people fail to show respect for their colleagues, or small problems become big problems. If things are not going well at work, it is okay to vent to a spouse, friend, or someone who is not related to your office situation. However, at the office you must find a way to work through the conflict. Put yourself in the other person's shoes and try to see the situation from that person's viewpoint. Conflict makes active listening very important. When discussing the situation with an antagonist, be sure to sit in a neutral position, find a quiet location, encourage the person to share his or her views with you, ask questions to clarify the situation, and keep a clear perspective as to the real importance of the situation.[19]

Other causes of office conflict include employees who do not adhere to the working hours. Breaks, lunch times, and specified starting and ending times, such as 9 to 5, should be observed. If an employee needs time off to handle personal affairs and these requests are infrequent, the supervisor may be happy to give his or her approval. When one person is consistently late or takes more time for breaks or lunch, others will feel they are not being treated fairly. When the behavior continues, other employees will view this as approval and will start taking extra time at breaks or lunch or coming in late as well.

People who have experienced conflict in office settings would probably agree that it is best to try to avoid conflict. In most office situations, conflict can be avoided by arriving early, being honest, admitting when you are wrong, refraining from foul language, and speaking favorably of others. Much of the office conflict could be diffused if people would practice good manners and would use such polite phrases as "thank you" or "I'm sorry" frequently. In addition, conflict can sometimes be avoided by regularly complimenting others when they do a good job. People tend to be ready to give criticism before they give compliments; giving compliments before criticism would be preferable. To be perceived as genuine, compliments should be sincere and specific. Learn how to accept compliments graciously. Do not reject a compliment by saying something negative about what a person said. Simply say, "Thank you; that means a lot to me." Also, learn to laugh at yourself and your mistakes, and others will laugh with you.

Communication is the key to avoiding office misunderstandings. If people would learn to soften their statements, particularly where criticism is involved, more office conflict situations would end up on a friendly, rather than on an unfriendly, basis. When you feel the need to criticize part of what someone has done, say "next time include..." rather than using the word "but." Criticism should also be done in private rather than in front of other people. When criticizing someone, give specific examples to help the person understand what you are suggesting. Changing the criticism to advice will often result in greater acceptance.[20]

How office conflicts are handled will determine if the working relationship can be salvaged or if it is lost forever. Before making a decision to end a working relationship, the decision needs to be made as to whether doing so is feasible or practical. If you have to work or interact with another individual, then you need to maintain a working relationship. Thus, whatever the problem is, it needs to be worked out. Understand that the decision to continue or discontinue the working relationship is yours, and you have to live with it. This is when the golden rule of treating others as we would like to be treated can be very helpful. At the end of the conflict, do not speak badly of the other person and continue to be positive and productive.[21]

SEXUAL HARASSMENT

While unwelcome advances do happen in the businessworld, you should not become paranoid and think that everything someone says is off color. Particularly if someone has been drinking, it is best to joke about the situation rather than make a big issue out of it. While everyone has a sexual orientation, it is not appropriate to discuss, make comments, or ask questions about one's sexual orientation in the work environment.

Because half of the people who are married met at work, sexual harassment can be a "can of worms." While sexual attraction is a natural phenomenon, sexual harassment is not. The best advice is to be very careful; if the other person says "no," respect "no" the first time it is stated. Bosses or supervisors should never ask subordinates out on a date; this invites criticism and may lead to charges of sexual harassment.

Sexual harassment is governed by Title VII of the Civil Rights Act of 1964 and has two forms. The first is Quid Pro Quo, which means "this for that" harassment. The harassee will be given something in return for a date or sexual favors, or the harasser threatens negative consequences if the harassee does not go out on a date or give sexual favors. The second type of harassment is Hostile Environment Claims and can include such things as unwanted flirting, touching, inappropriate comments, gestures, foul language, or comments on one's dress or appearance that are sexually suggestive. While harassers sometimes claim that they were only joking, it is important for everyone to realize that what one person finds humorous can be offensive to others.[22]

Sexual harassment is not only male against female; more cases of female against male are being reported. More homosexual harassment cases are also appearing. Some people have become so defensive about sexual harassment that they do not like to work with members of the opposite gender. If this happens to you, let the person know that you do not appreciate unprofessional comments and suggestive remarks.

The EEOC determines if complaints of sexual harassment are true. Such complaints generally take a long time to be researched and resolved. In many organizations, the Human Resources Department will try to resolve the complaint. Only when the company cannot resolve the complaint satisfactorily or when it does not take the complaint seriously does it go on to the EEOC. The EEOC will ask to see documentation to prove an EEOC case.[23]

Sexist language should be avoided; it includes failure to use the proper terms for men and women. When you say "men," then also use "women"; when you use "ladies," then also say "gentlemen"; and when you use "boys," then also use "girls." The only universal term is "guys," which refers to both men and women. Some titles have been genderized, such as

Use appropriate terminology to avoid suggestions of harassment. Terms of endearment sometimes used with family members and close friends, such as "honey," "baby," and "sugar," should not be used in the workplace. Likewise, assistants should not be referred to as "my girl" or "my boy." Say, "My assistant will call you," not "My girl will call you."[24]

businessman and businesswoman. As this area of genderizing titles is still changing, you will need to be careful about the appropriateness of the titles you use.[25]

If someone inadvertently makes an unwelcome comment and regrets it, an apology is in order. The apology should, of course, be sincere and be followed by no more inappropriate comments. Many times people have come from home or school situations where they were not corrected about such comments. Educate them about the inappropriateness of their comments. If they do not take the hint, take the situation to a member of management. Most unwelcome comments can be handled in a constructive manner without litigation.

Most sexual harassment can be avoided if people conduct themselves professionally at all times, treat others with courtesy, make no allusions to sexual matters, and watch what they wear in the work environment. As with other social sensitivity issues, considering how others may react before you say or do something is a good rule to follow.

OFFICE ROMANCE

Unlike employees who are unwilling targets of someone's romantic or sexual advances, some employees willingly become involved in a romance with a coworker. According to an American Management Association survey, over 40 percent of workers indicated that they have had an office romance; almost a fourth of the 500 supervisors surveyed admitted to having had an office romance. Many employees feel that the office is a good place to find a romantic partner; they maintain that the office is preferable to looking for love in bars and on the Internet. Working together gives both parties an opportunity to get to know each other in a safe environment.[26]

Since office romances are a reality of office life, it is important to establish guidelines for appropriate behavior. Some companies, in fact, have developed written rules for office romances. The first rule is to avoid becoming involved with someone on a different level, especially someone who reports to you. In the event this does happen and you are violating a company policy, it is wise to tell the person to whom you report. This person may be able to help you work out a solution that will be acceptable to the company, such as being transferred to a different division. Otherwise, a choice may have to be made between your job and your loved one.[27] Even romances between two employees on the same level can cause

The consequences of yielding to the temptation of having an affair with someone who is married can be loss of a job or a transfer to some remote location. According to Sue Fox, "There is no etiquette for illicit romances—just sad consequences. Do not do it."[29]

Among companies that have a policy on workplace romances, punishments include: transfers within the firm, 42 percent; termination, 27 percent; counseling, 26 percent; formal reprimand, 25 percent; and demotion, 7 percent. One-fourth have no punishments.[32]

problems. When the romance ends, continuing to work with the person can be rather awkward. An affair with someone who is married can be complicated and create numerous problems that may affect the operation in an office. The office gossips catch on pretty quickly when two employees who are married to other people often have lunch together, spend time together in each other's offices, and leave and return during the day in the same car.[28]

Another guideline for office romances is to be discreet, including arriving for work and leaving at different times. One couple who met at work and later married have continued to drive to work separately. They feel that it emphasizes their desire to keep their personal and professional lives separate.[30] An additional guideline is to avoid public displays of affection; do not send romantic e-mail messages. Finally, do not give each other special privileges. Other employees will notice such favors as longer lunch hours or extra time to complete an assigned project. Since one of the biggest problems with office romances is the perception of favoritism, those who have office affairs will want to be careful to avoid any appearance of favoritism.[31]

In summary, exhibiting socially sensitive behavior toward colleagues makes life more enjoyable for everyone. Although the rules for social sensitivity may not always be clear, people with good manners seem to sense what is appropriate to do or say in certain situations. They know that being known as a considerate, thoughtful, and helpful employee will probably be rewarded at raise and promotion time. As Hal Urban wrote in *Life's Greatest Lessons: 20 Things That Matter,* "I happen to believe that the overwhelming majority of people in the world are law-abiding, loving, and caring. They just don't get any publicity for it. Being good does not make the news."[33]

5

Electronic Communication Etiquette

Every day, it becomes more and more likely that someone's first impression of you will be received electronically. The first impression you make in the electronic world is every bit as important as the one you make in person.[1]

The nature of communication has changed in the twenty-first century. Online meetings, as well as e-mail and text-messaged communication, are replacing personal interactions. Speed and ease of communication are apparently more important than human contact. Some indications of how communication changes have affected behavior are listed in the box on the following page.

The number and complexity of communication tools continue to increase. Businesses use electronic mail, facsimiles, cellular telephones, and pagers in addition to telephones. Despite increased use of electronic communication devices, the telephone continues to be a significant vehicle for communicating in business situations. The human voice is still preferred over any type of written communication.[3]

TELEPHONES

Since about 70 percent of business is conducted over the telephone, good telephone manners are important. Businesses recognize that the manner in which employees communicate via the telephone plays a major role in the impression other people have of the firm. The telephone may be the only link between the company and customers and between

You know you are in the twenty-first century when you:

- Get up each morning and go online before making coffee;
- Use your cell phone upon entering your driveway to call someone inside your home for help with the groceries;
- Experience panic upon realizing that you left your cell phone at home;
- E-mail a business colleague who has the office next to yours; and
- Give as a reason for not staying in touch with family and friends that you do not have their e-mail addresses.[2]

the company and the public. Thus, it is important that proper telephone etiquette be stressed at all levels of an organization.

A major error many employees make is forgetting the rule that people who are visiting in person take precedence over answering a ringing telephone. In a monochronic culture, such as the United States, people do one thing at a time. Thus, answering the telephone when you have a visitor in your office is rude. Exceptions may need to be made occasionally, especially when expecting a call from someone of higher rank. When this happens, apologize to the visitor, answer the phone, explain to the caller that you have a visitor in the office, be brief, and promise to call back.[4]

Before placing a call, it is advisable to make notes about points to be covered. Failure to take this first step can result in the omission of items you had planned to bring up, making it necessary to call again. Keeping a notepad and pen by the telephone to record names, dates, and other pertinent information is recommended.[5]

First impressions are formed by the manner in which people place calls. Identifying yourself is the first step in making a favorable impression. Giving your full name and corporate affiliation is recommended. Callers who ask to talk with a specific person should speak clearly, distinctly, and slowly enough to be understood easily. Starting the conversation usually begins with such pleasantries as "Good afternoon" to avoid giving the impression of being abrupt that would have been conveyed had the caller gotten down to business immediately. If an incorrect number is dialed, it is polite to apologize before hanging up.

Generally speaking, people should place their own calls. Answering the telephone and having someone's assistant say, for example, "Please hold for Miss Lee," sends the nonverbal message that the caller's time is more important than the person who answered and is sufficiently irritating to cause some people to simply hang up. When asked to place a call for someone else, such as your supervisor, it is important to realize that this is a potentially negative situation and should make certain that the person will be ready to talk as soon as the telephone is answered.

Making the person on the other end of the line wait while you locate your supervisor is rude.[6] When it is necessary for one person to wait, proper etiquette dictates that a person outside the organization who is of lower rank be put on the line first; however, when placing a call to someone whose rank is equal to or greater than your supervisor, the supervisor should be on the line before the other person is called to the telephone.

Promptness in answering the telephone is just as important as identifying yourself. Giving your first and last name, as well as your position title or department, is helpful. Playing the game of "guess who you are talking to" is inefficient, time consuming, and bad manners. Making a good impression on the telephone also includes listening carefully, projecting courtesy, and being discreet in giving out information. When the person requested by the caller is unavailable, avoid saying, "I'm sorry, Mr. Sorrells is not available. Apologizing when someone is out of the office is unnecessary. Save the apologies for times when they are appropriate, such as when an error has been made in a customer's order. Rather than apologizing, simply say, "Mr. Sorrells is out of the office until May 7. How can I be of help?"[7] If the person receiving the call must look for information the caller has requested, the caller should be given the option of being called back later or being placed on hold. Callers who choose to be placed on hold should be given feedback on the progress of the search at frequent intervals and again given a choice of continuing to hold. For example, "We're still looking for the sales figures for last year. Would you like to continue to hold, or shall I call you back later?" Avoid such slang expressions as "Hang on." Before placing someone on hold, keep in mind that it tops the list of things that irritate people when conversing by telephone.[8] Companies should consider carefully whether to entertain callers who are waiting with music; some callers are annoyed, especially if they do not like the choice of music, while others seem to like it. Asking callers whether they prefer music or silence while they wait is considerate.[9]

Just as the beginning of the telephone call is essential to making a positive initial impression, closing the call appropriately is important to leaving a favorable final and often lasting impression. Remember, the one who places the telephone call should be the one who ends it. However, avoid closing the call too abruptly as this leaves the caller feeling annoyed or disappointed. The person ending the call usually signals to the other person that the conversation is coming to a close. Effective phrases for closing a call include, "Thanks for calling," "I appreciate your call," "It was nice talking with you," or "You have answered all my questions; thanks so much."[10] Ending with "Good-bye" is preferable to ending with some trite phrase, such as "Have a nice day." Another point of etiquette is that if you are disconnected during the telephone call, it is the responsibility of the one who made the call initially to place another call.

Michelle, who owned a small gift shop, was usually very friendly to customers and greeted them on the telephone and in person with warmth and enthusiasm. One day, however, she was abrupt and curt on the telephone to Greg, one of her regular customers. When Greg commented about her behavior, Michelle said, "I'm just too busy to be nice to anyone today." Greg did not call back; Michelle's gift shop eventually closed.[11]

Additional guidelines for all users of business telephones include speaking at a moderate rate, avoiding slang or terms of affection, limiting personal telephone calls during working hours, and smiling before placing or receiving telephone calls. A smile can be heard; it changes the voice tone and conveys friendliness. Finally, always be nice, regardless of how hectic the day may be.

SPEAKERPHONES

Speakerphones are very useful for bringing people together when it is not possible for them to get together physically. Speakerphones are also a good choice when you wish to bring others into the conversation. However, many people do not like to engage in a conversation with someone using a speaker phone. The nonverbal message is that the person using a speaker phone is too busy to devote full time to talking on the phone and is doing something else while talking. The first rule for using speakerphones is to ask permission before placing a person on speakerphone. When people object to the speaker phone, they may certainly say so and ask that the speaker phone not be used. The person who initiates the conference call on a speakerphone should introduce other participants; the reason for making introductions is that it is rude to listen in on conversations when others do not know you are listening. Participants should identify themselves each time they speak since recognizing voices is difficult because of sound distortion that is characteristic of speakerphones. In addition, when someone has to leave the call for any reason, that person should notify the others both when they leave and when they return. Speakerphones should be used in moderation since many people find them offensive.[12]

CELLULAR TELEPHONES AND PAGERS

Cellular (or wireless) telephones, once associated with affluence, power, and would-be players, have become commonplace for both personal use and business use. While cell phones are certainly a convenience, they are also a source of irritation. In one U.S. survey, 70 percent of those polled identified speaking loudly on a cell phone in public as a major irritant. Other rude behaviors identified were using cell phones in restaurants, meetings, movies, concerts, museums, and places of worship.[13]

Cell phones have been described as adult pacifiers. People who are glued to their cell phones and who apparently view them as a necessary wardrobe accessory seem to think they are "connected to a vital source of informational nourishment." Those who are the loudest and most ostentatious when using cell phones are typically people who are insecure and/or boastful.[18]

Using a cell phone while dining out is especially rude; it sends the nonverbal message that the person you are conversing with who is not there is more important than your guest who is there. In some restaurants, customers must leave their cell phones with the *maître d'*, who will inform them should they receive a call. When taking a call, leaving the dining area is expected.[14] Using a cell phone during business meetings and in public places such as movies and concerts is inappropriate; their usage in such situations is viewed as both intrusive (intruding on the space or sensitivity of another person in an annoying manner) and obtrusive (calling attention to oneself in a negative way). Using cell phones in places of worship is especially rude. In fact, Glassman suggests that using wireless phones in places of worship will "guarantee you a ride on the express to hell."[15] Using phones while driving is not only inappropriate but also unsafe. Carrying on a conversation on the telephone can distract the driver and increase the chances of an accident. In fact, a 1998 Canadian study found that those who talk on car phones greatly increase their likelihood of being involved in an accident.[16] In addition, car phones should not be used when conducting business, such as when using the drive-through window at a bank or a fast-food restaurant.[17]

To combat the rude behavior of cell phone users, many businesses are posting such reminders as "Please do not use cell phones or other electronic devices" or "Silence is golden." Quiet areas have been designated by airline clubs, and Amtrak has designated "Quiet Cars," where passengers may not use cell phones or other electronic devices and must speak in a low voice. International travelers may encounter "Quiet Cars" when riding on trains in other countries as well. Offenders will usually be reminded by fellow travelers. When the reminders do not work, the conductor will escort the offender to another car.[19]

In summary, cell phone courtesy involves following these guidelines: Use a standard ring tone—quirky ring tones are annoying; do not take or make calls during funerals, sports events, job interviews, worship services, classes, restaurants, courtrooms, and public events; avoid taking or making calls when in someone's company; be courteous to people around you by refraining from discussing personal matters when in earshot of others; keep your voice low; avoid making or taking calls while driving; and avoid confronting rude cell phone users—when it is necessary, admonish them diplomatically.[20]

Pagers or beepers, when used in inappropriate places, are also sources of annoyance to others. People who use pagers or beepers should remember to turn them off in public places. Fortunately, noisy pagers are now being replaced by ones with several alert options—a light, silent vibration or a low-volume tone. Use of silent vibration is preferable in meetings and public places; this provides voice mail and numeric or alpha messages. An alphanumeric beeper provides the entire message so that the recipient can determine if the call is an emergency. When the message is urgent, leaving the meeting quietly to avoid being disruptive is recommended.[21]

ANSWERING MACHINES AND VOICE MAIL

Positive or negative messages are conveyed by your use of answering machines or voice mail. For example, leaving a message asking the person to return the call without including your telephone number is indicative of a person lacking in social skills (or perhaps a person who is forgetful).

To convey a positive impression when recording a greeting for your business phone, keep it short; include your full name, the company name, and a request that the caller leave his or her name, company affiliation, telephone number, and a brief message. Negative impressions are often conveyed when recorded outgoing messages use humor or when messages state the obvious, such as saying "no one is available to take your call."[22] Before leaving the office for a few days, such as when going on vacation or making a business trip, it is advisable to change the recorded greeting to something like, "This is Jay Hutchings. I'll be out of the office until Thursday, July 19. Please call back then or call Rick Cole at extension 2140 if you need to speak to someone before I return."[23]

A couple in the market to buy a house called the realtor and heard this taped message: "We're not here right now, so leave your name and number after the beep." The realtor stated the obvious, failed to identify herself, and left a message that was curt as well as incomplete. Two days later the realtor returned the call and left this message: "This is Julie; call me at 385-4881." The realtor's lack of electronic manners made the potential buyers decide not to call back.[24]

When you leave a message, give your name, telephone number, and date and time of the call followed by a brief message that includes the purpose of the call. Remember to speak slowly. The message should be short and specific. "Please call me at 901-678-2884 to confirm our meeting at 10 A.M. August 10" is more specific than "Please call me at 901-678-2884 when you come in." End the message by repeating your telephone number.[25] State your name and number slowly; it is very difficult to understand numbers and names that are spoken rapidly.

When he realized he has just sent an e-mail message to his assistant who was seated near him, the CEO of a Georgia firm launched "no e-mail Fridays." Overdependence on e-mail at this company was associated with lower productivity and possibly with lower sales. Thus, the 275 employees were instructed to meet in person or talk with each other on the telephone on Fridays and to reduce e-mail usage on other days. Another CEO of a Chicago-based group also instructed his 350 staff members to curb e-mail usage and directed them to use e-mail only "to send a large document to read, or when written communication is absolutely necessary."[27]

ELECTRONIC MAIL (E-MAIL)

Electronic mail usage has increased to the point that it has almost replaced letters and memorandums in many organizations. This increased usage has raised new concerns related to proper usage of this popular form of communication.

When used correctly, e-mail increases productivity and eliminates telephone tag. E-mail users agree that this form of communication is fast and convenient and is an effective means of giving updates on current activities and assignments to colleagues and supervisors.[26] Excessive use and abuse of e-mail, however, has caused some companies to institute new policies related to its usage.

E-mail users should question how their personal relationships have been affected by excessive use of e-mail and should voluntarily decrease their e-mail exchanges and increase their personal interactions with their colleagues without waiting for their organizations to initiate rules to eliminate e-mail abuse.

When e-mail is used improperly, it can convey negative impressions ranging from a lack of professionalism to social insensitivity or tarnished credibility. Because both positive and negative impressions are formed via e-mail, using proper etiquette for sending messages is essential.[28]

A problem e-mail users report is the huge volume of unwanted messages. People experiencing this problem should tell offenders that the company has instructed employees to limit personal e-mail or should at least ask these persons to limit such messages. Another e-mail problem includes the writer's inattention to such basics of writing as spelling, punctuation, and word usage, which can damage credibility. The conclusion that will be drawn by the reader is that the sender is not well educated and/or has poor language skills. No one should aspire to being considered a *netwit* (a term presumably coined from network dimwit).

A graduate student at a Southern university sent the following e-mail message to his professor canceling an appointment: "I will be unable to make our 4:30 appointment this afternoon. Sorry for the incontinence."

In addition to checking spelling, grammar, and punctuation, the following additional guidelines are recommended to convey a positive image when communicating via e-mail:

- Use a separate account for personal and business e-mails; do not choose an e-mail address that may be considered offensive or that may reflect negatively on your professionalism.
- Honor the requests of colleagues, friends, and family members that no personal e-mails be sent to their work address.
- Check e-mail messages at least once a day; checking in the morning and again in the afternoon is recommended.
- Reply to e-mail messages within twenty-four hours, which is the same guideline for replying to telephone and other types of messages. When a request for information will require some research, reply to the e-mail and explain that you will send the information within a certain period of time.
- Include a subject line and make it as detailed and specific as possible; "Attached Agenda for June 14 Sales Meeting" is more specific than "Tomorrow's Meeting." Change the subject line when you reply to the writer on a different subject.[29] Resist the temptation to vent in a subject line: "You're an Idiot, Idiot! Get me off this list!"[30]
- Avoid the use of emoticons (a term formed by merging the words "emotion" and "lexicon," which is used for communicating emotions, such as ☺) and communicons (communication icons, such as BTW for "by the way" and FWIW meaning "for what it's worth") in business communications. While emoticons are intended to express humor, most people agree that humor in written communication simply does not work well. Their occasional use may not be annoying, but their repeated use in business communications is viewed as childish and immature; limit their use to personal messages. Commonly used emoticons are :-D (I'm laughing), ;-((I'm sad), and :-O (I'm surprised). When they are used, avoid creative emoticons, such as :*) for "I'm drunk" and the one humorist Dave Barry created to represent a woman who is not pleased with her breast enlargement surgery, :-{8.[31] An alternative to using emoticons is to state the emotion you wish to convey, i.e., "I'm just being sarcastic." However, for more formal business e-mail messages, avoiding jokes or sarcasm entirely is recommended.[32]
- Avoid keying the message in all capital letters as this denotes shouting (but do not key in all lowercase letters either); to emphasize a word or phrase, place it in asterisks (*...*). Also avoid flaming, which is sending personal insults, and spamming, which is sending unwanted messages.
- Address the receiver by name in the first sentence to personalize the message; when the message is going to several people, use "greetings" or something more informal, such as "Hi, Folks."
- Keep messages short but do not be abrupt; limit the length to two screens.
- Use quotation marks when quoting excerpts from the original message or other sources.

Pet peeves of e-mail users:

- Employees who resign via e-mail rather than facing the supervisor.
- People who use eighteen emoticons in one message.
- Signature footers longer than the body of the e-mail.
- Using too many exclamation marks—"That's so funny!!!!!!"
- Subject lines which are pointless—"Hi!"[36]

- Send attachments only with the receiver's permission or upon request; problems accessing attachments can be frustrating. In addition, the risk of infection by a virus makes some users hesitant to open them. Always warn users when the attachment is large by stating in the message the length and approximate download time. Rather than sending information as an attachment, some people prefer that the entire message be placed in the text.[33]

- Think carefully before forwarding a message. Remember that the contents of the message legally belong to the writer, not the recipient. Forwarding a message without the writer's permission is in violation of the copyright law.[34]

- Use the "Reply All" function with discretion. Sometimes only one person requires a response, not everyone on the distribution list.

- Avoid including confidential information or anything embarrassing or rude in e-mail messages; in addition, do not use e-mail for sending negative messages, such as a colleague's failure to get a promotion.

- Do not send newsletters, unsolicited advertisements, and announcements unless given permission to do so by the intended recipient.

- Use the "Out-of-Office" feature to notify others of a planned absence from the office.

- Include your signature at the end of messages; limit the signature footer to four lines; include your name and title, organization, and Internet address—street address and phone number may also be included.

- Avoid such sources of frustration as forgetting to include attachments, sending chain letters or virus hoaxes, and failing to delete messages so that a would-be sender encounters a full e-mail box.[35]

BLACKBERRY DEVICES

A BlackBerry device is a wireless PDA (personal digital assistant); this handheld device can send and receive e-mail and is also used to browse the web over a cellular network. Some BlackBerry models function as cell phones as well. This device has become very popular for mobile professionals.

The rules for polite behavior for use of a BlackBerry are the same as those for using cell phones and e-mail. Checking e-mail or phone messages on your BlackBerry while in a meeting or during an interview is impolite; those near you will probably take offense (and should). When the BlackBerry is placed on the table, people seated near you may be distracted by the vibration alerting you to the arrival of mail. Full attention should be given to the meeting or interview activities, not to electronic devices. BlackBerry devices are best left in the office; however, under certain circumstances, such as when waiting for important information, they may be brought to a meeting. In such cases, the person chairing the meeting should be alerted ahead of time that you may need to leave the meeting briefly; apologizing for the possible interruption is expected.[37]

FACSIMILE (FAX) TRANSMISSIONS

Although fax transmissions are still an important part of business today, they are used less frequently than e-mail. Faxes are useful in certain situations, such as for sending copies of drawings and drafts of brochures. In addition, they are useful in international communication where time is a main consideration and when written documentation is required. This method of message transmission can, however, be a source of irritation when used improperly, such as sending a lengthy report or a document printed on textured paper, which leaves black marks during the transmission process, making the message difficult to read.

The following guidelines for using fax communication are important to making a positive impression:

- Keep facsimile transmission short, usually fewer than five pages; when it is necessary to send lengthy documents, choose a time when the fax machine is not busy.

- Include a cover sheet that contains such information as name, telephone number, fax number, date, and number of pages (with the cover sheet counted as the first page). Some companies include a confidentiality notice on the first page. When a cover sheet is not necessary, a note with your name and telephone number may be placed on the first page of the document.

- Send clear copies on white paper; handwritten notes should be written in dark ink as pencil marks and light-colored inks are often too light to read.

- Photocopy documents that have been printed on colored paper or paper with a texture before faxing them; sometimes the colors darken considerably making the copy difficult to read, and textured paper may result in black markings throughout the document—both colors and textures make transmissions slower and costlier. In addition, photocopy documents on which correction fluid was used, as the areas on which the correction fluid was used transmit as a blotch and are not readable.

- Avoid sending confidential information; when it is necessary, include a cover sheet and write the word "confidential" across the sheet. As an added precaution, you may wish to telephone the intended recipients prior to sending the fax so that they will be nearby to receive the transmission containing confidential information.

- Call intended recipients to notify them of the intended fax transmission; the transmission should follow within fifteen minutes (this courtesy is especially important for people who have fax machines that share a phone line with a telephone).
- Notify the sender when the message is received (when the recipient does not confirm receipt of the fax within a short time, the sender may call to verify the message was received).
- Keep a copy of fax transmissions in case they are needed later to confirm that they were sent.[38]

In addition to not sending confidential information by fax, other practices to avoid are sending one copy and asking the recipient to make and distribute copies; sending advertisements for wide distribution; and sending such inappropriate messages as letters of appreciation, apology, condolence, or those containing negative information, such as news of a plant closing or company downsizing.[39] In addition, faxing a résumé is not recommended. Some companies not only tell applicants not to fax their résumés but actually throw away faxed résumés. Human resources personnel have even discarded mailed résumés from candidates who had disobeyed the no-fax rule.[40]

Impressions made electronically are just as important and lasting as those made in person. In fact, some would argue that electronic impressions are even more critical because of the lack of human contact. Use of proper manners when communicating electronically can ensure that your interactions will leave a favorable impression on customers, coworkers, subordinates, and supervisors. The person who observes such rude, inappropriate behavior as using a cell phone in a meeting may be in a position to promote or demote; thus, being considerate and well mannered when using the telephone, e-mail, and other forms of electronic communication can be important to career advancement.[41]

6

Manners for Special Occasions and Events

After three to five years on the job, there's less willingness to show concern, assist others, or even to act in a welcoming manner. We surmise that people just become more task-oriented and set in their ways.—Wayne Nemeroff, CEO, PsyMax.[1]

The special events of life are often celebrated in an office environment. People spend a great deal of time in the office, and social relationships help develop balance between work and play. According to David Zelman of Transitions Institute, we may "lose the sense of equilibrium that keeps us afloat and leads to feeling forever trapped on the treadmill" if we do not learn to step back from the work environment and socialize.[2] While some workplaces are very structured, others are unstructured and spontaneous; it is important to be able to decipher the workplace structure when dealing with special occasions and events.[3] Since people often feel less than confident in social/business situations, learning the intricacies of appropriate behavior when celebrating special occasions and events with coworkers and supervisors is important. How you interact during these social events can help make or break your career.[4]

BIRTHS AND BIRTHDAYS

Since many firms have written directives about birth and birthday celebrations on company time, it is important to check the guidelines of your company to make sure that your planned celebration is consistent with company policies. After all, births and birthdays are personal events,

After the arrival of one employee's daughter, the company held her position open for six months. Then after the employee and baby came home from the hospital, fellow employees sent her a beautiful pink blanket. The employee was impressed by the thoughtfulness of her supervisor and other people in her company.

and some businesses prefer that such celebrations be held at a location other than the company premises.

Baby showers are sometimes given to celebrate the arrival of an employee's child. The shower is typically given two to three months before the baby is due. In the past, only women were invited to showers; however, this tradition seems to be changing to include men. In most companies, baby showers are not given on the premises during work hours; baby showers should preferably be scheduled after work hours at a local restaurant or at a friend's home. If you are hosting the shower, you may wish to suggest to the mother-to-be that she register at a local department store or baby store so that guests will select gifts that she really needs. Appropriate gifts for the birth of a child are gifts such as rattles, bracelets, or other items that can be engraved with the name and birth date of the child. Other nice gifts include photograph albums or savings bonds. If the office is collecting funds for a large gift, then a stroller, a changing table, or some other large piece of baby furniture makes a nice gift.[5]

Milestone birthdays of business associates should generally be recognized. If you are a fellow employee, a card is sufficient; however, if you are the supervisor, then a small gift (under $25) would also be appropriate with the card. If you are friends in addition to being colleagues, you may wish to take your friend out for lunch in addition to sending a birthday card.[6] Sometimes the entire office may go together to buy a gift for the birthday person, especially if the birthday is considered a major milestone, such as forty, fifty, or sixty. Respecting the wishes of the person celebrating a birthday is important. Some workers enjoy receiving special attention; others are uncomfortable with such celebrations. An office tradition that is popular in some companies is to celebrate all birthdays within a month with one celebration on perhaps the last Friday afternoon of each month. Refreshments for these birthday parties often consist of cake and coffee or soft drinks.

A group of young secretaries decided to celebrate the nineteenth birthday of one of their new colleagues by taking her to a local restaurant. Everyone at the table was over twenty-one except for the honoree. The server appeared to be embarrassed after asking one of the secretaries who was twenty-four for identification before she would serve her wine and ended up serving wine to everyone at the table, including the 19-year-old birthday girl!

ILLNESSES AND INJURIES

When someone in the office is ill or has been injured, it is helpful to keep the person informed about what is happening at the office. Above all, be sympathetic and try to help the person. Your help could be offering to shop for groceries, providing transportation to doctors' appointments, picking up medications, feeding or walking a pet, or taking office work to the person if he or she is able to work.[7]

For people who are seriously injured or terminally ill, be sure to stay in contact with them. Continue to visit them and try to be upbeat and positive. Do not, however, say that they look great if they do not or continue to assure them that they will be fine when you both know that this is untrue. Resist the temptation to tell about other people you know who have had the same disease or injury, especially if the person did not survive. Follow the sick or injured person's lead in discussing the illness or injury.[8] The closer you are to the ill or injured person, the easier it is to talk openly about the situation. Some people, however, will not want to talk about their condition; others discuss their illness or injury openly and will appreciate someone who listens. Send cards and notes to assure them that you care and are thinking of them.[9] Before sending cards, be sure to read them carefully. They should be cheerful and uplifting and make the person feel good. Write a personal note of encouragement. Communicating with someone who is incapacitated is very important even if the person does not feel well enough to receive visitors.[10]

HOSPITAL ETIQUETTE

Hospital etiquette guidelines when you are the patient start with preparation before you check in. Check your insurance policy to make certain you are familiar with the hospitalization coverage your policy provides. In addition, married women should be sure to use the name used on the policy when checking into the hospital to avoid the unnecessary confusion that would result if you have used your maiden name at the doctor's office and your married name is on the policy. Bring appropriate clothing, including a bathrobe and slippers, as well as toiletries and cosmetics. Packing magazines, books, a pen, stationery, stamps, and an address book is also recommended. Do not bring jewelry, but you may want to bring cash for purchasing small items, such as the morning newspaper.[11]

If you are sharing the room with another patient, be considerate about limiting your telephone conversations, keeping the television/radio volume low, and asking visitors to speak in a low voice. Observe all hospital rules, including limits on the number of visitors permitted in the room at one time.[12]

Patients should remember to express their appreciation to nurses who cared for them when they leave. A platter of cookies or bowl of fruit that can be shared by all nurses is an appropriate gift; a gift certificate to the local deli will also be appreciated. Writing a note of appreciation to the nurses is a nice gesture as well.

Before you visit someone in the hospital, call ahead to find out the hospital's visiting hours and to make sure that visitors are welcome. A majority of hospitals prefer that patients have only one or two visitors at a time. Short stays of ten to fifteen minutes are appreciated; shorter visits are recommended when it is apparent that the patient is not well enough to carry on a conversation. If a doctor or nurse enters while you are visiting, step out into the hall to allow them privacy. Watch the level of your voice as there are other sick people around who need rest. When calling on the telephone someone who is in the hospital, keep the conversation short unless the patient indicates a desire to continue to talk. Ask the patient if there is anything you may bring to the hospital. When in doubt, ask someone in the family about the appropriateness of food items. A gift of a box of chocolate candy, for example, would be inappropriate for a patient who can eat no solid foods. Be careful about floral arrangements and plants, as many hospital rooms have neither the space to accommodate them nor the personnel to care for them. Another thing to consider before selecting flowers is the allergic reactions that some flowers trigger. Visitors should also remember that flowers are not allowed in the Intensive Care Unit of a hospital.[13]

Other considerations when visiting someone in the hospital are the gender and rank of the patient and visitor. A female assistant should question whether it is appropriate to visit her male supervisor when he is in the hospital. Her male boss, who is usually in a position of power and strength when in the office, is now in a vulnerable, weak position and is scantily clad. Likewise, a male colleague may feel uncomfortable visiting a female colleague who is connected to numerous tubes, one of which is attached to a highly visible bag that collects body waste.

HOLIDAY AND OFFICE PARTIES

Company parties, especially during the holidays, are times to share the positives of the year and forget the negatives. These social events that involve the entire company should be limited to one or two a year and should be rather short. When you are invited, make an attempt to attend. Be sure to talk to everyone, and try to greet everyone by name. If you cannot remember someone's name, just say "I think we have met before," then reintroduce yourself. Conversation topics should not be controversial or sensitive. Appropriate topics include a new book or movie, sports, or other light subject matter; stay away from discussions about politics, religion, or work-related problems. Since this is a good opportunity to make connections and to get to know people from other departments, take advantage of these opportunities to socialize. A good

A Nashville firm invited its two summer interns, Michelle and Donna, to the annual Labor Day picnic by the pool of one of the executives. Michelle's mentor had advised her to have only one alcoholic drink at the picnic; Donna received no advice. Employees, including upper management, drank too much; many jumped into the pool fully clothed. Donna had several drinks, danced on the diving board, and was sick in the Jacuzzi. Michelle, who had followed her mentor's advice, received a call on Tuesday morning from the president of the firm offering her a permanent position upon her graduation; Donna received no offer of employment.[15]

handshake, nice smile, and interest in the other person go a long way toward successful interactions and will be noticed by others. While it may be difficult to speak to people you do not know, a company party is the perfect place to make a special effort to do so. Getting to know others on a social basis can be very helpful to career advancement. Even though excellent food and a wide variety of drinks are usually provided, be sure to spend more time socializing than eating or drinking.[14]

While office parties can help us connect, build bridges, and develop balance in our lives, they can also lead people down the road to unemployment or unpromotability. Never drink too many alcoholic beverages at these events as this leads to problems with boisterous, loud, and inconsiderate behavior as well as a loss of credibility and respect. Drinking too much is probably the most common and most damaging offense at office parties. When people have too much to drink, they lose control; once control has been lost and things have been done or said that are harmful to others or to your own career, the damage can rarely be reversed.

In addition to excessive drinking, dressing and behaving inappropriately have contributed to the negative reputation of many office parties. Attire should be conservative; women should avoid wearing revealing or provocative clothing. If the event is casual or formal, dress accordingly. The corporate culture should be considered when choosing party attire.[16] Avoid all appearance of inappropriate behavior. Do not flirt with co-workers or supervisors, provide impromptu entertainment, or leave the party with someone who could bring your reputation into question.

Many companies have discontinued their office parties largely due to excessive consumption of alcohol, employees who became belligerent and out of control, or lawsuits due to accidents by employees on the way home from the party. Instead, some firms are now giving employees a half-day off for holiday shopping, donating money to charity, or having a picnic in the summer for the families rather than a holiday party for just employees or employees and spouses. It is important that all members of senior management attend the party and stay until its conclusion. Senior management members need to enjoy themselves and take part in any

The president of a corporation showed up for ten minutes at the office Christmas party. He did not accept a drink or eat any food. He explained to several people standing nearby that he would have to leave to attend his child's soccer match. After the president left, discussions began quickly about his short stay and about other key personnel who were missing. Employees were not impressed by the lack of corporate response.

activities that are happening at the party. If entertainment is scheduled, it should be quality entertainment.[17]

Be sure that significant others or spouses are invited before bringing them to company social affairs. Children are never to be brought to company parties. Company parties are good for building morale; however, it is possible to have too many events in a year. Events should be well thought out and planned so that they are meaningful to the employees who are attending.

Giving and receiving gifts at holiday times is covered in Chapter 4, "Social Sensitivity."

WEDDINGS AND WEDDING ANNIVERSARIES

Employees should not be surprised if they do not receive a wedding invitation to an associate's wedding or to his or her child's wedding as many people prefer to keep their work and personal lives separate. Also, when fellow employees do not know the child personally, they may feel that sending an invitation is primarily a request for a gift. You can, of course, choose to send a gift whether you are invited or not.[18]

If you are invited to colleague's wedding, reply to the invitation promptly. Buy an appropriate gift, and have it shipped to the address on the invitation. Today many web sites are set up to do this automatically for you. Most brides sign up at bridal registries at local stores or on web sites. Using the registries helps to prevent duplications and assures the buyer that the couple will receive items that they would really like to have. It is also permissible to give the couple money. Gifts of money should be accompanied by a token gift, such as a crystal bud vase or picture frame. Do not bring gifts to the wedding. Remember that the invitation will be addressed to those who are invited; do not assume that it is acceptable to bring a guest unless the invitation specifically states that a guest is also invited.[19]

If you are the one sending out invitations, include a stamped, addressed envelope and return card that can be marked and mailed indicating the number of people who will be attending the wedding and reception. The guest should not be expected to pay postage to return enclosure cards. While receiving money as a gift is permissible, it is not proper to include a request for gifts of money with the invitation.

Anniversaries are generally celebrated with family and friends at the mile-marker dates such as the twenty-fifth or fiftieth anniversary. Because people generally do not need anything at this point in their marriage, friends and family may pool their resources to purchase a vacation trip for the couple or for a special gift, such as a nice set of luggage, if a trip has already been planned.[20] Many couples will request that guests bring no gifts to their party.

BUSINESS RECEPTIONS, CONVENTIONS, AND TRADE SHOWS

Business receptions for customers or work associates need to have a work plan. If you are responsible for the event, start early. First, make a note of all details: how many people are expected to attend, where the event will be held, whether it is casual or formal, and the amount of the budget that has been allocated. Next, prepare a time line and lists of assignments, vendors you plan to use, and contingency plans.[21] Be sure key people are in open areas of the room so that the doorways are not jammed with people wanting to talk to key personnel. Business receptions should have a start and stop time.

A corporation was having a 100-Year Anniversary Party and decided to have a girl pop out of a fake cake as part of the entertainment. When it came time for the girl to pop out of the cake, there was no girl. No one had rehearsed that part of the program to see if the girl could fit through the top of the cake; you guessed it, she couldn't!

During business receptions, have plenty of business cards to hand out and follow up on the business cards you receive. People generally discuss business opportunities during these business receptions.[22] If there are going to be boardroom-type meetings, agendas should be prepared and reviewed before the meetings. If presentations are going to be made at meetings or meals, these should be rehearsed and outlined so that the person making them does not ramble and give the impression of being unprepared. If you are in charge of introducing a speaker, find out about the speaker prior to the event so that you can introduce the person properly.[23] Additional information is included in Chapter 10, "Meeting and Conference Etiquette," and Chapter 11, "Presentations," concerning the proper etiquette in these situations.

During business receptions, it is important to talk with everyone, not just the people with whom you are comfortable. To break the ice, simply introduce yourself to someone, extend your hand for a handshake, and ask a simple question about a product or make a comment about the food at the buffet or one of the presentations. Be sure to give your full attention when speaking to people; it would be rude to have your eyes wandering

At a large industry convention, the chief executive of a major automotive manufacturer was scheduled to give the keynote address. The executive chose to fly the morning of the presentation. When the airline cancelled the flight and there were no other options for him to arrive on time, he had to call and cancel. As a planner, you need to be prepared for such events. Whenever possible, of course, it is preferable to have a keynote speaker arrive the night before the presentation.

around the room or to be looking at your BlackBerry rather than giving eye contact to the other person. Since these are business meetings, you will probably be asked about your company or your company's products. Have some answers ready, and be sure you do not divulge confidential information.[24]

Because many of these events take place away from the office and often in other cities, a partying atmosphere develops after hours. Remember that whatever happens after hours, as well as what happens during the event, will find its way back to the office.[25] Being on time for opening ceremonies, for transportation taking you to events, and for meetings is important. Being late is disruptive and makes you and your company be viewed as less than professional. During most of these events, you will be asked to wear a name tag. Place the name tag on the right side about four inches below your shoulder.[26]

If the event includes a meal, consult other members of the group about what courses they would like to order before you place your order. All people at the table should order the same number of courses; it is rude to expect others to wait while you eat an appetizer or dessert when no one else ordered those courses. Likewise, if you have special dietary considerations, call the restauranteur ahead of time to find out what items on the menu fit your diet requirements. Generally, at business meals the meal is eaten before business discussions commence; however, it is important to follow the lead of a senior person at the meal. Indicate that you are to be given the bill by making a comment such as, "I would like my guests to order first." This will alert the server as to who is responsible for paying for the meal.[27]

Generally, if spouses have been invited to conventions, they are expected to entertain themselves during the day and perhaps some of the evenings. However, if the company has sponsored events for spouses, the spouses should participate. They should, of course, follow the same rules of good manners that are expected of the employees, including not overindulging in food or alcoholic beverages.[28]

PROMOTIONS AND RETIREMENTS

In some organizations, the person receiving a promotion, especially to a position of high responsibility, will have a party to celebrate the event with those in the organization who have played a role in his/her advancement. Such celebrations may be formal or informal depending upon the nature of the promotion and the type of party the person being promoted enjoys. When entertainment is part of the festivities, appropriate ideas include a review of the person's career using a slide show, anecdotes from colleagues, and photographs of highlights of the person's career leading up to the current promotion.[29]

Retirements may or may not be celebrated with a party depending upon the individual's preferences and the circumstances. Some employees look forward to retirement and welcome having a party to celebrate the event. Others prefer to retire quietly, especially if some unpleasant situation is associated with the retirement. Check with the retiree or with a close friend or family members before planning a big celebration. Even when no party is planned, employees who have been with the company for a number of years, such as thirty or forty years, should be given a card and group gift. The amount of money spent on the gift should be consistent with the number of years of service. Checking with a close friend or spouse before choosing a gift is recommended. Some ideas for gifts for a retiree include sports equipment for sports enthusiasts, music lessons for those who have expressed a desire to learn to play a musical instrument, gift certificates for visits to local spas or health clubs, a nice piece of crystal, computer equipment or accessories, an album containing letters of remembrance from colleagues, anything related to the retiree's hobby, or a charitable donation. Many times the company, in addition to the department, will present a retirement gift.[30]

It is proper for the firm to send out promotion and retirement announcement cards to keep people inside and outside the firm informed.[31] The retiree may wish to send postcards to business colleagues with whom he or she would like to keep in touch; postcards would include the home address, phone number, and e-mail address. The card can be informal and humorous. Retirees should never criticize the person chosen to replace them in public as this is viewed as very bad manners. Retirees should also resist the urge to return to their old place of employment. They should remember the saying: "When you're gone, you're gone." Retirement is a time to turn to new ventures and opportunities, not a time for revisiting the past.[32]

Upon her retirement, one employee received a number of automobile gasoline cards. Many colleagues knew that the retiree and her husband had planned a summer automobile trip. The gas cards were greatly appreciated and were appropriate for the retiree's situation.

FUNERALS

Condolences and support are the most important things you can give a business associate who loses someone close. Generally speaking, the closer the relationship, the longer the mourning process and the greater the need for emotional support. Patience is especially important for those who have just suffered the loss of a loved one. If you supervise a person who has lost a loved one, watch for signs of stress. The person may need a few days off from work. Redistribute the person's work load for a short period of time to help.[33]

Gifts of food are appropriate if a number of out-of-town guests will be attending the funeral. Check with a family member to determine what types of food may be needed. A card expressing sympathy and offering to help is always appreciated. Many times this help just means being there to listen. In addition to a sympathy card, a letter of condolence is comforting at this time.[34] Sometimes sharing a happy moment that happened between you and the deceased or recounting how the deceased touched your life can be very comforting to the person reading your letter. (Cards and condolence letters are discussed in Chapter 7, "Written Communication Manners.") Most people who have lost loved ones will tell you that they enjoy talking about them and that they are uncomfortable when friends and colleagues avoid talking about the deceased.[35]

> When a good friend lost his 22-year-old daughter, friends and family were very supportive by attending the wake and the funeral. A year later, however, he began handing out credit-card size pictures of his daughter with a poem on the back and a note requesting people to continue to talk to him about his daughter's life. His friends were at first shocked, then saddened when they realized that they no longer talked about his daughter with him.

Checking the obituary to see if the family wants flowers or would prefer to have donations made to a certain charity is advisable. If the obituary does not say whether flowers or charitable donations are preferred, feel free to do whichever you prefer. If the obituary says, "charitable organization of giver's choice," you may make a donation to one of your favorite charities or choose one that conducts research on the disease from which the person died.[36]

Although you may see all types of dress at a funeral, it is still proper to wear dark colors to funerals. A dark suit for a man and a dark dress or suit for a woman are the best choices. The actual funeral is a time for quiet and dignity for the departed. If there is a receiving line, you should shake hands with everyone in the line. If you do not know someone, introduce yourself and give your relationship to the departed.[37]

If the person is an executive with the company, it will be necessary for the company to place death notices in the industry publications and in the house organ. Generally, if the person is well known locally, there will be a column about the individual in the local newspaper as well as in the obituary column. Company executives should let the telephone operator know where to forward calls that may come in with questions about the funeral arrangements or who is going to take over the person's job responsibilities.[38]

Sometimes employees will want to set up a memorial to honor the deceased. If this is the case, it is proper for members of senior management to make a corporate donation to the memorial and for employees and senior managers who wish to make personal donations. The memorial should be used for education of the children of the deceased, scientific research, or other worthwhile objectives.[39]

While special events run the gamut of fun to serious, they are important times in the lives of the employees and the company. Even the happy events, however, need to be taken seriously. Sometimes the birthday or holiday celebration that was intended to be fun turns into something quite different, often because of drug and alcohol abuse. Behavior at these events can have negative consequences; an employee's career can be damaged irreparably. Thus, the knowledge of appropriate behavior at these special events can play a role in career advancement.

Written Communication Manners

> Today, most business executives bemoan good business writing as a dying art. In truth, good writing is not quite ready for burial but is definitely in need of resuscitation.[1]

First impressions are very difficult to change, including impressions formed through written communication. Messages that use an incorrect format, poor writing style, and incorrect grammar and punctuation convey a negative impression. Sloppy writing leads the receiver to think that not only is the writer sloppy but that products or services of the company the writer represents may be inferior as well. No one wants to deal with a company that does not present a good image. Image involves more than an attractive logo; it also involves the paper on which the communication is written and the writing style used in the messages.[2]

LETTER AND MEMORANDUM FORMATS

The two most common styles for arranging business letters are the block style, in which all lines begin at the left margin, and the modified block style, in which the date and closing lines start at the center of the page. Styles of punctuation that are commonly used are open punctuation, which features no punctuation after the salutation or the complimentary close, and standard or mixed punctuation, in which a colon is used after the salutation and a comma after the complimentary close. Letters should be centered, with equal left and right margins of 1 to 1½ inches and equal top and bottom margins; they should be printed on the company's letterhead. The personal business style, which is often used for employment messages, includes the writer's address just above the date and the writer's keyed and signed name below the complimentary closing. Do not use company letterhead for personal business letters; instead, use 20-pound bond paper of 25 percent rag content. When writing personal business letters, either the block or the modified block letter style may be used; either open or mixed punctuation is acceptable.[3]

Standard parts of a letter are the date, inside address, salutation, body, complimentary closing, and writer's name and job title. Letter parts that are used less frequently are special mailing notations, such as "Registered," attention and subject lines, and enclosure notations. Since many writers make a negative impression by using an inappropriate salutation, here are some reminders on proper salutations to use.

Salutations for all types of written correspondence differ depending upon the relationship between the writer and the reader. If you are on a first-name basis with the intended recipient, address the person as "Dear Susan;" however, if you do not know the person well, the salutation should be "Dear Mrs. Smith." At no time would a salutation include the first and last name of the addressee; thus, "Dear Susan Smith" is incorrect. All correspondence should be addressed using the correct title for the person or persons to whom the correspondence is addressed.[4]

Position	Title to Use
Personal	Mr., Ms., Mrs. Miss, Master, or Dr.
Military	Service rank is used, such as Captain or Major, in place of the personal title; the service abbreviation is used after the name
Political	Governor, Senator, or President is used in place of the personal title; the address would be "The Honorable" and the person's last name.
Religious	Archbishop, Reverend, or Rabbi is used in place of the personal title
Nobility titles	Prince, Queen, or Duke is used in place of the personal title
Judge	Replace the personal title with "The Honorable." The Chief Justice of the United States is addressed as "Chief Justice" and name
Lawyers	Add Esq. after the name with no courtesy title preceding the name

Many people have worked very hard to earn their titles and take offense when titles are not being used properly. You may wish to consult a desk reference manual when you have questions about the correct form of address.

While e-mail messages are replacing hard copies of memorandums in many companies, memorandums are used often enough so that you will want to be familiar with their format. The guide words "To," "From," "Date," and "Subject" (usually in that order although "Date" may precede "To") are keyed 1 to 1½ inches from the top of the paper. Double-space between the guide words and triple-space between the subject line and the first paragraph of the memorandum. Align the information presented after the guide words using a tab one inch from the left margin. Since a memorandum is an informal means of communicating with employees inside the company (although they are currently being sent to people outside the company), omit personal titles before both the sender's and the recipient's name; however, position titles, such as Director of Sales, may be placed after the name. No salutation or complimentary closing is used; writers may place their initials or signature after their names in the memorandum heading.[5] Electronic mail messages are set up as a memorandum in a predetermined format with guide words to indicate the information you are to provide. Guidelines for writing e-mail messages are provided in Chapter 5, "Electronic Communication Etiquette."

STATIONERY

The stationery a person chooses to use tells the reader about the sender. The stationery can indicate the sender's knowledge of etiquette and can also convey the sender's attention (or inattention) to details.

The company letterhead should have a matching envelope that fits the folded letterhead exactly and second sheets that match the first sheet in color and texture. Employees may use letterhead paper for personal notes of congratulations to other professionals; however, letterhead would not be used for purely personal correspondence. The best choice for important correspondence is watermarked, rag-content paper.[6] White or off-white paper with black ink for the lettering is preferred, especially for companies who conduct business with international clients. Many businesses, however, use other colors of paper and ink for their stationery. Generally, they will have specific reasons for using these colors. Business stationery is usually 8½ inches by 11 inches; however, businesses often provide monarch sheets, which are 7¼ inches by 10½ inches for writing personal business letters. Stationery that is 6½ inches by 8 inches, either with or without a letterhead, is also used for personal business correspondence.[7]

For social correspondence, such as for writing notes of appreciation, congratulations, and condolence that are not business related, women usually use half sheets, which are single sheets that fold in half to fit their matching envelopes, or monogrammed notes, which are note cards that are already folded and used for short messages. The most popular monogram style is probably a large center initial representing the first initial of the woman's last name. Another style is with all letters the same size; the initials then appear in order. Correspondence cards, which are heavy cards with matching envelopes, are used for informal notes. The person's name, monogram, or coat of arms may be included at the top. When using the card, remember to write only on the front side. Men use monarch sheets, half sheets, and correspondence cards; they do not usually use monogrammed notes.[8]

Many corporations spend a great deal of money for developing logos and graphics for their business stationery. Some corporations will use the design on all of their paper products, including stationery,

One corporate executive had all of his envelopes lined with paper printed in his family's tartan pattern. Anyone interested in projecting a unique image may use special colors of paper or ink.[10]

business cards, invoices, and other forms. When designing these logos and graphics, it is important to select fonts that are readable.[9]

WRITING GUIDELINES

Regardless of whether you are writing positive, negative, or routine messages, following these guidelines will help you project a favorable image and will make your business messages more effective:

- Write the way you talk. Your messages should sound like you; they should be conversational. The exception to this rule is that you should choose words and construct sentences more carefully than you would when you communicate orally. While use of the personal pronoun "I" is often used in conversations, in written communication the message should be directed toward the reader. Sometimes called the "you attitude," this reader-oriented approach is preferable to the "I" approach. For example, rather than saying, "I think your idea is excellent," say, "Your idea is excellent."

- Begin with good news whenever possible. When someone asks you to speak to a group, start by accepting the invitation. For example, say, "Yes, I will be happy to address your group on May 7." Avoid beginning with, "Thank you for your invitation"; this beginning is often considered trite and ineffective for many types of messages.

- Use humor with caution. Since the nonverbal aspect is missing, the reader may find no humor in what you thought was amusing. Your attempts at humor may be perceived as flippant or even insulting. Humor should never be used when writing to someone of another culture or to people you do not know.

- Use courtesy expressions at proper times. "Please," "thank you," and "appreciate" are examples of courtesy expressions to use frequently in written messages. Some writers who have not used courtesy expressions in the body of the message will end with "Thank you" or "Thank you in advance" when nothing has been done for which the reader should be thanked. Never thank people before they do something. When you have requested some action of the reader, simply end by expressing appreciation using future tense. For example, when you asked for delivery of a book by April 10, say, "Your sending me the book by April 10 will be appreciated."

- Use positive, specific statements for most messages. Rather than saying, "Don't forget to turn in your report soon," say, "Please turn in your sales report by Friday, June 11, at 4:30 P.M." The exception to the rule of being specific is in negative situations. For example, "I'm sorry you are ill" is preferable to "I'm sorry you broke your leg."

- Write clearly and concisely; avoid unnecessary words. Rather than using "At this point in time," just say, "now."

- Use contractions sparingly. While occasional use of contractions adds to a conversational tone when writing informal messages, they should be used with discretion. If you know the reader, it is acceptable to use them occasionally.

- Use a variety of sentence types and sentence lengths. Although most of the sentences you write for business messages will be simple sentences, the message should not be made up entirely of simple sentences. Using other types of sentences—complex, compound, and compound-complex—adds variety to business writing. While the average length of sentences should be from thirteen to twenty words, varying the length of your sentences adds to the overall effectiveness of the message.

- Use nondiscriminatory language. Job titles should be gender neutral. For example, use "fire fighter" rather than "fireman." Be sure that pronouns agree with their antecedents and that they are gender neutral. For example, say, "Managers may use their own judgment" rather than, "A manager may use his own judgment."

- Avoid a dictatorial tone. People respond more readily to a polite request (please) than to a dictatorial tone (must or should). Say, "Please order the software" rather than "You should order the software."

- Use correct grammar, word usage, punctuation, and spelling. Such errors can cause the reader to question the educational level or intelligence of the writer. Examples of these errors are lack of subject–verb agreement, run-on sentences, using the wrong word (raised for razed and affect for effect), comma splice, and errors in spelling.[11] Some errors are quite humorous, such as the sign on the door of the employee break room in one hospital that read: "Employee's lounge is being renovated." (The lounge is for only one employee?) You have to question the word usage skills of the people who wrote these statements: "I had such a feeling of utopia" (intended word: euphoria); "After that, I became a *persona au gratin*" (intended word: *persona non grata*); and "On this date in 1861, Mississippi succeeded from the Union" (intended word: seceded).

These freshly painted signs around the swimming pool of a large motel caused guests to wonder about the educational level of the person responsible:

- "Pool for registered guest only." (guests)

- "Absolutely no cut off jeans in swimming pool; the dye in jeans work against pool chemicals." (cut-off jeans; works)

- "Children must be accompanied by an adult to insure safety." (accompanied; ensure)

THANK-YOU NOTES

Handwritten notes to thank someone or acknowledge receipt of a gift are very important for business success. If handwriting is not an option because the person's handwriting is illegible, then a keyed note is acceptable. Thank-you notes should say more than "Thank you for the

A survey by Robert Half International found that 76 percent of executives consider candidates who write thank-you notes following job interviews more favorably than those who do not; however, only 36 percent of the people interviewed actually write thank-you notes.[12]

flowers" or "Thank you for the interview." They should be specific about what the expression of appreciation is for and should acknowledge the appropriateness of the giver's choice. If a gift of money is received, acknowledge it with the phrase "your generous gift" rather than the specific amount. Thank-you notes to interviewers need to say something specific about what was discussed at the interview or some aspect of the interview that you especially appreciated, such as being given a tour of the building or being treated to lunch.

A thank-you note to someone who gave a gift that was shared by departmental employees needs to mention how the gift was enjoyed by the staff. If you are working on a project, it is always nice to thank the people who have helped make the project a success. Little kindnesses such as thank-you notes go a long way in the business world; they are remembered long after the event.[13]

"Gratitude is the most exquisite form of courtesy."—Jacques Maritain, French Philosopher[14]

Being prompt in writing thank-you notes is important; they should be written within a week or ten days after the event. Thank-you notes are also written when you are someone's house guest, when you are invited to dinner at your supervisor's home, when someone has helped you with a meeting, and to express appreciation to invited speakers at business functions.[15] Verbal expressions of appreciation are appropriate for people who have done small favors or on any other occasion where expressing appreciation is appropriate.[16] However, anytime someone has spent more than fifteen minutes helping you, a handwritten or keyed thank-you note is in order. While handwritten notes are more appreciated, e-mail responses are acceptable; they are better than no "thank you" at all.[17]

One company has a rule that if an employee goes to lunch with a vendor, the employee pays for the vendor and the employee. If gifts are received and are items that could be shared by all office employees, such as candy or cookies, the gifts can be kept. However, the employee is not permitted to receive personal gifts or gifts of value from a vendor; such gifts are to be returned with a "thank you" but "no thank you" note explaining the company's rule.

In the business world, it is sometimes necessary to return a gift because the firm does not allow employees to receive gifts from vendors. In this case, thank them for the gift, explain why you cannot accept it, and return it to the giver.[18]

CONDOLENCE LETTERS

Sometimes personal tragedies, such as the death of a member of the family or a business colleague, are so traumatic that about the only help you can offer is an expression of condolence. Your expressions of sympathy can be in the form of making a personal visit, sending flowers, attending the visitation at the funeral home, contributing to a charity, sending a card, or writing a letter. Although letters of condolence are difficult to write, they are often the most appreciated. The main purpose of this letter is to let the person know of your concern. Whatever you do, do not simply ignore a person's death just because you find the situation uncomfortable. Doing or saying nothing simply adds to the sorrow the bereaved person is feeling and is, of course, very bad manners.[19]

In writing a letter of sympathy, acknowledge the terrible loss the person is experiencing, offer to help in any way, and speak well of the deceased, mentioning the person's character, accomplishments, or anything else that is praiseworthy. You might say something like, "Charles helped me so much when I was first hired. He was kind and had a great sense of humor, in addition to being admired for his competence."[20]

Statements you would wish to avoid when writing letters of condolence are:

- "Her passing was really a blessing; she suffered so much." (At this point, it is probably impossible for the bereaved to believe that the person's death was a blessing, regardless of how much suffering the person endured.)
- "Time heals all wounds." (People who have just suffered the loss of a loved one cannot possibly believe that in time their grief will subside.)
- "I know just how you feel; my own sister died two years ago." (People in mourning are not interested in your making comparisons of your loss to theirs.)
- "I was horrified when I heard how tragically he died in the automobile accident." (When the death is sudden and tragic, avoid saying how shocked or horrified you were.)[21]

Flowers, letters of sympathy, and gifts to charitable organizations in memory of the deceased should be acknowledged within about two months. Some mortuaries furnish printed acknowledgments that are appropriate to use, especially when you have numerous notes to write. Adding handwritten expressions of appreciation to each acknowledgment is recommended.[22]

CONGRATULATORY LETTERS

Letters of congratulations are easy to write. Most people are happy to recognize and to share in the accomplishments of their friends and colleagues.

Congratulatory letters are written when friends get promoted, when they receive recognition for their work, and when they are elected to office. When you see the person frequently, oral statements of congratulations are appropriate and are usually accompanied by a pat on the back and a handshake. These oral remarks may be followed by a written note of congratulations, especially if the accomplishment is significant. When you see the person infrequently, write a letter. Make your congratulatory remarks in the first paragraph, using some form of the word "congratulate." Even though these letters are typically short, make an effort to write more than one sentence. After the first sentence in which you express congratulations, try to mention something specific about the person's accomplishment. Your letter to one of your employees who has just been promoted could sound something like this:

> Congratulations! Your promotion to director of sales for Mid-South Manufacturing has just been approved.
>
> Your outstanding performance over the years, together with your excellent communication skills, professional manner, and loyalty to the company, is being rewarded. Your annual salary when you assume the duties of your new position on July 1 will be $91,000.
>
> I look forward to working closely with you in your position as director of sales.

Writing messages of congratulations can lift the morale of the reader and can make a favorable impression in a professional manner. People appreciate recognition; they enjoy receiving letters that they often share with family and colleagues. Such letters are often read repeatedly before they are discarded. In fact, people often save these letters for years.[23]

INVITATIONS

Corporate invitations look very similar to other formal invitations people receive. Invitations should begin at the top with the corporate name or symbol. The hosts are listed next, followed by the invitation phrase. The type and purpose of the party is then given followed by the date and time, as well as the location of the event, where to reply, and special instructions, such as appropriate attire. Both the date and time are written in words rather than numerals; dates are never abbreviated. Corporate invitations should not include any type of advertising slogans.

Special instructions and reply information are normally written at the margin at the end of the invitation. Phone numbers and/or e-mail addresses are sufficient for R.S.V.P.s (*respondez-vous, s'il vous plait*). While some people use the phrase, "Regrets only," this is not recommended because you may never know whether an invitation reached its intended recipient; whereas, if you keep a record of who has responded, you will know that you need to follow up on those who have not replied by a specific date.[24]

The meeting should determine the type of invitation that is issued. While informal meetings may only require a telephone or e-mail invitation, formal meetings dictate a written invitation. The larger the group being invited, the further people may have to travel; hence, the more notice will be required. Shareholder meetings and annual board meetings should have four to six weeks' notice. In-house meetings should have a minimum of one week. Since it is best to reconfirm the day before a meeting, make use of calendar-scheduling software for notification. Make sure the appropriate people for the meeting are invited.[25]

ACCEPTANCE OR REGRETS

Invitations should be responded to within a week of receipt. If an emergency develops, the host should be called immediately. If there is an enclosure card, this should be completed and returned to the sender. If there is a phone number, e-mail address, or fax number, then one of these would be the proper means of responding to the invitation. If this information is not provided, write your reply. Not replying is rude; it should not be necessary for the host to have to call to find out who is attending the event.[26]

In earlier times enclosure cards were not included with invitations; people receiving them were expected to write a reply on their own stationery. Use of enclosure cards began because of poor manners; people did not respond to invitations. Now it is correct to either include a response card or not. In the absence of a response card, it is still correct to write a response on your own stationery.

If there are extenuating circumstances to share, feel free to write a letter, fax, or e-mail explaining the situation. Since so many people today fail to R.S.V.P., the extra time you take to compose a short note will be appreciated and remembered. Those who do not have the good manners to reply but who show up for the party or those who said they would attend and do not show up are also remembered.

When you receive an invitation to join an organization, give a presentation, or receive an award or recognition, write a letter accepting the invitation or expressing your regrets.

At a recent wedding, the bride had not received reply cards from several people who had been invited and incorrectly assumed they would not be attending the wedding. A few minutes before the service started, the ushers were frantically setting up more chairs for guests who arrived unexpectedly. Because of the unexpected guests, there was insufficient food at the reception; twice as many people attended the wedding as had responded. A happy event became quite harried because people did not respond.

While the acceptance is straightforward with kind words about the organization, the message expressing regrets should include, in addition to your regrets and some kind remarks, the name and contact information of another person who may be able to make the presentation. When time is short, an e-mail or phone call may be the fastest way to respond.[27]

When responding to an invitation, you would not use the Jr., II, or III designations in the salutation. Mr. & Mrs. Stevens J. Martin, Jr. becomes Mr. & Mrs. Martin in your salutation. Also, if both hold doctor's degrees, the salutation is Drs. Armani. The inside address and envelope address would be Drs. Deniz & Andrea Armani rather than Mr. & Mrs. Deniz Armani. If the woman has a doctorate and the man does not, then it is Dr. Barbara and Mr. James Posner. If a wife maintains her maiden name, then the address is to Mr. George St. Clair and Mrs. Linda Holmes.[28] Boys are addressed as "Master" until age 18; they then become "Mr.," and girls are addressed as "Miss" until age 21; if they are still single at 21, they can begin to use "Ms."[29]

ANNOUNCEMENTS

A business often finds itself in the position of wanting to let customers, vendors, stockholders, and others of significance to the corporation know what is happening in the business. Formal announcements are the way to make such information known to those outside of the firm. Generally the wording of such announcements is formal.[30] Announcements should be simple; the point should be made quickly. The information is generally printed on a flat piece of heavy paper stock or light card stock in white or off-white with black lettering.[31] However, advertising or marketing firms may be more creative with paper and lettering color, as well as with the style of the announcement.

The types of information a business may want to let others know through the use of announcements include a move, a new address or phone number, the introduction of a new employee, the announcement of an employee's retirement or a formal meeting, or the death of a key employee.[32]

COMPLAINT LETTERS

James M. Kramon, author of *You Don't Need a Lawyer,* says that sending a well-written letter that is certified with a return-receipt request is more likely to persuade a company to help you. He also says that you are more likely to get the desired results with a letter than with a phone call, fax, or e-mail.[37]

While face-to-face conversations are preferable to writing a letter of complaint, sometimes a letter is your only means of communication.[33] Complaint letters are unique in that they concern a negative idea but are trying to persuade the reader to do something positive for the writer.

Complaint letters require time to write if the information is to be accepted by the recipient. They should not be written when angry, should have no apparent emotion, should be very factual, and should be grammatically correct.[34] They should contain only essential information and should be polite. If a letter is antagonistic, the receiver may not give it the attention it needs.[35] Make a phone call or visit the company's web site to find out to whom the letter should be addressed, and make sure the person's name is spelled correctly.[36]

Companies often have departments to handle complaint mail. The key to a company's retaining an unhappy customer is to stay calm, acknowledge the writer's viewpoint, and rectify the situation. If it is going to take a while to investigate the situation, inform the complainer that you are working on it and will be back in touch as soon as you have some answers.

Issues on the job that may warrant writing a letter of complaint include problems with coworkers, customers, groups, and sexual harassment. Complaining successfully is an art. No one wants to be seen as a compul-

A food processing company received a letter with a screw in it. The letter was written to tell the company that the screw had been found in a box of cereal; the writer very cleverly made jokes about the screw rather than complaining and being negative. The result was that the person who returned the screw received twice the usual number of coupons for free products and a letter thanking her for her lighthearted approach to the screw.

sive complainer; therefore, ask the following questions before registering a complaint: Is the problem worth complaining about and is this the right time? What is the best channel to use—e-mail, telephone call, or in person? Is the problem well documented? What is the best possible solution?[38]

If the problem is not resolved soon after the complaint is made, you will need to decide if the problem is worth pursuing. Minor complaints, such as problems with a new chair, are easily handled by an e-mail or memorandum. Serious problems, such as a lost security card, should be addressed immediately by telephone or in person. Many times it is smart to start with a face-to-face meeting before putting anything in writing to get a feel of how the supervisor is going to react. Be prepared to offer facts, rather than moral judgments or opinions, if they are requested.[39]

CARDS

Sending greeting cards for holidays, birthdays, Christmas, Ramadan, Hanukkah, or the Chinese New Year can be fun for the sender and the receiver. Cards should be in good taste; some time should be taken to choose the appropriate card. Cards should be mailed in time to arrive before the date of the holiday being observed. A nice touch is to buy holiday postage stamps rather than use the postage meter. Company cards should be signed by everyone with whom the receiver has interactions. Cards from the company should not include pictures of the executive's children. E-cards or e-greetings are also appreciated; some are rather elaborate and include sound effects and animation.[40]

All cards should be personalized with signatures and a special note. Such notes are energizing and can continue to provide enjoyment to the person for a long time after the event.[41] Cards are a quick way to let people know that you are thinking of them; they help to build and maintain relationships.

Remember that the letters, memorandums, and notes that you write provide a permanent record of your writing ability. Investing some time in polishing your writing skills will be well worth the effort.

8

Dining Etiquette

Working like a dog will get you promoted; eating like a pig will not.[1]

Etiquette mavens and image consultants have long emphasized the connection between good table manners and career advancement. Many employers will not let employees with poor table manners take prospective clients to dinner; they are well aware of the perceived relationship between good table manners and breeding, upbringing, education, and position within the organization.[2] People in higher positions in a company are typically presumed to have better table manners than those in lower positions. This presumption has been confirmed by research. In one survey, 80 percent of presidents, vice presidents, and board chairmen of major firms had excellent table manners, while only 40 percent of persons in middle management had polished table manners. In addition, 60 percent of top executives surveyed said they would not permit employees who did not have good table manners to represent their firm in public.[3] Even though that survey was conducted over twenty-five years ago, employers today still know that an employee's poor table manners can reflect negatively on the image of the organization.

Employees who are interested in gaining a competitive edge at promotion time will want to learn some basic guidelines for eating appropriately and practice these rules both at home and when dining with supervisors, colleagues, and clients at business meal functions. Knowing and using good table manners is an important social skill that can set you apart from others who are being considered for advancement in the company.

STYLES OF EATING AND PLACE SETTINGS

The "zigzag" style of eating is practiced by people of the United States. When using the American style, hold the knife in the right hand and the fork in the left with the tines down. After you cut a piece of food, place the knife on the upper right edge of the plate. Then switch the fork to the right hand, and eat the piece of food with the fork tines up. The term "zigzag" comes from the constant switching back and forth of the fork from the left hand to the right and back again.

Place settings vary somewhat based on the formality of the occasion, but the basic rule to follow when setting the table is to arrange the silverware so that the utensil to be used first is placed on the outside farthest from the service plate, with forks to the left of the plate (salad fork on the outside) and knives and spoons to the right of the service plate (soup spoon on the outside, then the entree knife, with the teaspoon closest to the service plate. This arrangement may vary; the soup spoon and teaspoon may be to the outside with the entree knife closest to the service plate.) You only have to remember to choose utensils from the outside and work your way toward the center. As soon as you are seated, determine which plates, glasses, and utensils are yours by remembering that glassware and cups are placed to the right of the service plate and the bread plate is placed to the left of the center of the place setting. The dessert spoon (handle facing right) and dessert fork (handle facing left) are placed above the dinner plate. Napkins may be placed in several locations, including inside the wine glass or coffee cup, on the plate, or to the left of the plate; however, they are never placed under the forks. Table settings are arranged for right-handed persons; no accommodations are made for left-handed persons.[4]

Indicate when you have finished eating by placing the knife with the blade toward you and the fork with the tines up parallel (fork inside) at approximately the ten o'clock and four o'clock position. To signal that you have not finished eating, place the knife and fork in the center of the plate.[5]

Molloy conducted an experiment in Maui to determine the effect of dress on restaurant service. He sent six groups of executives to different restaurants and varied the dress of each group from suits to very casual attire. Those who wore jackets and ties were given better treatment, better seats, and more attention than the executives who dressed casually.[6]

BASIC GUIDELINES FOR BUSINESS DINING

Basic guidelines for dining etiquette in business and social situations include the following:

- Dress appropriately for the restaurant. Inappropriate attire may result in a table near the kitchen or some other undesirable location even with a reservation. Most good restaurants have a minimum dress requirement; to get a desirable table, be well dressed.

- Know where to sit when entertaining and being entertained in a restaurant. The host takes the least desirable seat; guests should wait for the host to indicate where they should sit. In addition, a male host sits across from a female guest, and a female host sits across from a male guest.

- Place the napkin in the lap immediately upon being seated; do not shake the napkin out or wave it. Small napkins are opened fully; large napkins remain folded in half on the lap. Do not use the napkin as a bib, as a substitute handkerchief, or to wipe the mouth (simply dab the corners of the mouth). In addition, do not tuck your napkin into your shirt, waistband, or belt. If it is necessary to leave the table during the meal, which should be done only between courses, place the napkin in the chair seat. Return your loosely folded napkin to the left of the plate only when everyone at the table has finished eating.

- Order the same number of courses that others at the table have ordered when dining in a restaurant; diners should pace themselves so that everyone finishes at about the same time. When only one person orders a dessert, for example, the others have nothing to eat and must simply watch the person eat or sip a beverage.

- Request a glass if a beverage is served in a bottle or a can; in business and social settings, always drink beverages from a glass.

- Begin eating only after everyone at the table is served. (For larger tables seating more than eight, wait to begin eating until those seated near you have been served.)

- Remember rules for cutting or breaking food before eating it: cut sandwiches in halves or fourths; break off a small piece of bread before buttering and eating it; and cut only enough salad greens for two or three bites. When cutting a food item, such as a piece of meat, hold the fork in the left hand with the index finger pointing down the handle to steady the meat, then hold the knife in the right hand with the index finger pointing down the blade to pull the knife blade through the meat. Cut outside the fork tines, not between or below them; cut only one or two pieces of meat at a time.

- Know the rules for passing food. Pass food in a counterclockwise direction (to your right) without serving yourself first; pass the salt and pepper shakers together (even if the person asked for only one of the condiments) and place them on the table rather than passing them from hand to hand. (Remember to take only one roll or two small crackers when they are passed.)

- Use your fingers only for eating finger foods, such as *crudités* (raw vegetables) and pickles. Remember that when eating *crudités,* dip the vegetable into the sauce only once; dipping the bitten portion in the sauce a second time is unsanitary. No double dipping is the rule. Fried chicken and French fries are typically considered finger foods and are served at home or at casual dining functions, such as a picnic or a tailgate party. When fried chicken is incorrectly served at more formal meal functions, a knife and fork are used to get as much meat off the bone as possible.[7]

- Taste food before adding salt or other seasoning.
- Order soup only if you know how to eat it correctly; eat soup quietly; use the soup spoon to dip the soup away from you.
- Leave a small amount of food on your plate; the nonverbal message you send when you clean your plate is that you do not get enough to eat. This behavior is inconsistent with people who live in the United States of America, often referred to as the "land of plenty."
- Return utensils to their service plates after use; for example, return the spoon used to stir coffee to the saucer. Do not place used utensils directly on the table.
- Maintain good posture throughout the meal.
- Leave one hand in your lap while eating; you may rest your hand and wrist on the table between courses.

In addition to the preceding guidelines to observe in dining situations, avoid the following behaviors so that you will not be labeled as socially inept:

- Avoid ordering hard liquor with your meal; order water or wine with your meal and coffee after a meal.
- Avoid doing two things at once, such as holding a cracker in the left hand while eating salad or taking a sip of water with the right hand.
- Avoid tasting food from someone else's plate or sharing dishes in business situations.
- Avoid inappropriate behaviors while dining, such as placing elbows on the table while eating, applying lipstick, using a cell phone during the meal, taking medicine or vitamins in full view of others at the table, rocking back in your chair, or using toothpicks at the table (or walking out of the restaurant with the toothpick in your mouth). Talking with food in the mouth and chewing with the mouth open are considered the top dining mistakes people make.
- Avoid turning your glass or cup upside down when you do not wish a beverage; simply place your hand over the class or cup and say to the server, "No, thank you." If the server fills your glass or cup anyway, simply leave it untouched.
- Avoid ordering foods that are difficult to eat, such as lobster, French onion soup, spaghetti, and ribs, when you wish to make a good impression.
- Avoid removing the foil encasing a baked potato; simply slit the foil to access the potato; eating the skin of a baked potato is acceptable.
- Avoid eating too much; have a snack before leaving home to avoid eating ravenously. Do not ask for a doggie bag; some people say it indicates that the person rarely goes out; others say it indicates someone of low class.[8]

One employee, early in her career, ate so much during one business meal event that her belt popped open and fell to the floor noisily when she stood up. When she bent over to retrieve the belt, she burped loudly. Needless to say, she was totally embarrassed and wanted to crawl under the table.[9]

- Avoid placing objects, such as a purse, keys, cell phone, or glasses, on the table; a woman should carry a small purse when dining out and place it in her lap with the napkin placed on top of the purse.
- Avoid carrying on lengthy conversations with the server; the others at the table deserve your full attention.
- Avoid stacking your dishes, brushing crumbs from the table, or pushing your chair back when you have finished eating.

- Avoid offering to pay for the meal or leave the tip when someone invites you; the person who extends the invitation pays for the meal, the tip, valet parking, and for checking items.
- Avoid arguing over the amount each person owes when one check is presented at the end of "dutch-treat" meals. (Separate checks should have been requested before the first person ordered to avoid such awkward situations.)[10]

Although following the preceding guidelines will cover most situations, problems sometimes occur that require you to handle them with tact and diplomacy.

PROBLEM DINING SITUATIONS

When dining in a restaurant, problems involving seating, the food, the service, or mishaps, such as a dropped utensil, occasionally happen. People with good social skills know how to handle these situations graciously.

Problems with seating should be resolved by the host before the guests arrive. Getting to the restaurant early to check out the seating is recommended. The host waits either near the entrance for the guests' arrival or at the table when it is near the entrance. Hosts who choose to wait at the table should refrain from drinking or eating anything and should not disturb the table setting before the guests arrive.

Problems with the food should be handled discreetly. When the food is not what was ordered, the server should be asked to correct it. When food is cooked improperly, such as steak that is served medium rare when the order was for medium well done, quietly call it to the server's attention and explain how you wish it cooked. (This should be done after eating only one or two bites; eating over half of a steak before complaining and requesting another one is very bad manners.) Be assertive but polite; do

When a supervisor treated two of his female colleagues to lunch, it soon became apparent that the server had problems with body odor. After the server took the order, the supervisor remarked, "It looks like we have a problem here; can we put up with this or should I speak to the manager and request another server?" His colleagues indicated that they could tolerate the situation. After returning to the office, the supervisor called his colleagues to report that when he telephoned the manager, the manager expressed appreciation for the information and assured him that the situation would be resolved.

not make a scene or talk down to the server. If a foreign object is in the food, do not announce "There's a hair in my soup." Simply mention to the server that there is a foreign object in the soup and ask for a replacement serving, without identifying the object.

Complaints about poor service make up about three-fourths of all restaurant complaints.[11] To get the server's attention, raise your hand and say "Waiter" or "Waitress" (or "Miss"); do not clap your hands or snap your fingers. Use "Please" when requesting service and "Thank you" when the waiter has performed a service. Should you wish to substitute one food item for another and the rules of the restaurant are "no substitutions," do not vent your frustration on the server. If you were given a glass with lipstick smudges or an unclean utensil, ask the server for a replacement. When the service is poor or the server incompetent, make your complaint known to the server in most cases. If the problem with the server persists, or if the problem with the server is of a personal nature, such as lack of proper hygiene, it is appropriate to ask to speak to the manager. Sometimes diners prefer to leave a small tip and call the manager to report the problem upon their return to the office.[12]

Other problems include beverage spills, dropped utensils, and removing inedible items from the mouth.

- If someone spills a beverage, use a napkin to wipe up the spill; then call the server for additional help.
- When you drop a utensil, simply motion to the server and ask for a replacement. Do not retrieve it, wipe it off, and use it.
- To remove something inedible, such as a piece of bone, from your mouth, remove it the same way it entered your mouth. If the bone entered your mouth on a fork, use a fork to remove it and place it on the edge of your plate. If you placed an olive in your mouth with your fingers, remove the pit with your fingers. (Some advise hiding the discarded items beneath the garnish.) Do not spit the object into your napkin.
- Some problems should be handled by excusing yourself and going to the restroom. These include removing food that is stuck in your teeth, blowing your nose, applying lipstick, and removing or replacing orthodontic appliances.[13]

MANNERS FOR DIFFICULT-TO-EAT FOODS

While the best advice for business dining is to order foods that are easy to eat, occasionally food is served that requires special knowledge. Most of these difficult-to-eat foods can be categorized as fruits, vegetables, shellfish, or pasta.

Fruits

Fruits are generally cut in halves or quarters, pitted or cored, and eaten with the fingers. When eating a banana, peel it and cut it into small pieces with the fork before eating it. When eating grapes, take a small bunch and place it on your plate; then eat the grapes whole using your fingers. Blueberries and cherries are eaten with a spoon; remove the cherry pits with the spoon and place them on the service plate. Oranges or tangerines are peeled with the fingers or a knife; sections are pulled apart and eaten with the fingers or a fork.[14]

Vegetables

Vegetables that require special skill include artichokes, asparagus, cherry tomatoes, and peas. Artichokes are steamed and served whole on special dishes containing a small well designed to keep them upright. Small dishes containing melted butter and lemon or a special sauce will be served with the artichokes. To eat this vegetable, pull off the outer leaves one or two at a time with your fingers, dip the base into the sauce, and pull them through the teeth with the meaty portion down, scraping off the tender parts of the leaves. The leaves are discarded on the side of the plate. When you get to the base of the artichoke, scrape off the spiny tips and cut the heart into small pieces with a fork and knife; then dip the pieces into the sauce before eating them. Asparagus is considered finger food in informal settings, but at more formal occasions, cutting the stalks with a knife and fork is recommended. Cherry tomatoes are eaten in one bite; do not attempt to cut them with a knife and fork. Peas are eaten with a fork; crushing them slightly will make them easier to manage.[15]

Shellfish

Shellfish and mollusks are sometimes difficult to eat neatly. Clams and oysters are often served on the half shell; mussels are served in the shell. An oyster fork is used to dislodge the meat; the meat is then dipped in the sauce provided and eaten in one bite. In an informal dining situation, you may suck the meat off the shell while holding it with the fingers. Lobster and crab, which are served at informal dinners, require a bib since they are quite messy. They are eaten with the fingers. If you are unsure of how to eat lobster and crab, you usually have people nearby, either the host or other guests, who are happy to give advice on how they should be eaten. Generally, the claws are twisted off, cracked with the utensil provided, and an oyster fork used to remove the meat. The tail is then broken off the body; the fork is used to access the meat; then the legs are twisted off and the meat sucked out. Steamed shrimp served in their shells are also eaten with the fingers. Since they are messy to eat, a bib and extra napkins are recommended. The shells are placed on your plate if a separate bowl or plate has not been provided. When eating escargot (snails), use a cocktail fork to remove the snails and dip them into the sauce provided. If you really enjoy escargot but do not want to deal with the mess, you may want to ask the server before ordering if the shells have been removed since they are much neater to eat when they are served in a special sauce without shells.[16]

Pasta

The pasta that is most difficult to eat is spaghetti; it is eaten by using a fork to twirl a few strands at the edge of the plate. A place spoon may be used as well; just wind a few strands of spaghetti on the fork, place it into the bowl of the spoon, and twirl the fork until the strands in are in a neat ball before placing it whole into your mouth. Do not suck spaghetti strands into your mouth. While some people consider it acceptable to cut the spaghetti into small pieces with a fork, Italians rarely use this method so it may not be a good idea at an Italian restaurant.[17]

CULTURAL VARIATIONS IN DINING ETIQUETTE

When dining in other countries, first consider whether certain animals or insects are viewed as food, pets, or something else.

Since numerous intercultural encounters involve dining, it is important to be aware of cultural variations in eating styles, table manners, and food customs.

In European and Latin American countries, as well as in many other countries of the world, the Continental or European style of dining is used. With the European style, the fork remains in the left hand with the

- Dogs are a delicacy in Korea and a number of Eastern countries; they are considered watchdogs or hunting dogs in the Arab world but pets in the United States.[18]

- Rats are rarely killed in India; they are viewed as sacred and would not be eaten.[19]

- Grasshoppers are considered pests in the United States, pets in China, and an appetizer in Northern Thailand.[20]

- Horse meat is on the menu in many restaurants in Belgium, France, and Japan; U.S. people would never knowingly eat a cowboy's best friend.[21]

tines down for both cutting and eating the food. U.S. people who have traveled in foreign countries sometimes prefer the efficient European style of eating and have wondered if it is acceptable to use this style after they return and are dining in the United States. According to etiquette experts, using the European style of eating in the United States is acceptable only for foreigners who are visiting this country and those who are foreign born; for everyone else, it is perceived as an affectation. People should not pretend to be something they are not.[22] To signal that they have finished eating, people who use the European style align the knife and fork (tines down) in the upper right portion of the plate with the knife on the outside, blade facing the center of the plate. The Continental resting position involves placing the knife with blade toward the center of the plate crossed with the fork in the center with the fork on top of the knife blade. Place settings vary as well. Since people of other countries usually eat the entrée before the salad, the larger fork and knife are placed on the outside. Because Europeans typically serve more courses than people of the United States, they have additional utensils for the added courses, such as a fish fork and knife.[23]

Other styles of eating do not involve the use of knives, forks, and spoons and may be encountered when traveling abroad. In some African communities, as well as in India and Middle Eastern countries, for example, you are expected to use the fingers on the right hand to eat from one serving container. Refusing to eat with the fingers from a common platter would be an insult. Researching the special nuances of eating with the fingers is recommended, as in some parts of a particular country the entire hand is used for scooping food (southern India) and in other areas the fingers are placed in the food only as far as the second joint (northern India). In addition to the use of the fingers for eating, in China, Japan, Korea, and Vietnam, chopsticks are used, which vary in shape, length, and material (ivory, bamboo, or plastic). Soup spoons, in addition to chopsticks, are provided in Korean and Chinese cultures.[24]

Cultural variations exist in what is considered proper table manners. For example, in some countries people are expected to clean their plates, but in other countries they are expected to leave some food. While people in the United States, England, Costa Rica, and Colombia do not customarily clean their plates (indicating that they get enough to eat), in many European countries, including Denmark, France, Germany, Norway, and the Netherlands, and in some South American countries (Bolivia, Peru, Panama, and Guatemala) cleaning your plate is customary. Leaving food is viewed as wasteful. Sampling everything offered, which is expected in the United States, is also customary in most South American countries. The appropriateness of making noises while eating also varies with the culture. Though slurping and making other noises while eating is considered rude in the United States, in most Asian countries, including Japan and Hong Kong, people slurp their soup and smack their lips

U.S. people should consider how they look when eating corn on the cob—butter dripping down their chins and pieces of corn wedged between their teeth. Visitors from other countries are no doubt thinking: "He not only serves animal food, but he also looks like an animal when eating it."[26]

to indicate enjoyment of the food. Saudi Arabians and people in the Philippines belch and make other noises to express appreciation for the food. In Thailand and China, however, making such noises would be viewed as uncouth.[25]

Food customs of people in some cultures are viewed with surprise or disapproval by people of other cultures. In the United States, for example, eating corn on the cob is not uncommon. However, in some countries it is considered food for animals only.

Additional U.S. foods viewed as unusual by people of other countries include marshmallows, popcorn, crawfish, sweet potatoes, grits, and pecan or pumpkin pie. Dog meat, which is never eaten in the United States, is viewed as a desirable meat in Taiwan (though now illegal).

The American taboo against eating dog meat surprises some Asians, since dog meat is viewed as a delicacy in many Eastern countries. Out of respect for this American taboo, Korean restaurants in Seoul removed from their menus dishes featuring dog meat during the 1988 Olympics.[27]

Other foods considered unusual by people of the United States include snake meat (Korea), sheep's eyeballs (Saudi Arabia), and sea slugs (Hong Kong). In addition, the ant eggs, flying bedbugs, and toasted grasshoppers that are eaten in Mexico do not appeal to people of the United States. Sometimes the surprise is not so much the food that is served but how it is served.

One Swiss visitor to Japan decided to try raw fish when dining in an elegant Tokyo restaurant. What he did not expect was being served a live fish which was still flopping on the serving platter. The maitre d' then sliced the live fish and served it.

Since you are expected to eat what you are offered, it is important to learn about special foods that you may be served in the country you are visiting to avoid being caught off guard. Making derogatory comments about a country's food customs is rude. The best advice when served food with which you are unfamiliar is to cut it into thin slices, pretend it is chicken, swallow quickly, and never ask what it is.[28] In addition, cultural and religious consumption taboos should be respected. For example, Muslims do not eat pork; Hindus

A visiting professor from Java, when he first came to the United States to teach, was invited by his American colleagues to their homes. When they offered him something to eat; he always refused the first offer. Even when they asked their visitor again, he declined. Only later did the U.S. colleagues learn his country's custom of waiting until the third invitation to eat before accepting.[30]

do not eat beef; some people in India and Pakistan are vegetarians; some Puerto Ricans do not combine pineapple with other foods; Catholics do not eat meat on Ash Wednesday and Good Friday; and Orthodox Jews do not consume pork or shellfish—many do not eat meat and dairy products at the same meal.[29]

A food custom that is a surprise to people of the United States is the practice in some countries of refusing food when it is first offered. In fact, people of Korea and the Philippines not only refuse food the first time it is offered but often wait until food is offered for the third time before accepting. When guests refuse food offered by U.S. hosts, the assumption is made that the person is not hungry or that the international visitor does not like U.S. food; U.S. hosts do not typically offer food a second or third time.

In summary, because dining is an integral part of conducting business, it is essential that you learn table manners and practice them both at home and in business and social situations. Employees who aspire to higher levels in the organization will want to change Oscar Wilde's lamentable statement, "The world was my oyster, but I used the wrong fork," to "The world is my oyster; I used the right fork." [31]

Business Entertaining

How well you handle yourself at the dinner table, a party, a golf course or tennis court, a business associate's private club, or the theater says much about who you are.[1]

Entertaining colleagues, clients, and potential clients has long been recognized as an important part of doing business. Companies that conduct business internationally are especially aware of the role that entertaining plays in building a successful business relationship. Whether business entertaining is conducted at the host's home or country club, at a golf course, or at a restaurant will depend upon a number of factors, including the preferences of the host and guests and the occasion.

RESTAURANT ENTERTAINING

Restaurant entertaining continues to be popular; breakfast and lunch seem to be preferred times for U.S. business meals. While dinner is also a good time for restaurant entertaining, it is usually associated with special occasions, such as meetings of professional associations, visits by out-of-town clients, or interviews with applicants for important positions in an organization. The purpose of dinner entertaining is usually to build relationships, to show appreciation for someone's contributions, or to honor a special person. Breakfast and lunch are primarily for discussing business. The roles of host and guest are equally important.[2]

Business executives often arrange and host business meals; thus, knowing appropriate behavior for these occasions is important. The following guidelines are helpful when one is hosting business meals:

- The host reconfirms the meal appointment with the guest and restaurant the day before the scheduled event—or the morning of the event for lunch or dinner.
- The host either selects a restaurant that is convenient for everyone or offers the guests a choice of two restaurants. Lunch or dinner at a private business club is a good choice if your company has a membership.
- The person hosting a business meal makes reservations and arranges for paying in advance. Whoever does the inviting does the paying; this includes charges for drinks, the meal and tip, checking hats or coats, and valet parking. Hosts should know the correct amount to tip. The usual tip for the meal is 15–20 percent, depending upon the type of restaurant and the service. For cocktails consumed in the bar before being seated, the bartender receives a tip of 15–20 percent. A *sommelier* (wine steward) who was helpful in making a wine selection receives 15 percent of the wine bill. The valet receives $2–5, and checkroom attendants should receive about $1 for each item checked. When the service is excellent and the restaurant is one you visit frequently, tip the *maître d'* as you leave.[3]
- The host should always arrive a few minutes early to confirm reservations and arrange for seating; the host takes the least desirable seat.
- The host may order first or permit guests to order first; the host usually offers suggestions on menu items and the number of courses, thus giving guests an idea of the approximate price range the host has in mind. The host should order the same number of courses as the guests.
- The host has the responsibility of seeing to the guests' comforts, including asking guests if they are satisfied with their food and requesting beverage refills.
- The host initiates small talk at the beginning of the meal and business discussions toward the end of the meal.

Guests also have responsibilities during business meals to assure that the occasion is pleasant.

- Guests should be punctual; if they are late, they should call the restaurant and request that the host be informed of the delay.
- Guests should order quickly and avoid appearing indecisive; they should order food that can be eaten neatly and should avoid corn on the cob, crab legs, or a club sandwich, unless the sandwich will be dismantled and eaten with a knife and fork.
- Guests should take into consideration what other guests have ordered and order the same number of courses. If the host suggests an appetizer or dessert, however, it is acceptable to order it; otherwise, stay with the basics of a salad, entrée, and beverage. When the host does not give suggestions on menu items, guests would order something in the mid-price range rather than ordering the most expensive item.
- Guests should excuse themselves and go to the restroom if they start coughing, sneezing, or choking.
- Guests should wait for the host to initiate business discussions.

- Guests should handle problems with the food quietly.
- Guests should leave their cell phone at the office or in the car unless they are expecting a very important call.
- Guests would not offer to leave a tip or pay for valet parking and should accept graciously when the host offers to pay all expenses.
- Guests should thank the host for the invitation in person, then send a handwritten note of appreciation.

WINE AND TOASTING ETIQUETTE

Selecting a correct wine for the meal and the occasion can be a challenge, especially for those with limited knowledge of wine selection. Fortunately, the *sommelier* who takes the order will offer suggestions upon request. Since wine is selected after the meal order has been placed, the host tells the *sommelier* what has been ordered so that the wine complements the meal. If price is a consideration, mention the price range within which you would like to stay. Another option is to ask guests their preference or give the wine list to a guest who is knowledgeable about wines. After the wine has been selected, the *sommelier* will present the unopened bottle of wine to the host to confirm that it is what was ordered; it will then be uncorked and the cork given to the host for inspection. While it is acceptable to squeeze the cork to check for moistness or to sniff it to make sure it does not have the smell of vinegar, people often simply look at the cork and, if it is moist, say something like "I am sure it is fine." The host is then poured a small amount of wine for tasting and approval; this tasting ritual is not intended to determine if the host likes the wine; it is to determine whether the wine is acceptable—that is, it does not have the smell of vinegar or some other odor suggesting that it is spoiled. After the host tastes the wine and signals approval, the *sommelier* then serves each guest; the host is served last. Refilling the wine glasses is usually done by the server, but the host may refill the guests' glasses when the server does not; guests do not refill their own glasses.[4]

People who are not connoisseurs can learn some basic guidelines so that they can do an acceptable job of ordering wine. In the past, the rule was that white wine was served with white meat (chicken or fish) and red wine was served with red meat (beef, pork, and game). This rule is now considered more of a suggestion, as some people have a strong preference for either red wine or white wine with whatever meal they order. Additional points to remember are that white wine is usually served chilled in a long-stemmed glass; the glass is held by the stem to avoid warming the wine. A red wine is usually served at room temperature in a glass with a larger bowl and shorter stem; the glass is held close to the bowl as the heat from a person's hand actually improves the flavor of the wine.[5]

Candidates for the position of dean of the business school at a large university were taken to dinner by members of the search committee. One candidate ruined his chance for serious consideration when he ordered two drinks of scotch and water before the meal, two glasses of wine during dinner, and a martini after the meal. Another candidate was eliminated from further consideration when he ordered four bottles of beer and drank one before the meal, two during dinner, and one after the meal—all consumed from the bottle. Both candidates had excellent credentials but failed the drink test.

When drinking wine or any other alcoholic beverage, both the host and the guests should avoid excessive consumption. What is excessive depends somewhat on the person, as some people become tipsy after one glass of wine. The alcoholic content of the drink, amount of food consumed, and medicines taken are also factors in how a drink affects the body. Do not be the only person ordering an alcoholic drink, and do not drink, of course, if you are driving. Some people who usually imbibe socially do not drink in business situations, because even a moderate consumption of alcohol can loosen the tongue and result in a person's saying something that would be viewed negatively by business colleagues. Becoming inebriated at business meal functions is no way to make a positive impression and will be remembered when hiring and promotion decisions are made.[6]

Toasting is a charming custom that makes a meal more festive. Toasting should not be limited to such social occasions as weddings and anniversaries; it is certainly appropriate at business meals as well. Toasting at meal events is especially recommended when entertaining colleagues from other countries. Although U.S. toasts of "Cheers" and "Bottoms up" are widely understood, toasting in a person's language, such as *skol* when toasting someone from Denmark, is a nice gesture. Toasting to a person's health is always appropriate; just say "To your health" when toasting in English. The host usually proposes a toast of welcome to visitors at the beginning of the meal and another toast to honor the guest of honor. The guest of honor then responds by toasting the host.[7] Toasts should be brief; they can be amusing, as the following example illustrates: President Kennedy, during a White House dinner honoring Nobel Prize winners, proposed this toast: "I think this is the most extraordinary collection of talent, of human knowledge, ever gathered at the White House, with the possible exception of when Thomas Jefferson dined here alone."[8]

Errors to avoid when proposing a toast include reading the toast, clinking glasses, and drinking when you are being toasted. In addition, guests who do not drink alcohol may toast with another beverage or may use an empty wine glass. Toasting with a glass of water, especially when international visitors are present, is unwise as it is viewed as disapproval of the toast in some cultures. Do not be surprised if U.S. people toast with a glass of water; earlier beliefs that toasting with water is bad manners or unlucky are not universally accepted.[9]

ENTERTAINING AT PRIVATE CLUBS, SPORTING EVENTS, AND THE THEATER

Private clubs are excellent choices for business entertaining. Tennis courts, swimming pools, and golf courses are often available and offer numerous opportunities for company executives to relax with their customers. The morning or afternoon of golf or tennis usually ends or starts with lunch. When a game of golf is scheduled, the green fees are usually charged to the member. Guests should offer to pay their own green fees or at least pay for caddie fees for both. Checking the tipping practices of the club is recommended as some clubs forbid tipping; if tipping is permitted, tip the caddies and locker-room attendants who perform a service. Private clubs have certain rules of etiquette that must be observed. In some clubs, for example, no cash is used; all expenses are charged to the club member's account. Some clubs have rather strict dress codes; the guest should be informed ahead of time of such rules. In many clubs, jackets and ties are required for men in the dining area. Women should dress conservatively and should not wear revealing attire.[10]

The host at a spectator sport orders the tickets and arranges for transportation well in advance. The guests will inquire as to appropriate attire; they will follow the host's lead in conversation and in rising when other spectators stand during the event. Guests should offer to buy drinks and snacks for the host and other guests; they should not leave during the game unless absolutely necessary.[11] Etiquette for specific sports is included in Chapter 12, "Sports Etiquette."

Inviting guests to a theater is appreciated by those who enjoy plays, concerts, or ballets. The host would ask guests their preferences regarding the type of entertainment they prefer and would purchase tickets far enough in advance to get good seats. Being on time to the event is very important; late arrivals are disruptive as they locate their seats and squeeze past others who arrived promptly. The host takes the aisle seat after allowing the guests to enter the row first. The host and guests should dress appropriately for the event.

Proper behavior during a theater event includes remaining silent during the performance. When people near you are talking, it is appropriate to ask them politely to keep their voices down so that you can hear the performance. Leaving the cell phone at home is expected; in an emergency,

Dressing up when you go to the theater shows respect to the actors and indicates that you are able to differentiate between ballpark attire and theater attire.[12]

bring the cell phone and place it on silent vibration. Refreshments are enjoyed during intermission only and are not brought into the auditorium. Knowing when to applaud is important; avoid applauding the set when the curtain rises. If you are unsure about when to applaud, wait until the other members of the audience do so.[13]

COCKTAIL PARTIES AND RECEPTIONS

Many companies choose cocktail parties and receptions to entertain employees and customers; they provide an opportunity for people to become acquainted in a relaxed atmosphere. The invitation will indicate the degree of formality of the event by specifying the type of attire—business professional or business casual dress. Guests should understand that business professional dress does not mean that a man may wear any color of suit and tie; a dressier look, such as a dark suit and silk tie, is expected. Women should wear a dressier business suit, dress, or pants suit than they would wear to the office. When the invitation states business casual attire, men would know that, although they are not expected to wear a tie, they should wear a nice jacket, dress slacks, and a solid-color shirt or turtleneck. Women would likewise understand that business casual dress for cocktail parties does not imply shorts or khakis and a T-shirt—it usually means a conservative pants suit.

Cocktail parties usually last about two hours, beginning and ending between 5:00 and 8:30 P.M. Alcoholic and nonalcoholic drinks are available as well as hot and cold hors d'oeuvres. Since guests expect to stand throughout the party, few tables and chairs are provided. Cocktail buffets, held between 6:00 and 9:00 P.M., offer more substantial food than that provided at cocktail parties. Guests are able to sample a variety of foods and cuisines at the food stations located around the room; tables and chairs are provided for those who prefer to sit while eating. Cocktail receptions are usually held to honor special guests and are more formal than cocktail parties. Black tie or dressy business attire is expected. These receptions are held either before or after evening events. When scheduled before the evening event, the time is 6:00–8:00 P.M.; drinks (including champagne) and hors d'oeuvres are served. When scheduled following an evening event, the time is 10:30 P.M. to midnight with more substantial fare provided.[14]

Proper behavior at cocktail parties and receptions includes holding the beverage with the left hand to keep the right hand free for shaking hands. No one appreciates being offered a hand that is cold and wet. In addition, avoid piling your plate with food and select food that is easy to eat. When standing, do not attempt to eat and hold your drink at the same time. Since the purpose of a cocktail party is to meet people, spend only about ten minutes with each person or group of people before moving on. Talking with the same person during the entire event defeats the purpose of the cocktail party.[15]

HOME ENTERTAINING

Entertaining colleagues or customers at home conveys the message that they are special. Home entertaining is more personal than inviting guests to a restaurant; it affords guests an opportunity to gain insight into the host's personal life, including family, pets, interests, and taste in architecture and decorating. Visiting in a person's home is conducive to getting to know people on a different level than what is experienced in the office.[16]

Whether you have decided upon a backyard cookout, Sunday morning brunch, an open house, or a sit-down dinner, you will want to plan ahead to make the event as enjoyable as possible. The amount of money you can afford to spend is a consideration in deciding upon the type of social event to host and the number of people you will invite. Cookouts on the patio and Sunday morning brunch are great for entertaining a group of friends or business colleagues; an open house works well around the holidays when you wish to invite a larger group; and a sit-down dinner is more formal and an excellent way to entertain the supervisor, an out-of-town guest, or an international visitor. When deciding upon the guest list, consider the reason for the event and for including some people and not others. Having a reasonable explanation for leaving certain people off the guest list is advisable but not necessary; most people who attend will know that the reason that two persons in the department were not invited is because they never have a positive word to say about anyone in the office.[17]

Invitations for a picnic or brunch are usually informal; they may be issued in person, by telephone, or by e-mail. More formal events usually call for a written invitation. If the guests may bring their children, spouses, or roommates, that should be indicated when the invitation is issued. In addition, give directions to your home and suggestions for parking; just include a card or a sheet of paper containing the directions with the written invitation. When the guests will be parking on the street, inform your neighbors of the possibility that your guests may be parking in front of their homes during the time of the event. (By the way, inviting the neighbors is a good idea!)[18] Additional information on invitations is included in Chapter 7, "Written Communication Manners."

When you are hosting the event, getting organized is important. A few weeks before the party, decide who to invite, send out the invitations, plan the menu, and make arrangements for extra tables and chairs if needed. (Renting or borrowing extra furniture that you need is recommended.)

If you need to hire someone to help you, make appropriate arrangements. You may find that college students who have experience as servers in local restaurants will be happy to help

You need not spend a fortune on your parties. "Time, creativity, and imagination can substitute for money spent. Food does not have to be elaborate; it just has to be abundant."[19]

you serve and clean up after the party. Just be sure to pay them fairly and to indicate how they are expected to dress. (The women usually wear a black skirt or slacks, white shirt or blouse, and perhaps a white apron; men wear black pants, white shirt, and tie.)[20] For informal parties, you may have a friend who will come over the day before and help with the food preparation and/or serve as the bartender at the event. A few days before the party, call those who have not responded; make sure glasses, dishes, and cutlery are clean; buy food and beverage supplies; prepare and refrigerate dishes that can be made ahead of time; and make arrangements for cleaning the house and yard.

As the guests arrive, greet them, introduce them to others standing nearby, and offer them something to drink or indicate the location of the bar. An associate or spouse may help in greeting guests as the party gets underway. As the host, you are responsible for ending the party. When the guests stay too long, simply stand up, thank the guests for coming, get their wraps, and move toward the door, while making some comment such as, "I'm so pleased you could come."[21]

Guests have certain responsibilities, too. If they want to continue to be invited to someone's home, guests should behave appropriately. They should respond promptly to invitations and should be punctual in arriving at the party—within about fifteen minutes of the starting time specified on the invitation. Guests who have special dietary needs should inform the host in advance. When invited to someone's home, a gift of wine, chocolates, or a green plant is appropriate. Guests should not assume that they may bring another guest or their children. For picnics, brunches, and other informal events, guests may wish to offer to bring an appetizer or dessert. At the party, guests should mingle with the others and never monopolize the host. Well-mannered guests do not make negative comments about the host's home, decor, the food, or the guests who were invited. They do not drink to excess or call attention to themselves in a negative way.

As the ending time indicated on the invitation approaches, guests should thank the host for being invited and leave promptly. In addition to an oral expression of appreciation, sending a thank-you note to the host after the event is considerate.[23] Suggestions for writing thank-you notes are included in Chapter 7, "Written Communication Manners."

Showing your wild side when attending business events is a no-win situation. Acting like a fool or getting drunk is no way to make a positive impression on business colleagues.[22]

ENTERTAINING INTERNATIONAL VISITORS

When deciding whether to entertain visitors from other countries in a restaurant or in your home, consider the customs of the visitor's country and the length of the relationship.

When Letitia Baldrige, etiquette maven and former Chief of Protocol in Washington, asked a French official during a luncheon honoring the President of France what was the worst thing about doing business in the United States, he said, "Doing business at breakfast! You Americans with your endless meetings at the breakfast hour—it kills us!"[26]

Australians, Canadians, and New Zealanders, like U.S. people, often entertain business associates in their homes. People of Latin America, Asia, and most European countries (except England and Denmark), on the other hand, entertain business colleagues primarily in restaurants; they entertain in their homes only after a personal relationship has been developed.[24]

To entertain international visitors successfully, take into consideration differences between when your visitors and U.S. persons typically eat, as well as differences in what is customarily eaten. (Additional information about cultural variations in dining etiquette is contained in Chapter 8, "Dining Etiquette.") In addition to breakfast, lunch, and dinner (or breakfast, dinner, and supper), people of the United States have added brunch (usually a weekend meal), which is unknown in most other countries of the world. Thus, brunch might be a good choice when introducing foreign visitors to U.S. meal customs. A business breakfast is not a good idea as this practice is uncommon abroad.[25]

An important point for U.S. hosts to remember is that in most countries the main meal is served at midday rather than in the evening. (Since "midday" does not always mean noon in other countries, asking guests their preference on when they wish to eat their main meal is considerate.) Another choice is to select a restaurant where both options are available. The evening meal in the United States, which is between 6:00 and 8:00 P.M., may not be a good choice for international visitors who usually have only a light meal of perhaps cheese and fruit in the evening.[27]

U.S. hosts may wish to entertain their international visitors with an outdoor barbecue featuring steaks, hamburgers, or barbecued chicken. This would not, of course, be a good idea if the visitors are from countries where dietary restrictions include eating no meat. In these situations, entertaining at restaurants that are accustomed to accommodating special food preferences is recommended. Selecting a restaurant known for excellent steaks is usually appreciated by Europeans and Asians; people in these countries do not customarily receive the quality and quantity of meat served in U.S. restaurants. U.S. hosts who live in coastal areas may wish to select a good seafood restaurant as fresh seafood is appreciated by people in most cultures. Inviting your visitors to restaurants that specialize in their native cuisine is not recommended, as the U.S. version is quite different from what is served in their country. People in most cultures understand that when entertaining in a restaurant, the person

A Korean visitor to a U.S. businessman's home observed that the wife was preparing the meal. He said to his host: "We hope you will permit your wife to join us for dinner." In Korea, a wife's place is in the kitchen.[29]

who extends the invitation pays for the meal, the tip, and additional expenses, such as valet parking. Since dress customs in restaurants vary, remember to let your visitor know what attire is appropriate.[28]

In addition to entertaining your international guests in restaurants, inviting them to your home is often appreciated. Visitors usually enjoy seeing how their U.S. hosts live, including the fact that the wife usually prepares the food; this practice is often in contrast to having servants who prepare and serve meals in the visitor's home country.

Serving food buffet style may not be a good idea, depending upon customs in the visitor's country. Many people from El Salvador, for example, serve food more formally and do not expect guests to serve themselves. The host fills plates and gives them to each guest; not doing so is perceived as impersonal and uncaring.[30]

When you entertain international guests, remember the Platinum Rule: Do unto others as they would have done unto them. In other words, try to accommodate the visitor's customs, preferences, and needs as long as they are not in conflict with what you feel is ethical or moral. Competing successfully in the global marketplace often involves entertaining international visitors. Thus, developing an awareness of cultural differences in dining and entertaining is essential.[31]

In summary, business entertaining provides an excellent opportunity to get to know business colleagues on a more personal level. Building personal relationships, especially with international visitors for whom personal relationships are essential to conducting business, can often tip the scale in favor of a successful business relationship.

10

Meeting Etiquette

Meeting etiquette is like stage lighting. You only notice it when it's bad.[1]

Meetings are a very time-consuming part of business. Estimates are that upper-level managers spend over half of each week in meetings, while middle-level managers spend over a third of each week attending meetings.[2]

Although meetings are time consuming, they are a necessary part of doing business. They are a major vehicle for creating and maintaining impressions of credibility, power, efficiency, and effectiveness. Meetings represent opportunities to acquire and disseminate valuable information, develop skills, and make a favorable impression on superiors, colleagues, and subordinates.[3] People who manage meetings successfully can win recognition for their savoir-faire and respect for their professionalism. Professionalism includes knowing and practicing good manners and is important for making meetings productive rather than time wasters.[4]

Employees who have a negative attitude toward meetings often perceive them to be a waste of time. This perception is validated by studies that indicate that over half of the time people spend in meetings is wasted.[5] The negative attitudes toward meetings can be changed when meetings are conducted properly, with special attention being given to following correct procedures and practicing good manners. When meetings are well planned, brief, and productive, participants leave with positive feelings.[6]

To ensure that meetings are successful and achieve their intended purpose, attention should be given to meeting planning and preparation, seating arrangements, responsibilities of the chairman and participants, refreshments, and follow-up activities. Additional guidelines should be followed for virtual meetings and for intercultural meetings.

MEETING PLANNING AND PREPARATION

The first step in planning a meeting is determining the purpose. The next step is deciding the approximate length of the meeting to accomplish the stated purpose. The length may range from less than an hour to several days. What becomes extremely irritating to attendees is dragging out a meeting to two hours when the purpose could have been accomplished in thirty minutes or have been handled by e-mail. Next, determine the amount of time the meeting should take, considering the preferences and other commitments of those expected to attend. Then select a location, considering the degree of formality or informality appropriate for the occasion. A formal setting suggests that the person chairing the meeting will wear professional business attire, use a lectern, and have the room arranged in a classroom or theater arrangement. An informal setting suggests that the person presiding will dress in business casual attire, speak without a lectern, and have the room arranged in a U or in groups of small tables to encourage group interaction. Finally, announce the meeting by e-mail, telephone, voice messaging, facsimile, or memorandum. Include in the announcement the date, time, approximate length of the meeting, topics to be discussed, and identification of people scheduled to make oral presentations. You can also ask for a response by a certain date, especially if knowing the number planning to attend is important.[7]

Meetings will only be productive if you follow certain basic guidelines and procedures. These guidelines include minimizing the number, frequency, and length of meetings; scheduling meetings only when necessary; selecting a date and time that is convenient to most people; announcing and adhering to a beginning and ending time; and preparing a detailed agenda, with an indication of who is responsible for each item as well as the approximate length of time allotted to each topic.[8]

When selecting a meeting site, it is important to choose an area that will be comfortable for all participants, including comfortable seating, ventilation, and temperature level. The lighting should be good and the layout arranged so that those attending can see the visuals and hear what is said.[9] In addition, make sure you have side tables for refreshments or handouts. Provide bottles or pitchers of water and glasses; consider providing writing pads and pencils for participants as well.[10]

In the site selection process, keep in mind that for a meeting of employees who are considered equals, a conference table in neutral territory is considered appropriate. For informal sessions, someone's office would be appropriate. Which office you select is also a consideration; for example, a meeting would not be held in an employee's office if the supervisor were delivering bad news. When the desired impression is authority or power, the boardroom is a good choice.

When choosing the site, take into consideration the needs of physically disabled persons. For example, if someone using a wheelchair is attending, remove chairs as needed to make sure the person has adequate space to get around easily. Participants who have difficulty hearing should be given a seat near the front with a clear view of the speaker.[11] After the choice has been made, the availability of the room should be determined and the appropriate reservations made.

INTRODUCTIONS AND SEATING ARRANGEMENTS

Making introductions is the responsibility of the meeting chairman, who should arrive early and take the initiative in introducing people. In addition to introducing newcomers, the chairman greets regular participants as they arrive and shakes hands. Rules have changed over the last decade; the guest now takes the initiative in extending a hand first. Special guests should be introduced at the beginning of the meeting to alert those attending to the role the guest will play. In the absence of an early introduction of a special guest, participants start assuming that bad news is imminent, such as layoffs.[12]

Seating is an important aspect of meetings. When you are a participant, select a seat to the immediate left of the most influential person, who is not necessarily the one chairing the meeting. Sitting next to an empty chair is not a good idea as this tends to detract from your influence.[13] Arrive early so that you have a choice of seating; however, permit a person who outranks you to select a seat first. Avoid sitting across from a person with whom you expect a confrontation; this position is symbolically confrontational. Sit on the same side of the table as the person with whom you anticipate conflict, but not right next to the person. When meetings are conducted over lunch, choose adjacent chairs rather than chairs across from each other, a confrontational position.[14]

The importance of seating was illustrated in the 1972 United States/Vietnam Peace Conference. Prior to the conference considerable time was spent discussing not only seating arrangements but the shape of the conference table as well. These two factors were viewed as important to successful negotiations.[15]

The person in charge of the meeting takes a seat of central authority. The head of a rectangular table that is farthest from the door, commonly referred to as the "power perch," is widely recognized as the position of greatest authority. Although the person chairing the meeting could sit in the center seat along the length of the table, this position commands less attention and authority. The seat to the right of the chairman is typically reserved for an assistant to the chairman or for the person next in importance to the chairman. Placing a folder on the table is usually sufficient to reserve this position. The person who is considered next in the line of authority or importance would be seated to the left of the chairman. People invited to make special presentations should wait to be seated until regular attendees have taken their seats. The person chairing the meeting will usually indicate where the guests are to sit. Care should be exercised in choosing the position at the opposite end of the table from the chairman as this location is sometimes viewed as confrontational. Remember that rank, rather than gender or age, is a consideration in seating and participation in meetings.[16]

Henry Ford used a rather eccentric technique at his staff meetings to symbolize his control. He sat in the only chair; all his employees stood. This technique also kept staff meetings short and to the point.[18]

To avoid the seating dilemma in meetings, you can remove the chairs from the room and have everyone stand up. The meetings will no doubt be very short.[17] Of course, if you wish to emphasize your position of authority, you may decide to do what Henry Ford was reported to have done and have the only chair in the room.

CHAIRING RESPONSIBILITIES

The person chairing a meeting would be wise to review what a recognized authority in meeting management has identified as "Dumb Things Meeting Leaders Do": makes a poor initial impression, is boring and dull, stands in one spot, has a poor facial expression and weak eye contact, does not involve the audience, shows no enthusiasm, has an inaudible voice, and uses poor visual aids or uses them incorrectly.[19] Etiquette authors have identified these additional behaviors as being characteristic of a leader with poor meeting manners: failure to start or end on time; failure to introduce self or participants; and failure to follow the agenda, keep control of attendees, and schedule breaks.[20] In a survey of Mid-South employees to determine their perceptions of proper meeting manners, respondents identified these additional inappropriate chair behaviors: Recapping the information covered for meeting participants who arrive late and bringing one's own refreshments to a meeting.[21]

To chair a meeting successfully, the person in charge should schedule it well in advance and choose a date and time that is convenient for most of the expected participants. Meetings scheduled early or late in the day should be avoided as well as meetings on Friday afternoon (especially when bad news or criticism is on the agenda), Monday morning, or the afternoon before a holiday. Just before lunch may not be a good choice unless lunch is being provided. Asking those expected to attend their preferences on dates and times is usually appreciated as it shows consideration for others.[22]

The meeting chairman should distribute the agenda a few days in advance of the meeting; this agenda should include not only the date and location but also the beginning and ending times (most routine meetings should not exceed an hour) and topics to be discussed. In addition to listing each topic and the person responsible for leading the discussion, notations such as "for discussion only" or "for decision today" should be added to let those attending know what is to be accomplished on each item. If the meeting is scheduled near lunchtime and refreshments are planned, include a statement on the agenda that light luncheon fare, such as sandwiches and cookies, will be served.[23]

An effective chairperson will decide which visual aids to use. These visuals may vary from handouts to projected computer-driven displays. Although overhead projectors were popular in the past, they have been replaced by such projected computer-driven displays as PowerPoint. PowerPoint slides are quite easy to prepare and require only a computer and the appropriate software.[24] Since using poor visuals or using visuals incorrectly has been identified as being characteristic of an ineffective chairperson, those who lead meetings should become knowledgeable about which visual aids are appropriate for specific types of meetings and should learn to use them correctly. Additional information about visual aids is presented in Chapter 11, "Presentations."

Before starting the meeting, the person chairing it should place on the door a sign that states "Meeting in Progress" to avoid interruptions. The chairperson should avoid recapping information for late arrivals; this tends to give the impression of condoning tardiness. In addition, the chairman should follow proper parliamentary procedure using such references as *Robert's Rules of Order* and *Jones' Parliamentary Procedure at a Glance* to assure that the minority is heard but that the will of the majority prevails.[25]

The meeting chairman is also responsible for maintaining control of the meeting, including anticipating issues that might cause conflict or disagreement. The chairman can simply make a statement that persons should limit their comments to a couple of minutes to allow sufficient time for all participants to express their opinions.

Other responsibilities of the chairman include thanking people who made presentations and recognizing those who contributed in any way to the success of the meeting, including those who compiled figures, prepared charts or handouts, and arranged for refreshments. Above all, the chairman should start on time and end on time. While going beyond the stated ending time by five minutes is acceptable, extending the meeting longer than that is rude.[26]

PARTICIPANT RESPONSIBILITIES

Proper participant behavior is also essential to the success of meetings. Participants should arrive three to five minutes early since punctuality is essential in this culture.[27] (The United States is considered a five-minute culture when it comes to punctuality. You are allowed to be five minutes late, but even then an apology is expected.) Arriving too early is also inappropriate. Arriving more than ten minutes early creates an awkward situation for persons in charge of the meeting who may be attending to last-minute details or discussing meeting procedures with a colleague or supervisor. They do not appreciate being scrutinized by participants. Participants who arrive early and see that people are busy with last-minute preparations should step outside and wait until the announced time of the meeting.[28]

Participants are expected to introduce themselves to others and shake hands when the person presiding does not introduce them. Visitors should remember that they extend their hands first; they should wait for the chairman to be seated and to indicate where they are to sit. As a participant, you should bring along a pad and pen for taking notes. Sit erectly and lean forward slightly to indicate interest in the discussion. Give appropriate eye contact, and give your full attention to the speaker. Asking questions or making comments is certainly appropriate; however, do not dominate the discussion, interrupt, or be argumentative. Stay for the entire meeting; leaving during the meeting is disruptive and rude. If a prior commitment necessitates your leaving early, the person presiding should be informed before the meeting starts. In such cases, sitting near the door to leave without being disruptive is considerate.[29]

When you are a meeting participant, do not engage in distracting behaviors, such as doodling, playing with rubber bands, chewing gum, or sucking on mints or candies. Do not engage in any activities that are unrelated to the meeting, such as reading mail. (Since the United States is a monochronic culture, doing only one thing at a time—participating in the meeting—is expected.) Carrying on side conversations is rude and gives a negative impression. Avoid bringing a laptop, PDA, or Black-Berry to a meeting; turn off cell phones or set them to vibration mode. Keep your clothes on—jackets and ties should not be removed. Be aware of your gestures and posture; crossing your arms in front of you is indicative of a closed mind or hostility. Do not place elbows on the table, and keep your feet on the floor rather than propping them on an adjoining empty chair.[30]

At the end of the meeting, thank the person in charge and shake hands with the chairman and other participants as they leave. After attending an out-of-town meeting, write a note to the chairperson to thank and compliment the person on doing a great job.

REFRESHMENTS

Offering refreshments at meetings is considered a gracious gesture and is appreciated by persons attending. Good manners dictate that refreshments be provided when a meeting is expected to exceed an hour and a half. These refreshments should be available at a nearby table and arranged so that participants can serve themselves. The person who makes arrangements for refreshments should keep these guidelines in mind:

- Provide a tablecloth (a paper covering is acceptable) and napkins as well as small plates and eating utensils as appropriate. Provide small plates when serving more than a single item and plastic utensils as needed.

- Furnish glasses and/or cups; drinking from a can or a bottle both in business and social situations is indicative of a person with poor social skills.[31]

- Provide ice in an ice bucket or large bowl with a scoop to transfer ice to glasses for those who prefer iced beverages.

- Offer an assortment of drinks to accommodate various preferences, i.e., soft drinks, juices, coffee, tea, and bottled water. Also keep in mind that 2-liter bottles of drinks which participants are expected to share are inappropriate. (In an individualistic culture, such as the United States, each person wants his or her own drink.) In addition to a variety of beverage options, choices in sizes should also be made available—provide both 12- and 8-ounce sizes of bottled water, soft drinks, and juices. Try to provide both regular and decaffeinated coffee and tea.[32]

- Select food that is appropriate to the time of day—muffins, fruit, and/or bagels for morning meetings and popcorn, pretzels, cheese, cookies, or finger foods for afternoon meetings. (Doughnuts, once popular at breakfast meetings, have been replaced with more healthful choices. The high-sugar doughnuts provide quick energy but an equally quick energy crash; bagels, which provide complex carbohydrates, are preferable). Avoid crunchy, greasy foods, such as chips, and messy foods that are difficult to eat, such as pizza. Also try to accommodate vegetarians.[33]

All persons attending the meeting should remember that when serving themselves, they should take only one muffin or cookie (or two small ones) until all attendees have been served. Later, they may choose to go back for seconds. Those attending meetings should also remember that bringing their own beverages or food to a meeting is rude.[34]

FOLLOW-UP ACTIVITIES

The meeting should end with the chairman's summary of what the meeting has accomplished, reminders to participants of any tasks for which they have volunteered or have been assigned, and a determination of the date of the next meeting.[35]

Handling follow-up activities is the responsibility of the meeting chairman and his or her administrative assistant. These activities include being sure that the meeting room is left in good order. Leaving behind used cups and plates, for example, leaves a negative impression and will not be appreciated by the next person who uses the room. The chairman should send a summary memorandum to all participants indicating their assignments and deadlines for completing these assignments. While this informal memorandum is adequate for thanking participants, more formal letters of appreciation should be sent to those who made presentations or special contributions to the meeting. Other follow-up activities include arranging for preparation and distribution of the minutes. Distribute minutes within two days of the meeting; they need not be arranged in a formal style but should list principal accomplishments, assignments, actions taken, and the date of the next meeting.[36] An important part of the follow-up procedure is to review and evaluate the success of the meeting immediately upon its completion. By analyzing each aspect of the meeting, such as the agenda, accomplishment of stated objectives, and conflict resolution, areas needing improvement can be determined.[37]

BUSINESS MEAL MEETINGS

Business meals have become commonplace in the United States. Dressing and behaving professionally during business meals is even more important than would be true of corporate, nonmeal functions on the company premises. At business meals your table manners are scrutinized in addition to your conversational skills; these skills leave a positive or negative impression of both you and the firm you represent.[38]

In many organizations breakfast meetings, which are usually scheduled 6:30–8:00 A.M., are making the workday longer. Many of these breakfast meetings are conducted in-house with caterers providing refreshments; in other cases, the person in charge provides simple fare such as muffins and coffee. Some employees resent this intrusion on what they may consider their personal time; they must get up earlier than usual and select clothing and do their homework for the meeting the night before.[40] Breakfast meetings are popular because they are less expensive than lunch or dinner meetings and because the regular workday is interrupted only slightly if at all. In some companies, business lunches are preferred to breakfast meetings. These lunches are

A successful business owner, known for hiring excellent managers, said that part of the interviewing process was inviting the person to lunch. Interviewees who salted their food before tasting it were not hired. To the business owner, this behavior was indicative of poor manners.[39]

usually short—lasting from one to two hours—because employees must return to work. They are more informal; employees do not feel that their personal time has been infringed upon. Business discussions are begun after the main course; the person of highest rank or the one in charge of the meeting begins the business discussion. The person who issues the invitation, regardless of gender, pays the bill, including the tip. The business dinner is more formal and longer since employees are not rushing to return to their offices. Often the business dinner is to honor an employee who is retiring or perhaps to entertain an out-of-town client. The purpose of such meetings is not usually to discuss business but to thank an employee for long years of service or to build a positive working relationship.[41] When you are invited to a business breakfast, lunch, or dinner, remember to send a thank-you note to the person who invited you. Special guidelines for business meals that are part of the job interview are covered in Chapter 1, "Job Interview Etiquette"; other aspects of business meal meetings are included in Chapter 8, "Dining Etiquette," and Chapter 9, "Business Entertaining."

CONVENTIONS

Conventions bring together professionals who share common interests. Conventions usually last from two to five days and involve travel to another city or country; they also involve scheduled and unscheduled social events. Those attending conventions must remember that, while fun and merriment are an accepted part of conventions, their conduct is being observed by others. Such conduct reflects on the organization they represent as well as on the individual.

Specific suggestions for conveying a professional image include wearing appropriate attire, participating in business sessions, drinking and "partying" in moderation, being courteous and respectful to hotel employees, and paying your share of meals and entertainment. When not attending meetings, convention goers may dress casually but should choose attire that is appropriate for the occasion. A conservative bathing suit while poolside, for example, conveys a more favorable impression than a revealing bikini. Attend all sessions that relate to your job since this is primarily a business event. If a spouse or child accompanies you, make sure they understand that business comes before play, especially when the company pays your expenses. Drink moderately; dancing the night away in a local nightclub may not be a good idea when sessions are scheduled for the following

Will Rogers, known for his American cowboy wit, had this to say about the importance of proper behavior at conventions: "There is no better place in the world to find out the shortcomings of each other than a conference."[42]

morning. Be very polite to hotel personnel; losing your temper in public leaves a bad impression. Finally, pay your own way. Do not expect others to pay for your drinks, meals, or entertainment.[43]

VIRTUAL MEETINGS

Technology has had a significant impact on the way meetings are conducted. Since meetings are so costly for companies, they are looking for ways to cut down on the time and money involved in travel to and from meetings. Many companies are now exploring the use of virtual meetings as an option to traditional face-to-face meetings. Virtual meetings involve having employees connected by computers, satellites, or telephones.

Virtual meetings have an advantage of employees' being able to share information, discuss options, and make decisions in the comfort and privacy of their offices. Thus, the time and money required for travel is saved. In addition, the likelihood of adversarial discussions is reduced; people tend to be more focused since the distractions of traditional meetings are removed.[44] Although virtual meetings do not eliminate all face-to-face meetings, they do result in a savings to the organization. Some employees have even expressed a preference for virtual meetings; they feel they get more accomplished than when they attend traditional meetings, and they also feel freer to express their opinions.[45]

Despite the advantages of virtual meetings, they also have some disadvantages. The primary disadvantage is perhaps the absence of nonverbal communication. How something is said is often as important as what is said. Another disadvantage is the slower pace of making decisions since time is required to collect information from all participants before making a decision. Finally, confidentiality of information is compromised as well as the ability to build a team spirit.[46]

Proper etiquette for virtual meetings includes adhering to agreed-upon guidelines, replying to messages promptly, avoiding negative attitudes or implied criticism, avoiding the use of humor (even use of emoticons is not advised when communicating electronically), and taking necessary precautions to protect confidential information. Further, it is important to use plain language and to explain special terms. In addition, researching issues and being thoroughly prepared is essential to the success of virtual meetings.[47]

MULTICULTURAL MEETINGS

Business meetings involving people of different cultures can vary greatly from typical U.S. business meetings. Many things must be taken into consideration, including cultural variations in opening and closing the meeting as well as variations in how discussions are conducted, the use of language, and nonverbal communication. In addition, cultural

During World War II, a misunderstanding arose between American and British representatives over the verb "to table." In Sir Winston Churchill's memoirs, he reported a discussion with their American allies over whether to "table" an issue. When Americans "table" an issue, they mean setting it aside for consideration later; when the British "table" an issue, they mean placing it on the table for discussion immediately. Churchill stated that the two sides had quite a bitter argument until they discovered their two cultures had different meanings for the same term.[48]

differences exist in the meaning of certain terms when following parliamentary procedure.

In the United States building a relationship prior to getting down to business is not important. In Latin America, Central and Eastern Europe, Asia, and Arab countries, however, personal relationships are important. Opening talks start promptly in the United States with a brief period of time spent in light conversation. In Finland, on the other hand, there is no small talk as they prefer to get right down to business. Agendas are important in the United States but are not necessary in Latin America, the Middle East, and some Asian countries, especially Japan.

Discussions, which tend to be unemotional in the United States, may be rather emotional in Argentina. Meetings with the French can be quite lively as they enjoy debating issues. In discussions with Asians, it is important to remember that smiling usually conveys lack of understanding. In addition, when the Japanese say "Yes," the actual meaning may be "Yes, I understand."[49] Silence should not be misinterpreted when meeting with the Japanese. Unlike people of the United States, the Japanese value silence and use it to contemplate what has been said. The Japanese are indirect, whereas people of the United States are direct and to the point.

Cultural variations in seating should also be considered. In U. S. meetings, participants usually sit across the table from each other, but in the Arab culture, participants are arranged by age and status. Meetings end differently also; U.S. meetings end with a plan of action, including commitments from those attending. Japanese meetings end with no commitment; Arab meetings end with a promise to continue the business relationship.[50]

Other suggestions when participating in multicultural meetings include the following:

- Avoid telling jokes as U.S. humor is hard to understand in other cultures.
- Avoid the use of slang.
- Ask permission to speak English if you do not speak the local language (or use an interpreter).
- Accept any refreshments offered.

A Swiss executive who had moved to the United States was asked by his new boss how he was adjusting to the U.S. business culture. He replied that the most difficult adjustment was related to U.S. business meetings. In his country, meetings are announced two weeks in advance, an agenda is distributed one week in advance, and the door to the meeting room is locked one minute after the stated beginning time of the meeting. Latecomers are not permitted to enter, and pagers and cell phones must be turned off. No one leaves the meeting early; meetings always end on time.[51]

- Dress conservatively in professional business attire.
- Do not use gestures.
- Follow the lead of people in the host culture regarding greetings, business card exchange, and gift giving.

Additional information related to intercultural etiquette is presented in Chapter 14, "Global Manners."

Since meetings are a necessary yet time-consuming part of business life in the United States as well as in other cultures, they should be designed carefully to assure that time is used wisely and that optimum results are achieved. Knowledge of proper meeting etiquette, whether as a meeting leader or participant, will be noticed and may be an asset in promotion decisions.

Presentations

> You can shape the audience's perceptions of you and your message by
> the way you dress, stand, project your voice, and speak with authority.[1]

The ability to make an effective presentation before an audience is a
key business skill that is often associated with career advancement.
Presentation effectiveness is not only related to what the speaker says
but to elements related to nonverbal communication and good manners
as well. Speakers' dress, their eye contact and body language, their vocal
characteristics, their use of visual aids, their apparent preparation, and
their use of time when speaking to a group largely determines both
personal and organizational credibility.[2] In addition to speaker behavior
and etiquette, other important aspects of presentations that require
knowledge of good manners are presenter introductions and audience
etiquette.

EYE CONTACT, POSTURE, AND GESTURES

The most important nonverbal communicator when speaking to an
audience is eye contact.[3] With direct eye contact, the speaker appears
more confident and more accepting of audience feedback. Eye contact,
accompanied by a smile, gives the audience the impression that the
speaker is happy to be there. Experts advise connecting with individuals
rather than letting the eyes sweep over the audience without making
eye contact with anyone in particular. A good technique to use is to select
a person in the audience who is smiling and nodding in agreement and to
talk directly to that person, then choose another, focusing on each person
about three to five seconds.[4] With large groups, it is important to make
eye contact with people seated in different parts of the room. Speakers

should, in fact, strive to maintain eye contact with the audience about three-fourths of the time. Since this is almost impossible to do when reading from notes or the screen, presenters should be well prepared. Speakers who are prepared have an easier time maintaining eye contact with the audience.[5]

In addition to eye contact, your posture is important to projecting a positive image when making a presentation. Posture should be erect but relaxed. Being too stiff suggests uptightness, being too loose conveys sloppiness, and being hunched indicates low confidence and self-esteem. You should stand erectly with weight balanced on both feet to convey an aura of confidence.[6] While some presenters feel that sitting or leaning on a table or desk gives the impression that they are relaxed, this type of posture is often viewed negatively. Leaning on the lectern is to be avoided since this may be interpreted as needing something for support.[7] In addition, leaning on the lectern conveys informality and a lack of forcefulness.[8] Another negative association with the lectern is sometimes referred to as "the death grip," which indicates extreme nervousness and lack of confidence.[9]

Gestures are helpful for a speaker; they complement, clarify, and intensify the spoken message. Speakers who use some gestures appear more at ease than those who use no gestures. Gestures may be voluntary or involuntary and may support a point or call attention to the speaker's discomfort. Natural relaxed movements communicate self-confidence; to appear natural, however, gestures should coincide with specific points but should not distract from the presentation.[10]

Speakers who seem to smile naturally make audience members feel comfortable. They can create instant rapport with the audience. Of course, smiles should be used at appropriate times; smiling at inappropriate times can undermine the intended message. Giving the audience a reassuring smile is certainly preferable to the stone-faced look that is more appropriate for delivering a eulogy.[11]

PRESENTATION ATTIRE

People form impressions of others within about a minute; much of this initial impression is based on such nonverbal elements as dress and appearance. Successful speakers recognize that appropriate attire conveys expertise, trustworthiness, and dynamism. Being dressed appropriately will boost a speaker's confidence and make him or her more at ease before a group. How a speaker dresses is also related to respect. Some listeners will make judgments about the message based on their interpretation of the respect being shown them by the speaker's choice of attire.

When speakers wear very casual attire, the audience may feel that the presenters do not consider them sufficiently important to warrant

After the third week of classes, a graduate assistant remarked to her major professor that she was planning to drop one of her courses because she did not think the instructor knew the subject. Her conclusion that the instructor was incompetent, it seems, was based upon the fact that he wore the same torn jeans, soiled T-shirt, sandals, and white socks to every class.

wearing more professional attire. Regardless of the business situation, people who wear suits, whether male or female, are perceived as more professional than those who wear any other type of attire.[12] Speakers who wish to be taken seriously should wear very dark suits in gray or navy blue with white cotton shirts for men and medium-range blue or navy suits with white blouses for women. Women should avoid bright reds and oranges as these colors detract from the face. Unusual patterns can be distracting so solid colors generally work best.[13] Women should also be careful of the hem length especially if they will be sitting on a stage; longer hems and longer sleeves are recommended.[14]

Presenters should dress so they stand out, not stick out; they should remember that presentation attire includes not only their clothing but their hair style, grooming, and accessories as well. Shoes are especially important to presenters; they should be well shined and in good repair as the audience will scrutinize them. Men should remember to wear hose that are long enough so that no bare leg shows when they are seated. Accessories should be conservative; jewelry should be kept to a minimum and should not be distracting. Distracting jewelry is jewelry that sparkles, dangles, or makes a noise.[15] Hair should be clean and styled conservatively; nails should be clean and well trimmed. In short, speakers should dress in a way that does not distract the audience and detract from the message.[16]

VOCAL CHARACTERISTICS

Vocal image is important in establishing a speaker's credibility. Varying the rate, pitch, and volume enhances a person's image. Speakers with a smooth and clear vocal image, with good volume, and with a varied speech rate free of hesitation are thought to be more dynamic and trustworthy.[17] Weaknesses in vocal image include speaking at a steady, even pace; speaking in a monotone; maintaining one level of volume throughout the presentation; and improper use of pauses. Presenters who speak too slowly or in a low voice, as well as those who mispronounce words and use poor grammar, damage their credibility.[18]

One of the most common speech problems is speaking with a nasal voice. Excessive nasality is not peculiar to a specific region or culture. Because it can be distracting, speakers should make an effort to correct this habit. Other voice problems include harshness, speaking in too high a pitch (associated more with women than with men), breathlessness, and use of filler words to avoid silent pauses. Using a lower pitch makes the speaker sound more confident and calm; both men and women should strive to lower the pitch of their voices.[19]

Silent pauses are desirable; they allow time for the audience to get the full impact of what the speaker said. Pausing is useful before changing the subject or for emphasizing a point. Vocalized pauses and fillers, however, can be distracting. A vocalized pause is a pause a speaker fills with "uh," "um," or "okay." When vocalized pauses are used frequently, listeners become distracted and start noticing these fillers and lose sight of the message content. These vocalized pauses can, in fact, be just as distracting as slang and regional peculiarities in speech.[20] Speakers who have picked up local accents and speech patterns must make a real effort to lose them, especially when they move to another part of the country where such regionalisms can be distracting. In addition to these fillers, some speakers use speech tics that are popular at the time, such as "like," "you know," "really," "basically," and "actually."[21]

You should be aware of foods or beverages that affect the voice. Water at room temperature with lemon is a good choice for nervousness; the lemon clears mucus. Presenters should avoid milk, ice cream, or yogurt before presentations as these foods cause phlegm that will necessitate constant clearing of the throat. Coffee and tea should be avoided as caffeine dries the throat and sometimes makes the voice crack. Sodas are not good choices because of the carbonation, which can cause burping. Alcohol should be avoided; the results are somewhat unpredictable depending upon the person and the amount of alcohol consumed.[22]

PRESENTATION ORGANIZATION

After determining the subject of the presentation, the speaker should follow this plan: *tell what you are going to tell, tell it,* and *tell what you have told.* Following this plan will result in a talk with three sections: introduction, body, and conclusion.[23]

In the first element of the introduction, the speaker attempts to get a favorable reaction from the audience. While some speakers think they can get a positive reaction by telling a humorous story, others prefer to avoid humor. Additional ways to gain the listeners' attention are beginning with a startling fact, reading a short quotation that introduces the topic, giving a related statistic, or asking an appropriate question.[24] A second element of the introduction is providing background information to help the audience understand why the topic is important; for example, "During the past year absenteeism has increased 20 percent; today we are going to examine the relationship between absenteeism and employee morale." A third element is the scope, which sets boundaries of the talk; for example, "This morning I will discuss employees' business casual attire; business professional attire will not be addressed at today's meeting." The fourth element is defining terms with which the audience may not be familiar; for example, "I assume everyone knows the meaning of the term *crudités*. If not, what do you call a platter of raw vegetables cut into small pieces and served with a dip?" Finally, plan the presentation; tell the audience what topics will be covered; for example, "We will discuss four ways to improve the ethical climate at our company." This fifth element is the final part of the introduction; it provides an effective transition to the body of the presentation.[25]

In the body of the talk, the speaker should remember to limit the body to a maximum of five main points. The body can be organized by importance, with the most important topic presented first; by component, which means presenting information by geographical location, department, etc.; by chronology, which means presenting information in the order of occurrence; or by cause/effect/solution, which is self-explanatory.[26]

The conclusion of a talk is just as important as the introduction. Closing remarks are so important that memorizing them is recommended. When presentations end on a weak note, because they are either too lengthy or too abrupt, audiences tend to remember that fact.[27] In the conclusion, summarize the main points, make recommendations, restate the purpose, motivate the audience to action when appropriate, or end with a quotation from a recognized authority to emphasize the importance of the topic.[28] Closing remarks should be followed by an expression of appreciation for the audience's attention.

HUMOR

Humor is often used in U.S. presentations to build rapport with the audience and to provide a bit of levity. Speakers know that people enjoy a good laugh and that they tend to like presenters who are humorous. When they like a speaker, audience members are more likely to listen carefully.[29]

Starting a presentation with a joke, a common practice by U.S. presenters, is actually a questionable way of beginning a talk, especially when audiences are made up of people of different cultures. Often the speaker tells a joke that is unrelated to the topic or that unintentionally offends someone in the audience. Alienating audience members is not an effective way to begin a presentation.[30]

When deciding upon the type of humor appropriate for the occasion, follow these guidelines: Make sure the humor is related to the topic; use humor the audience can understand; and avoid sarcasm, embarrassing anyone, profanity, and jokes or anecdotes related to gender, politics, ethnicity, religion, or jokes with sexual undertones. While self-deprecating humor is appropriate, making fun of other people is not. Speakers who do not feel comfortable telling humorous stories may simply include them on their slides or transparencies. Finally, when you are in doubt about the appropriateness of humor to a specific audience, it is better to leave it out.[31]

VISUAL AIDS

Visual aids can be very useful for gaining attention and for helping audience members retain information. Since people remember half of what they both see and hear, as opposed to only one-fifth of what they hear and about one-third of what they see, visual aids are helpful for both increased comprehension and retention. Visual aids give a polished touch to presentations; they are evidence of preparation and enhance the speaker's credibility. Visual aids are especially useful in multicultural audiences; people whose first language is other than English can follow the presentation easier with well-prepared visuals.[32] Visuals can also be useful for keeping the speaker well organized and can replace the speaker's notes; they serve as an outline to keep the speaker on track.[33]

To design effective visual aids, use the KISS and the KILL Methods. KISS stands for Keep It Short and Simple. Limiting the information to one idea per visual is recommended. The KILL Method means Keep It Large and Legible. When using presentation software, such as Power-Point, a large font size should be used: at least 24-point font for text and 28- to 42-point font for titles. To increase legibility, a sans serif font (no strokes or "feet" after letters) such as Arial, is recommended. In addition, the number of bullet points per slide should be limited to five, and the structure should be parallel. The "build" effect (revealing only a single bullet point at a time) is effective but should not be overdone. Clip art should be used sparingly if at all. The same color scheme should be used throughout the presentation.[34]

When visuals are used incorrectly, the effect may negate the impact of an important message. Bear in mind, therefore, that visual aids should be two things: *visual* and *aids*. To make sure that the visual aids are *visual*, avoid standing between the visual and the audience and use a font size that is sufficiently large that persons at the back of the room can read the

The president of a large shipping company spoke at a conference where he was given an opportunity to gain new customers for his firm. During the presentation he inadvertently pressed the wrong buttons on the remote control; the slides did not correspond to what he was saying. He was embarrassed and knew that his opportunity for new customers was disintegrating before his eyes. He knew that the audience would conclude that they would not trust a shipping company whose president did not even know how to operate visual-aid equipment.[36]

Winston Churchill always had notes with him when he delivered a speech; however, he seldom used them. When questioned about this, Churchill replied, "I carry fire insurance, but I don't expect my house to burn down."[37]

slide or transparency. Too much information on visuals, as well as an excessive number, will reduce the effectiveness of the presentation.[35] To assure that the visual aids are *aids,* be well prepared so that you do not have to read from your slides or transparencies. Reading suggests a lack of preparation and a lack of confidence. Also remember that visuals should not be too overpowering so that audience members are concentrating on the visuals rather than on the content of the message.

Some presenters feel more comfortable with notes. Notes enable the presenter to speak conversationally to the audience and are preferable to memorizing a talk. Speakers who take along notes do so to provide reassurance in case of memory failure.

When notes are desired, note cards (4 by 6 inches or 5 by 7 inches) are easier to handle and are less conspicuous than full sheets of paper. The cards can be numbered to keep them in correct order; the notes should be large and clear enough to see at a glance. Using only one side of a card is preferable. Put no more than two or three notes on each card; each note should prompt about a half minute of speaking time. When using note cards, speakers should look at the audience before looking at their notes. Quotations should be read; audience members will understand the importance of quoting material correctly.[38]

Presenters who use notes should be aware that their use can interfere with effective delivery of the message. Use of notes may be interpreted by the audience as lack of preparation; reading from notes may result in a loss of the attention of the audience. In addition, the constant movement of the speaker's eyes from the notes to the audience can be annoying.[39]

PRESENTER ETIQUETTE

Speakers should be on time. Punctuality in a time-conscious culture such as the United States shows respect for the time of people in the audience. Tardiness indicates that a person is inconsiderate, disrespectful, and disorganized.

Begin your presentation by making a self-introduction when you were not fully introduced; then acknowledge dignitaries present and thank the person who issued the invitation. For example, "Dr. Hunt, Judge Freeman, and members of the Junior League, thank you for inviting me to speak to you today." Although some speakers start with a humorous story, this is not always a good idea. It is more important to appear pleasant, interesting, likable, warm, and sincere.[40]

At a conference for business educators in the Mid-South, one of the featured speakers was a teacher who had recently been named "teacher-of-the-year" by the local school system. The title of her presentation was, "How to be an Effective Teacher." When she arrived twenty minutes late and breathlessly explained for ten minutes why she was so late, the audience was neither amused nor sympathetic. In view of her topic, nothing she could have said could make up for her tardiness. Her suggestions for being an effective teacher fell on deaf ears as audience members, who were also teachers, knew that tardiness was not the mark of an effective teacher and that "Actions Speak Louder than Words."

Studies show that the maximum time the average person can listen attentively to a speaker is about twenty minutes. Thus, the classic reminder from Mark Twain that "no sinner is ever saved after the first 20 minutes of a sermon" is probably good advice for presenters.[42]

Being well prepared is essential. Audiences will remain more alert and interested when the speaker has organized, practiced, and timed the presentation. Inadequate preparation, which soon becomes evident to the audience, shows a lack of consideration for people who have taken time out of their busy lives to listen to what they had assumed would be an enlightened, stimulating presentation.

Speakers who are not well prepared spend an excessive amount of time looking at their notes rather than at their audience. When presenters are ill prepared, they often exceed the expected time limit; then audience members will leave either mentally or physically. Speakers should ask someone to monitor the time and signal them when they are approaching their allotted time so that they do not have to glance at their watches. Smart speakers will start on time and end on time even if they have to omit parts of the presentation they had intended to cover.[41]

DISTRACTING OR ANNOYING PRESENTER BEHAVIORS

To increase their speaking effectiveness, presenters should attempt to understand what behaviors are distracting or annoying to audience members to the extent that they interfere with the intended message. A survey of trainees in an international airfreight company with world headquarters in the Mid-South was conducted to determine what presenter behaviors were most distracting or annoying during their training sessions. The following behaviors were viewed as most distracting or annoying (in order, starting with most distracting or annoying):

- Wasting valuable learning time by straying from the topic;
- Saying "uh," "um," "you know," or "okay" repeatedly;

- Blocking the audience's view by standing in front of the screen;
- Mispronouncing words or using poor grammar;
- Not allowing feedback or questions from the audience;
- Having nervous mannerisms, such as clicking a pen or clearing the throat;
- Speaking too slowly or too rapidly or in a low voice;
- Reading the presentation or having participants read from their materials;
- Speaking in a monotone; and
- Using no gestures and standing motionless behind the podium.[43]

When trainees in this survey were also asked to indicate the extent of their agreement with the statement that distracting or annoying behaviors have a negative impact on their understanding of the intended message and on the trainer's credibility, they indicated agreement with the statement.[44] Other distracting behaviors speakers should avoid include talking toward the visual rather than toward the audience, standing near and touching the screen, and making comments about lack of knowledge of the operation of the equipment, such as, "How do you focus this thing?"[45]

A speaker's gestures are often distracting to the audience. Gestures to be avoided include rocking or pacing back and forth, placing hands on hips, folding both arms across the chest, clenching or rubbing hands together, and repeated removal and replacement of glasses (or looking at the audience over the top of reading glasses). Other gestures that may prove distracting include touching the face, ears, or hair; adjusting articles of clothing; and repeated use of the same gesture.[46] Distracting gestures men are sometimes guilty of include jingling coins or keys in the pant's pocket and standing with hands in pockets while speaking. Women sometimes twirl their hair or wear jangling jewelry that can be both a visual distraction and an audio distraction.[47]

PRESENTER INTRODUCTIONS

People who introduce speakers should remember that introductions should be short and simple. The introducer should appear to be friendly to set a positive mood for the event. The person asked to introduce the speaker should request a short biography prior to the scheduled presentation. The points to be included should be of interest to the particular audience.[48] Sometimes the person introducing the speaker will say that he or she needs no introduction, implying that the speaker is well known to the audience, and then proceed with a lengthy summary of the presenter's qualifications. Such statements should be avoided; simply give enough information to interest the audience and to provide the needed credibility. The audience wants to know that the presenter is qualified to speak on the topic. Thus, the speaker's formal education, current position, awards and recognitions received, book and journal publications, and memberships in organizations related to the topic should be included in an introduction which should last about three to five minutes.[49]

The person making the introduction will probably need note cards, since details of a person's education, publications, honors, and memberships would be difficult to remember. Writing out the complete introduction is recommended; after some practice, glancing at the notes should be sufficient. Humor may be used provided it fits the occasion. However, telling a joke ostensibly to create a relaxed atmosphere would be inappropriate. Avoid including dates when giving a person's academic degrees or telling how long a person has been with an organization; women are especially sensitive to information that would reveal their approximate age. Saying, "Ms. Green received her Master's degree thirty years ago and has been with Mid-America Hospitality for over twenty-five years" has some audience members doing some quick math and is not a welcomed introduction, especially for women.

In a discussion with the speaker before the scheduled talk, the introducer would have determined whether the speaker will answer questions at the end and will indicate this to the audience, including the specific time period, which is typically about ten minutes. The introducer may suggest a question to a member of the audience ahead of time to get the question-and-answer session started. The person who introduced the speaker is responsible for bringing the questioning period to a close; this is usually done by saying that enough time remains for only one more question. During the question-and-answer session, should an audience member disagree with something the speaker said (very rude behavior), the introducer may wish to step in and suggest that debating the issue should be saved for another time. At the conclusion of the session, the person making the introduction stands, leads the applause, thanks the speaker, and dismisses the group or turns the program over to the person in charge if additional sessions are scheduled.[50]

AUDIENCE ETIQUETTE

Since most people are in the role of audience member more than in the role of presenter, it is important to know audience etiquette. Proper behavior for audience members includes being punctual, being quiet, maintaining good posture, appearing attentive, and asking appropriate questions.

Speakers appreciate it when audience members arrive on time. Latecomers may interrupt their train of thought causing them to forget what they had planned to say. In addition, those who arrive late may be disruptive as they chat momentarily with the person seated next to them in an effort to determine what has already been covered. A quiet demeanor is much appreciated by the speaker; use of a laptop computer,

PDA, or BlackBerry should be avoided. Cellular phones should be left in the office or set to vibration mode. Audience members should stay for the entire session as leaving and returning is very disruptive. Maintaining a good posture and a pleasant facial expression, giving eye contact, and exhibiting other listening behaviors are marks of considerate audience members. When questions are to be saved for the end of the talk, avoid interrupting during the presentation. Avoid making a statement that implies disagreement with what has been said as this is rude. When the speaker is not charging a fee for the talk, criticizing the speaker or what was presented shows very bad manners.[51]

Daniel Webster once said, "If all my talents and powers were to be taken from me by some inscrutable Providence, and I had my choice of keeping but one, I would unhesitatingly ask to be allowed to keep the power of speaking, for through it I would quickly recover all the rest."[53]

In closing, one of the most important things to remember when making a presentation is credibility. Audiences are more forgiving of an imperfect presentation if the speaker possesses high credibility. When a speaker has low credibility, delivering a perfect presentation will not matter. To enhance credibility, speakers should have character, competence, composure, likability, and extroversion. Character, which refers to the speaker's fairness, honesty, and trustworthiness, is probably the most important element of credibility. Competence, which refers to knowledge of the topic, educational background, and experience, is next in importance. Composure, likability, and being moderately extroverted appear to be linked to credibility as well. To enhance their credibility, speakers should associate with high-credibility organizations, should dress well, should admit when they do not know something, and should remember that actions speak louder than words. Speakers should also make sure that the person introducing them includes their credentials, including college degrees, honors and awards, experience, and publications. You can also work your credentials into the presentation to elaborate on certain points, such as mentioning living abroad when giving a presentation on intercultural etiquette.[52]

Seeking opportunities to speak before an audience will help presenters improve their oratory skills since practice, with knowledge and appropriate feedback, develops self-confidence.

Sports Etiquette

Sportsmanship is etiquette with an application of perspiration.[1]

The goals of all sports are "to win, to provide valuable exercise, and to entertain while others watch."[2] In accomplishing these goals, players and spectators should practice good sportsmanship. "Being a good sport" is actually about showing kindness and consideration to others. Sportsmanship involves following the rules.

Rules of the game exist for a reason; they prevent chaos and give structure and direction to the game being played. While some sports rules are for safety and courtesy of the players, there are also rules that govern the spectators.[3] Since most businesspeople will entertain either by participating with their guests in a sporting event such as golf or by being spectators together with their guests at a spectator event such as a basketball game, it is particularly important to understand the importance of sports etiquette to business. Businesspeople will be evaluated on their demeanor during such events, and a determination is often made on their suitability as potential business partners during these social outings.

RULES OF ETIQUETTE FOR ALL SPORTS

Being a good sport means playing by the rules, giving others the benefit of being correct, playing safely, dressing in appropriate attire, and graciously winning or losing.[4] The rules that affect all sports are the following:[5]

- Arrive on time whether you are playing or watching a game.
- Cancel as soon as possible when circumstances necessitate a cancellation.

- Shake hands with each player or with fellow spectators and greet them upon arrival.
- Wear the correct attire to play or watch the game.
- Take lessons before trying to play a game.
- Be honest about your ability to play the sport.
- Do not brag.
- Avoid ruining your image by using profanity, vulgarities, or drinking to excess.
- Do not criticize other players, the club, the court, or the surroundings.
- Do not complain when you play a poor game.
- Avoid making others wait while you answer the phone unless you have an emergency; cell phone calls are not considered emergencies. (Many venues are banning them because their use is rude and disruptive.)
- Do not play the victim when you lose or score badly.
- Do not argue about the score or the referee's call.
- Keep your voice at the correct loudness for the game.
- Bring your own equipment; do not borrow someone else's equipment.
- Do not blame your partner for a lost game.
- Avoid hissing or booing at the referee or the other team.
- Congratulate the winners by shaking hands and thanking them for a good game.
- Write a thank-you note if you are a guest.

These additional rules apply to invitations to private clubs:[6]

- Identify yourself to the guard at the gate or the doorman upon arrival and give them your host's name.
- Wait for your host to arrive in the reception area.
- Order food and drink when your host offers; order something similar to what your host orders.
- Do not offer to pay as private clubs allow only the member to pay.
- Obey all posted rule signs.
- Wear attire appropriate for the event; if you are unsure, ask your host about the appropriate attire.
- Tip only with your host's approval.
- Reciprocate by inviting your host to another event unless the outing is strictly business related. In both situations, however, a thank you-note is appropriate.

Being a good fan means consideration for other people. Do not use bad language or throw items at the players or at other fans. There is a joy in competition; there is also a gracious way to win and a gracious way to lose. The ticket to the event does not give anyone the right to "offend, berate, or belittle anyone."[7] It is helpful for both the coach and the players to show signs of moral decency. Research shows that the more the coach exhibits proper behavior and expects players and fans to behave correctly, the more likely everyone will be able to enjoy the event without unnecessary violence.[8]

The cult of victimology or the death of personal responsibility is caused by a society that blames other people when individuals do not get their way. Unfortunately, during sporting events this leads to throwing debris at officials and players, yelling, and threatening referees, players, coaches, and other fans.[9] According to fan etiquette, it is the ethical responsibility of each fan to allow everyone at the event to enjoy the experience and to feel safe.[10]

HANDBALL AND RACQUET SPORTS ETIQUETTE

Tennis, squash, and racquetball are the most common racquet sports. Handball is also popular. As with other sports, before accepting an invitation to play, learn the rules of the game and take some lessons. In addition to following the rules of the game, also follow the rules that are posted by the club where you are playing. Some other etiquette rules include not walking across someone's court to get to yours or to retrieve your ball. Balls should be returned to their owners during breaks in play so as not to interrupt the game. Prior to beginning the game, check the height of the net to be sure it is at the proper height and adjust it if necessary since net balls are an important part of the game.

During the game, watch your voice, as voices carry across tennis courts. Compliment people on nice plays, but keep conversation to a minimum on the court. If you are playing with an official, respect his or her calls. Questions should wait until after the game. Without an official, the players are responsible for line calls on their side of the net. At the end of the game, always shake hands with your opponent.[11]

Steve often played handball at noon at a local athletic club and had never worn protective glasses. One day he returned to work with ten stitches over his eye where the ball had hit him and broken his glasses. The whole area around the eye turned beautiful shades of purple. Needless to say, thereafter he wore protective glasses.

When playing racquetball or handball, be sure to wear shoes that do not have black soles; many clubs do not allow black-soled shoes. Eye protection may not be required, but it is highly recommended. A common complaint of racquetball and handball players is that the opponent does not move out of the way fast enough. Be sure you are physically fit to play this demanding game.[12]

Many times those we play racquet games with may be stronger or weaker players. If you are a weaker

A number of years ago, Jimmy Connors was playing in a tennis tournament at the Memphis Racquet Club. It was near the end of Connors' career, and he had knee braces and elbow braces on because every joint hurt from his years of playing tennis. Connors' opponent was younger and a better player. So Connors started using psychology on his opponent and the crowd; it was working. Connors so frustrated the young player that his game suffered. His opponent finally yelled to the crowd that they were stupid and that this was not how tennis was to be played. The young player was correct, of course; Connors was not following the accepted rules of the game.

player, let your opponent know your skill level. Asking for advice from an accomplished player is flattering to the better player. Likewise, if you are the advanced player, make the game fun for less accomplished players rather than destroying them.[13]

GOLF ETIQUETTE

Golf has become a major sport for businesspeople to pursue. If you do not know how to play golf and want to learn, there are numerous courses offered by universities, community colleges, and golf schools. The Professional Golf Association has an easy-to-read rule book and CD concerning the rules of the game that every player needs to follow.

Golf and business go together. Golf can be an icebreaker and deal-maker. However, golf can also be frustrating and is a test of a person's stress-management abilities. People do not have a good round of golf every time they play.[14]

Some business rules of golf that may be helpful are:[15]

- Try not to outplay the boss or client.
- Talk business only after everyone is playing comfortably with each other.
- Keep dirty jokes to yourself unless you know everyone in the group very well.
- Avoid business discussions during tense shots.
- Avoid betting unless your boss or client suggests it. If you win, do so graciously; if you lose, pay immediately.
- Do not cheat.
- Remember that tipping is done by the host; however, personal caddies may be tipped by a guest.

In addition to the preceding business rules of golf, here are some general rules of golf that you should follow:[16]

- If men and women are playing together and the women are playing from the women's tees, then the men will hit first since their tees are further back and the women's tees are forward.

- The person who hits the lowest score on the previous hole hits first on the next hole. However, men will always hit before the women because of the tee positions.
- Talking or moving while another person, either in your group or in another group, is hitting a ball is inappropriate; also make sure your shadow does not interfere with someone's play.
- Cell phones should be turned to vibrate and should only be answered if it is an emergency.
- Slower groups allow faster groups to play through.
- If someone loses a ball, everyone in the group looks for it. If it is your lost ball, only look for a minute, then take a penalty stroke, and drop another ball to keep the play moving.
- Players should be ready to take their shot and should not take too long to take a shot.
- Players should leave the golf course immediately upon finishing play.
- Trash should not be left on the course; receptacles and water are usually available on the course.
- Players who make a divot (a ball indentation in the turf) should repair it.
- Players who hit out of a sand trap should always rack the sand smooth.
- Players should use a ball marker on the green so that others do not have to be concerned with hitting another player's ball while putting.
- Players should offer to tend the pin when the hole is a long way from where the putter is standing.
- Players should remember to avoid stepping on the imaginary line the ball is to traverse on the putting surface.

Cheating in golf, as in other sports, is not allowed. In golf, however, it is unthinkable as players keep their own scores. Golf enthusiasts can probably recall when Tom Kite, an American golfer, once called a penalty on himself when his ball moved, though no one else saw it. "The informal penalties for cheating are worse than disqualification. Players who are caught cheating can be blacklisted for the rest of their lives," according to Eddie Merrins. Some good players have, in fact, been blacklisted. "If baseball were golf, the community would have ostracized the guys on steroids."[17]

Since golf is a game that can reveal someone's personality, it is best to be on your best behavior—throwing clubs, swearing, excessive drinking, or other childish activities have no place on the golf course. Many businesspeople take potential clients to play golf so they can tell what they are really like and to determine if this is the person with whom they wish to do business. While playing golf, refrain from giving other people advice on their game, unless they ask for the advice.

How people act on the golf course often transfers to the business office. Whether it is a temper, higher

A person's true character will be revealed on the golf course. "Golf tells no lies," says Suzanne Woo, founder of BizGolf Dynamics, a company that helps executives better understand the nuances of the game. She further states that golf "puts you under this weird pressure and expectations—and in this competitive mode"; that is why Chief Information Officer careers are often made or broken on the golf course.[18]

expectations of others than themselves, or erratic behavior, it is assumed this is also how these same people will act in business.

A good game to play for an organized business event is "best-ball"; it helps relieve stress and helps everyone socialize. Playing quickly is important; therefore, if you hit the ball ten times, pick up your ball and go to the next hole. If you come close to hitting someone on the course, be sure to yell "Fore!" If you hear someone yell "Fore!" take cover. Everyone who plays golf likes to be congratulated on the good shots they hit; they also appreciate it when other players pretend not to see the bad shots.[19]

WATER SPORTS ETIQUETTE

Water sports include swimming, sailing, and water skiing. Most swimming pools will ask that all swimmers take showers before they swim. Also because water will carry germs readily, it is best not to go swimming in a pool with an open sore of any kind or with a communicable illness. When swimming in a lap pool, swim on the right side so that faster swimmers may pass on the left.[20] If the pool is used for aerobics or general swimming also, each group has its own area in the pool. Check with the lifeguard to be sure where the groups are to do their swimming.

Sailing and motor boating can be wonderful opportunities to do business. If you have never sailed before, be honest about this fact; otherwise, your helping may result in an unexpected swim. Whoever owns the boat is the captain and is considered the law on the boat. If it is your boat, let others know what they should wear for the day. If it is someone else's boat, the owner should let you know what to bring for the day. Seasickness is preventable with medication so if you are not sure about your sea legs, you may want to get a prescription before going. Definitely wear deck shoes so you do not slip and fall.[21]

GYM OR HEALTH CLUB ETIQUETTE

While working out at a gym or health club is a personal routine, courtesy is necessary so that everyone can enjoy working out. Take two towels, one to wipe your brow and one with which to wipe the equipment. Your towels and other supplies, such as water bottles and charts, should be kept out of the walk ways so that people do not trip over them. Also, keep the locker room neat and clean by not leaving items in front of other people's lockers or on the floor. Leave the shower area clean; do not leave behind empty shampoo bottles for locker room attendants to dispose of.[22] Be considerate of others who may also wish to use mirrors or other accessories provided for the use of all members. When using the steam room or sauna, do not take up excessive space by lying down when other people need a place to sit. After leaving the steam room or sauna, always take a shower before entering the pools.[23]

When going through a rotation of exercise equipment, always return the equipment to the starting position and never leave weights where others can trip over them.[24] In addition, remember to wipe perspiration and body oil off of the equipment. Since equipment is not always supervised (particularly in hotels), if a piece of equipment is not working properly, notify someone at the facility.

If the exercise room is busy, take turns on each piece of equipment; no one should hold up the rotation of people through the equipment circuit. It is not appropriate to jump ahead to the next machine or to talk to others when people are waiting for their turn on the machine. Should you need to leave briefly, it is considerate to tell the next person waiting in line that you will be back shortly. Also, do not count aloud as this will be distracting to others who are counting as well. Since making grunting and moaning sounds can increase your blood pressure and put strain on your respiratory system, do not indulge in these theatrics.[25]

Dressing for the gym should include comfortable, stretchable clothing and shoes that will not slide easily. Skimpy clothing has no place in a gym. Wearing appropriate footwear is important as wearing inappropriate shoes may result in a broken toe or foot.[26]

Do not bring young children to the health club or gym unless a babysitting service is provided. The exercise floor is no place for children to play; it can be dangerous. Their presence can also be distracting to members. In addition, do not use a cell phone as this is disruptive to others. (In fact, many health clubs do not allow them.) Avoid excessive conversations with others who are exercising; save the chitchat for after the exercise session.[27]

When you use the personal trainers provided by the gym, you should give them twenty-four hours' notice to cancel an appointment; otherwise, the appointment should be paid for. While the trainer should be in control of the workout, you should let the trainer know immediately when you are in pain. When arriving for an appointment, if a trainer is with another person, it is only polite to wait until the trainer finishes helping that person rather than interrupting.[28]

HUNTING AND FISHING ETIQUETTE

Hunting and fishing generally require the purchase of a state or federal license from the authorities where you plan to hunt or fish. Again, there are rules that the state and federal agency have established that should be followed.

Hunting and fishing are both quiet sports because of the desire to not scare the game. Be careful with the equipment; fish hooks, arrows, and bullets can all hurt and kill. Be sure the people you hunt with know the rules of hunting and are excellent at following the hunting protocol of not shooting at noises. If new to hunting or fishing, be sure to have a compass. Many people who are inexperienced at hunting and fishing have gotten lost. If you do not know how to shoot, take a Hunter Safety Course offered by the National Rifle Association at one of the sporting clubs in your area.

RUNNING, BIKING, AND ROLLERBLADING ETIQUETTE

A number of businesspeople are starting running clubs or joining existing running clubs. Joining these clubs is a wonderful way to network and get to know other people. Wearing reflective clothing when running is recommended; if you run alone, be sure someone else knows the route. Since runners are generally gone for an extended period of time, it is a good time to talk about business.

Biking and rollerblading can be good sports for business as one can talk with a fellow biker or rollerblader and bike or rollerblade at the same time. As with runners, there are generally local biking or rollerblading groups; and these are an excellent way to meet other business people.

Running, biking, and rollerblading also have their rules. Knowing the proper etiquette and rules is necessary for these sports. Wear proper attire, and have proper equipment for each sport. Wearing the proper clothing will help you to enjoy the sport and let others know that you are serious about it. Wear protective gear with these sports to protect your body. Since these sports tend to take place where other people may be walking or driving, it is important to respect and follow the rules of the road. If on a bike, go with the traffic. Bikes are legally subject to the rules of the road. When biking, pedestrians have the right of way. If running or rollerblading, go against the traffic. Running when it is dark is dangerous since it is very difficult for drivers to see you.[29]

SPECTATOR ETIQUETTE

Spectators' responsibilities are to enjoy themselves without bothering other spectators or interfering in any way with the play. While it is expected that people will yell for their teams, it is inappropriate to

A spectator at an Indiana Pacer's and Detroit Piston's game in November of 2004 was heckling a player and threw a glass of liquid at the player. The player went into the stands after the spectator. The player was suspended seventy-three games (losing nearly a year's salary), and the spectator was barred from future games in the arena.[33]

criticize the other team. Applauding a missed shot is poor sportsmanship on the part of the spectator. Many times you may have a business guest who is a fan of the opposing team, and you always want to make a good impression. If your guest's team wins, offer your congratulations. If your guest's team loses, offer kind remarks about the team.[30] Two points of etiquette are of special importance: the use of cell phones and national anthem responsibilities.

Do not be one of the many cell phone users who is oblivious to others, self-centered, loud, boring, and discourteous by talking on a cell phone during a sporting event. Research has shown that many people are reporting negative results of taking work calls at home and home calls at work; lives are becoming blurred as to the line between work and home.[31] This can be extended to between home, work, and extracurricular activities.

The national anthem, the "Star-Spangled Banner," is sung at most sporting events. Everyone should rise and sing the national anthem. It is improper to walk, try to locate your seat, eat, smoke, or otherwise move while the anthem is being played. Men and boys should remove their hats and place them over their hearts. During the Pledge of Allegiance, place your right hand over your heart and recite the Pledge.[32]

Heckling players is not an act of sportsmanship and should be avoided. While many players will ignore most verbal heckling, it is a little more difficult to avoid items that are being thrown.

Former NFL quarterback, Warren Moon, said that "noise is an adrenaline rush." Noise is considered a big advantage by a home team's athletes and coaches. In the game of golf, however, noise is disrespectful. Davis Love III told reporters in 2002 after a noisy tournament that, "I'm certainly not going to go out and disrupt a business person in their business life, and they shouldn't disrupt our game."[34]

Noise is acceptable at certain spectator events and taboo at others. However, dealing with noise is a challenge for athletes.

Men tend to avoid asking women along to sporting events because they become irritated by the dumb questions many females ask, such as the difference between a linebacker and a running back. However, when a woman does know the sport, many men enjoy having a woman along. Women should take advantage of opportunities to join men at sports events; it is a good time to check their manners.[35]

A coaching career was ruined when the coach lost control and knocked out a player on the other team. Anyone who has followed football remembers Woody Hayes, the venerated coach of Ohio State University, making that fateful error in 1978. There were other minor altercations with the press, and yelling at his players and referees was second nature to Hayes. However, touching a player cost Hayes his job, even though he had won 205 games, two national championships, and made eight trips to the Rose Bowl. While we like to see people believing passionately in what they do, that passion does need to have limits.[37]

Spectators have begun running out on fields and floors after their teams win. While this was previously done only when you were ranked and playing a ranked team, it now happens for no apparent reason. A bit of advice for fans, "Try winning like you've done it before."[36]

Coaches should not interfere with the play, neither should fans interfere with play. The following story describes how a Chicago Cubs fan cost his team the game and more: On October 14, 2003, a Chicago Cubs fan caught a ball that was not foul and that would not have made it to the stands. The fan reached out and caught the ball as it was falling into his team's outfielder's mitt. By catching that ball, the fan cost the Cubs a chance at the World Series that year. Needless to say, there were and continue to be very angry blogs on the web about the situation. Fans must remember the rules of the game, and in baseball that includes not reaching out to catch a ball that is in play no matter how much adrenaline is in your veins.[38]

While many find brawls in the stands or on the playing surface offensive, there is an element of society that seems to appreciate such Neanderthal activities.

While fighting has become commonplace at professional hockey games and the brawls tend to bring in fans, if a player establishes a career as a fighter on the ice he is forced into that role at all games. However, if a player does not establish himself as a fighter on the ice, he is generally left alone. The National Hockey League knows that at the professional level fighting sells tickets.[39]

Dr. J. Wesley Robb has developed a four-step model for being a good fan. First, consider your motive for attending an event. Second, consider how your conduct at the event is viewed by others and how you want to be perceived. Third, consider the consequences. If you are acting unprofessionally, consider the results of your actions and how significant people in your life will be affected. Fourth, consider the legality or appropriateness of what you are doing.[40] If people consider their actions before engaging in certain behaviors, perhaps everyone could enjoy sporting events more. Although some fans try to blame their bad behavior on alcohol, excessive alcohol consumption is not an excuse for bad spectator manners.

Just because there may be fighting on the floor, arena, or field, however, does not mean it is acceptable for the fans to get into brawls with players, coaches, or other fans. It is always advisable to keep this question in mind: "What will my business associates think of the way I am behaving?" If you want to be successful in your business career, always practice proper etiquette. This advice is especially important in those situations that go beyond the office environment, specifically, when you are a player or a spectator in sports situations.

13

Travel Etiquette

I have found out that there ain't no surer way to find out whether you like people or hate them than to travel with them.—Mark Twain[1]

Travel is often very stressful, whether traveling for business or pleasure. This stress can cause people who are usually well mannered to behave rudely and to display bad manners. When you travel to another culture, polite behavior is especially important. People will judge you based upon how you act, without taking into consideration your lack of sleep, the delays and inconveniences you have experienced, and the inconsiderate behavior you have endured from others. You will have a much happier trip if you remain flexible, patient, tolerant, and adaptable. Regardless of where your travels take you and regardless of whether you travel by plane, automobile, train, bus, or cruise ship, be polite and courteous to all you meet.[2]

SUGGESTIONS FOR BUSINESS TRAVEL

When you travel on business, keep detailed records of all expenses to receive reimbursement. You will want to have a specific place to keep receipts. A large envelope works well for this purpose. Place boarding passes, documentation of all business expenses, and anything else that is germane to the trip in the envelope. Paying with a credit card will give a second source of documentation should it be needed. These suggestions will make getting reimbursed later easier. Business travel is work, and it is not unusual for the days to be long. Many hotels have swimming pools or workout rooms. You may wish to pack appropriate clothing to take advantage of these exercise opportunities. Exercise will help you relax after spending hours sitting in meetings.[4] While you will be surrounded

The importance of courtesy to airline personnel, especially to travel clerks, is illustrated in the following story.

A passenger standing in line at an airline ticket counter listened to a person ahead of him yelling at the ticket agent. After the mad, rude customer left, the passenger complimented the ticket agent on his patience, attitude, and calm demeanor. The clerk replied, "Thank you for your kind words, but don't worry, it's all right." The passenger asked, "How can it be all right?" The clerk answered, "It's all right because, you see, that man is going to Cleveland, but his luggage is going to Singapore."[3]

by strangers, it is still very important to practice good manners in order for everyone to have a good trip.[5]

AIR TRAVEL ETIQUETTE

With continued threats of terrorist activity, security is very tight at airports. The easiest thing to do is to take what you will need during the flight in your carry-on bag and check your large suitcase. Items you may need on the plane include laptops, papers, prescription medications, and books or magazines to read during the flight.

When packing your carry-on bag, be sure to place all cosmetics, liquids, toothpaste, etc., in a quart-sized plastic bag; items should be in bottles that are labeled as 3 ounces or less. Many people who formerly purchased liquor and brought it aboard with their carry-on luggage must now put the liquor bottles in their checked luggage because the bottles exceed the 3-ounce limit. With soft luggage, this practice is probably not very practical. All luggage needs to have an identification tag. In addition, you may want to tie a colored ribbon to your checked luggage to make it easy to locate in the baggage claim area since so many pieces of luggage are similar in appearance.

Since passengers are usually asked to remove their shoes when going through airport security, it is wise to wear slip-on shoes that are easy to take off and put on, thus speeding up movement through the line. Likewise, you will be asked to empty your pockets and remove heavy jewelry, jackets, and coats before approaching the security table. Do not attempt to carry on items that are prohibited. If you are not aware of what is prohibited on an airplane, check the Transportation Security Administration website: www.tsa.gov.[6] People who do not follow these simple rules cause themselves and others needless delays in getting through security.

If you use curbside check-in, tip the skycap $1–2 per bag. Many airlines are now charging for curbside check-in; however, this expense is not a tip but a charge by the airline. So be prepared to tip in addition to the airline's charge. Have your ticket, boarding pass, and tip ready for the skycap to expedite the curbside check-in.

After boarding the plane and locating your seat, step out of the aisle to let other passengers pass. When there is a break in the traffic, put your carry-on bag in the overhead compartment or under the seat in front of you. Once you are seated, do not use your cell phone as no one is interested in your personal conversations. If you are discussing business, you may have a competitor sitting near you who would be very interested in your business conversation. Public areas are always problematic when talking on a telephone or using a laptop. In addition to overhearing confidential information when you talk on the telephone, people near you can read what is on your laptop.

Some of the faux pas people commit that should be avoided include the following: filling the overhead compartment with numerous packages so there is insufficient space for items of other passengers seated nearby; hitting people with bags as they walk down the aisle; asking the attendants for items that are not available; complaining to flight attendants or treating them with disrespect; using the telephone in the seatback loudly; staying in the restroom for a prolonged period of time and failing to leave it clean; and dressing slovenly.[7] If you are being met by a business colleague, traveling in an old T-shirt, ripped jeans, and flip-flops does not make a good impression.[8]

Passengers seated together are not expected to greet each other, nor do they introduce themselves.[9] When everyone is seated, it is acceptable to make a comment or two to your seatmate, especially if you would like to engage in a conversation. If the seatmate starts reading or takes out working papers, this is an indication that he or she does not wish to chitchat. When you are the person who does not wish to converse, just say that you have some work to do or that you need to relax. Since many flights today have very little room between rows, reclining your seat when traveling in the main cabin is impolite, unless you first ask permission of the person seated behind you. Also be careful that you do not invade the space of the passenger seated next to you by spreading out your newspaper or working papers. In addition, remember the rule for who uses the armrests in rows with at least three seats. Passengers seated in a window seat use the armrest next to the window; those who are seated in the aisle seat would use the armrest next to the aisle, thus leaving the two remaining armrests for the passenger occupying the middle seat.[10] Because air travel generally requires people who do not know each other to sit closer together than U.S. people are comfortable with, be considerate of other people and give them as much space as possible.

Because many people are allergic to certain fragrances, you will want to show consideration for other people

A frequent business traveler found that she is upgraded more regularly than her colleagues; she attributes this to the fact that she always travels in business attire. She has observed that when flights are overbooked, ticket agents look over passengers in the waiting area before deciding who to upgrade. She feels that dress plays a role in their decision.[11]

by not wearing strong fragrances. Also practice good hygiene; make sure that your hair, body, and clothing are clean. If it is a long flight, carry a breath freshener to use during the flight. Be sure to wear comfortable clothing that will stretch, as it is common to have some swelling during flights. If you are traveling for business, travel with clothing that could be worn to meetings at the destination in case your checked luggage does not arrive with your flight.

When the plane has landed and the flight attendant has given permission to unbuckle your seat belt and move about the cabin, gather your belongings so that when it is time for your row to disembark, you will be ready. Making others who are ready to leave the plane wait while you retrieve your belongings from the overhead compartment is inconsiderate. If you cannot reach your items before people start deplaning, remain seated and wait until there is an opportunity for you to do so without holding up other people.

If plane connections are close, sometimes flight attendants can help you deplane quickly; however, if the plane is arriving late and many passengers are trying to make connections, then they generally cannot help. To assure that you have a seat, even when flights are overbooked, try to get a seat assignment before you leave. Generally, seat reservations can be made and boarding passes printed 24 hours before departure using the airline's website. Although airlines overbook because some passengers do not show up, sometimes everyone shows up for the flight. Those who arrive late will not have a seat on the plane. If you are the one who is late, practice your best manners. If you are polite, the gate agent will be very helpful in finding you a seat on the next plane and may give you a hotel and/or restaurant voucher or perhaps a coupon for a specific dollar amount that may be applied toward another flight. If you are rude, however, the gate agent is not obligated to do anything more than get you on the next available flight.

A cross-country flight was overbooked, and the gate agent asked for volunteers to take a flight three hours later. One couple who did not have a pressing engagement decided to accept the offer. After everyone boarded the flight, the agent called the couple to the counter to make the ticket changes. As she worked, the couple chatted and joked with her. After the agent finished the booking, she commented on how nice the couple had been and gave them complimentary passes to the members' lounge and vouchers for a meal at any of the restaurants in the airport. The lesson to be learned: When you are nice to others, they will be nice to you in return.

Flight personnel are not tipped. You should, however, remember to thank the flight crew as you deplane. Such expressions of appreciation from the passengers are welcome by pilots and flight attendants.

The privilege of riding on a corporate jet can be exciting. When riding on a corporate jet, allow plenty of time so that you are there well before the scheduled departure. Board the plane after the flight attendant has arrived and boarded. Carry your own bags unless the crew directs otherwise. When refreshments are offered, accept graciously what is offered; avoid making special requests. Since corporate jet crews are generally the same people on each flight, thank them at the flight's conclusion. Send a note of appreciation to the person who arranged your travel. If you are lucky enough to fly on a corporate jet on a regular basis, during the holidays sending a card and gift to the crew is appropriate.[12]

BUS, TRAIN, AND MASS TRANSIT ETIQUETTE

Buses and trains are also used for travel, often after arriving at your initial destination by plane. Manners for those who ride a bus are similar to those who take a train. Get in line while waiting to board a bus or train. Do not engage in such impolite behavior as pushing other people or trying to get ahead of others who arrived before you. Age, gender, or rank is not a consideration when waiting in line in the United States. The rule for lining up is first-come, first-served. Enter the bus or train only after passengers are permitted to exit. Choose your seat quickly after boarding. Confine your belongings to one seat unless there are plenty of empty seats; make room when someone asks to sit down next to you. Speak in a low voice, including phone conversations when you take a call on your cell phone. Before you open a window or lower a shade, ask permission of those seated near you. When traveling across the country by bus or train, you may choose to talk with other passengers or to simply read a book or watch the scenery. Since you are often expected to carry your own luggage, travel light. While bus drivers are not tipped (unless they drive tour buses), you are expected to tip for food when in the dining car of a train just as you would at any nice restaurant.[13]

Chartered buses are an excellent way to see the major attractions in a city in a short period of time. Some bus tours include a tour guide, who is very knowledgeable about the tourist sights. Do not carry on conversations or listen to a radio using earphones when the tour guide is speaking. Stay with the group during stops for lunch or for photo-taking opportunities at popular tourist attractions. Sometimes the tips for the driver and tour guide are included in the tour price; when they are not, the group may either pass the hat or each person may tip the driver and tour guide individually.[14]

In many cities mass transit is the fastest way to get around. Be sure to buy your ticket and transfers if you must transfer between lines or buses. It is generally cheaper to buy transfers than to purchase individual tickets for each segment of the trip. Many mass transit systems have passes that are good for one day, three days, or a week. For many automated sites, exact change will be needed to purchase a ticket. Also, most bus drivers are not prepared to make change, so exact change will be needed to ride the bus. Be sure to keep the ticket until your ride is completed. So as not to hold up others, be ready to exit and enter the bus or train in a very efficient manner. Many people may nap if they have a long train ride home after work. If the person seated next to you is napping and you know that the next stop is theirs, a nudge would no doubt be appreciated. Noise should be minimal, and cell phones should not be used.[15] Keep in mind that most people on trains or buses are not sociable.[16]

AUTOMOBILE ETIQUETTE

When traveling by automobile, be sure you know exactly where you are going and how to get there before you leave home. Look at the maps and directions to be sure they make sense; if they do not make sense, stop and ask directions. Whoever drives is liable for the passengers.

Be courteous to other drivers. Follow all the rules expected of polite drivers, including using turn signals, moving to the right to allow faster traffic to pass, and allowing others to merge. When another driver permits you to merge, always give a "thank-you wave." The radio should never be on loud enough for someone in another car to hear it. Loud music can also be dangerous for the occupants of the car since passengers will not be able to hear what is happening outside of the car. Since driving laws vary from state to state, be sure to review the laws of the state in which you are driving.[17] Since U.S. people are not good at dual tasking, do not talk on a cell phone, put on makeup, or read maps while driving. If any of these activities is necessary, pull off the road. If you have an accident, do not become rude. Get the other driver's name, address, and telephone number, as well as the car license tag number and insurance information. Depending on the state, you may need to call the police. If you hit a parked car that has no driver, leave your information. Treat others as you wish to be treated.[18]

If you are renting a vehicle, you should have a reservation confirmation similar to an airline ticket. Check the car when you pick it up for scratches, dents, and other damages and mark them on the contract you sign. This will protect you when you return the car, since the rental agency expects the car to be returned in the same condition in which it left the agency. Generally, the charge for gasoline is very high if the agency fills the tank when you return the vehicle; therefore, it is advisable to fill the tank close to the return point for the car. Also, renting cars may be difficult for newly hired executives just out of college as many rental agencies will not rent to someone under twenty-five years of age. As with hotel reservations, you can use your credit card to hold a car rental reservation. Insurance coverage may be included with your personal automobile insurance policy; check this out before you leave home.

If you are not sure whether your personal automobile policy covers rental cars, buy the rental company's insurance.

Who should ride in which seat is sometimes questioned; however, there is a simple rule to follow. The lower ranking executive should take the least desirable seat in the car when riding with higher ranking executives; the lower ranking executive should ask where he or she should sit rather than make assumptions.[19]

TAXICAB AND LIMOUSINE ETIQUETTE

While limousines are generally arranged for in advance to arrive at a specific time, taxicabs are normally found at taxi stands, outside of hotels, or on the street. (Of course, you may call the cab company to arrange for a next-day pick-up, especially when you have an early morning flight to the airport.) If you are in an area where taxicabs are unavailable, you may call for a cab to pick you up at a specific place and time. As soon as you enter the back seat of a limousine or taxicab, give the driver instructions on where you are going. While most drivers will not suggest that you buckle your seatbelt, it is wise to do so.

Limousine drivers will normally open the doors, and you should allow them to do so. Taxicab drivers may or may not open the doors for you. When you are the host, get in first so that your guests do not have to be inconvenienced by sliding across the seat to the other side. The junior executive, never a guest, should sit in the front seat of the cab if there is insufficient room in the back seat. Being seated next to or behind the driver is the proper place for the person who will be giving the driver directions and paying for the ride.[20] Tips to taxicab and limousine drivers depend on the length of the ride and if the driver has given extra services. Gratuities may be $10 for a ride to the airport or across town; they may exceed $100 if the driver spends the day taking you shopping or sightseeing, running errands, carrying packages, or doing other requested services. A tip of 10–20 percent of the trip cost is sufficient. If a limousine is provided, be sure to ask the driver what the rules are and follow them.[21]

Most cities have taxi commissions who take complaints and compliments concerning drivers. If you need to file a complaint or you wish to give a compliment, be sure to get the driver's name and taxi license

A traveler to Tijuana who hailed a cab had grounds for making a complaint. The taxi ride was a lengthy one through highway overpasses and alleys. When the traveler finally reached his destination, he thanked the cab driver and paid him. As he looked around, he saw that his destination was only a short distance from where he had gotten off the trolley and hailed the taxi. The traveler had definitely been taken for a ride.[23]

number, which will be displayed for the rider's benefit as required by law.[22] You may want to write down this information in case you need it later to make a report.

CRUISE SHIP ETIQUETTE

Cruise ship travel is becoming increasingly popular for vacations; many people view taking a cruise as the epitome of luxury. Before booking a cruise, however, you may wish to consider whether your personality and preferences lend themselves to life on the ocean. Some people have realized too late that the confinement, the constant expected socializing with strangers, and the cramped quarters are simply not to their liking. More recently, cruises are being used by companies for business purposes. Cruises provide employees numerous opportunities for relaxation after completing the day's meetings. Becoming familiar with onboard etiquette is essential before embarkation.[24]

On one cruise, the ship became "dead in the water," which means it was not moving but drifting with the current. The computers had shut everything down. What was surprising was how thin the walls were. You could hear everyone talking in the rooms next to you and in the hallways as well! The white noise that the engines and air systems supplied helped to cover up conversations, so it became necessary to talk softly in the staterooms.

Patience is needed when boarding ships. Passports are required and will be checked. A pen will be needed for completing the numerous forms, and arriving early may help avoid long lines.[25] After your initial packing, repack leaving half of what you had originally planned to take at home. Space is very limited on ships. Be sure to tag your luggage; generally, you will be given special tags to put on your luggage to facilitate the boarding process.

Maritime law requires that the ship have safety drills. These drills are for everyone's safety. If you do not show up for the drill, all passengers will be held in the drill formations until you are found and brought to your roster station.

Generally, there will be some formal events aboard ship; appropriate formal dress should be worn. Otherwise, dress aboard ship is rather casual. Some people prefer to dress for dinner, and some prefer more casual dress for dinner. Many ships also have formal dinner seating as well as buffet dinner seating. If you are traveling for business, dressing too casually would probably be frowned on by the executives. Modesty is important; passengers will need to wear a cover-up with a swimsuit for meals. Since the evenings on board may be cool, a shawl or jacket can be useful. You will also want to wear shoes that are appropriate for slippery decks. Guidelines for proper attire are included in the pre-boarding materials that are provided by the cruise line.

Cruise ships are known for their entertainment and dining. When the cruise is for business, it is important to remember that business is completed before beginning the fun. Most ships have smoke-free areas, or the ship may be entirely smoke free. Another rule of cruise ships is that nothing should be thrown over the side of a ship into the water.[26] While the cost of the cruise generally covers your accommodations, meals, entertainment, and use of sports facilities, there will be items that require cash or a credit card, such as wine, liquor, beauty salon visits, dry cleaning, massages, and premium dining.[27]

The ship's crew should be treated with the same respect given to other travelers. The captain is addressed as "Captain"; the other officers are addressed as "Mr.," "Mrs.," or "Ms." and their last name, except for the ship's doctor who is addressed as "Dr." If you are invited to sit at the captain's table, consider it an honor. Arrive promptly and wait to order until the captain arrives. Introduce yourself to others at the table and make appropriate small talk.[28]

Tipping is expected on cruise ships and is normally not included in the price of the ticket. Many times you can add gratuities to your account and designate the staff members to whom the gratuities are to be given. As in a hotel, give the steward who brings your bags to the cabin $2 per bag. Give the room and dining stewards $3 per day per person in the cabin. If they do an outstanding job, add $25 to their gratuity at the end of the cruise. For services that are purchased on board, such as haircuts and massages, the person performing the service should be given 15–20 percent of the bill as a gratuity.[29]

HOTEL MANNERS

Hotels are ranked and vary from simple accommodations to deluxe. Some hotels are known for their restaurants that feature well-known chefs; other hotels feature famous entertainers or elegant clothing boutiques. Luxury hotels often provide such extras as minibars, terry cloth robes, hair dryers, coffee makers, and an assortment of toiletries in the bathroom. Well-mannered travelers know that they should not take the terry cloth robe, towels, soap dishes, or other hotel property without asking the clerk at the front desk. The clerk will then charge your room for the items you wish to take with you. The best way to find a good hotel is by asking someone who has traveled to the destination city.[30]

Make your hotel reservations well in advance of your trip. Most hotels will guarantee rooms for late arrival with a credit card. If there is a major convention or several small conventions in town at the same time, or if a major holiday falls during the requested dates, there may be a shortage of rooms. Convention rates are also generally good up to a certain date;

then the full room charge will apply. When it is necessary to cancel a room, remember that you have a minimum number of days or hours before the reservation is to start in which you may cancel without being charged for the room. When making a reservation, be sure to ask for the desired bed configuration: single, double, queen, or king. In addition, be sure to ask for a smoking or nonsmoking room, whichever is your preference.

Arriving at a hotel before check-in time is the problem of the guest, not the hotel. When you arrive before check-in time, hotel personnel are usually happy to place your bags in a holding area. You are then free to attend a meeting, shop, or go sightseeing until the room is ready.[31]

Be courteous to guests in the rooms next to, below, and above you by not having the television or radio on loudly at any time but particularly late at night or early in the morning. Likewise, watch your voice volume, as many times voices will carry if the walls are not sufficiently sound-proofed. Remember to walk with light rather than heavy feet. If people in other rooms are being loud or rude, it is advisable to call the front desk to let the hotel handle the situation.[32]

In the United States it is proper to tip the concierge and bellman a couple of dollars each time they help you. The usual tip to the bellman is $1 per bag; room service is $1–5; the valet parking attendant receives $1–3; and the doorman who hails a cab is given $1–2.[33] Increase the amount of the gratuity when hotel personnel give you special service or when you are at an elegant resort where larger tips are expected. Have a number of $1 bills available for tipping; giving coins is impolite.

As most hotels are not responsible for valuables, be sure to put them in a safe or keep them with you rather than leaving them in the room. Many times locking items in your suitcase is an alternative if a room safe is not provided. Leaving expensive jewelry in the room, however, is unwise unless it is placed in a locked safe.

Hotel bedrooms are not suitable for business meetings. If you have a suite with a living area that is separate from the bedroom, then the living area is suitable for same gender meetings or for mixed gender meetings of several people. Hotel lobbies or hotel restaurants are also appropriate locations for meetings.

Checking out of a room is done in a number of ways today depending upon the hotel. In some hotels, guests still check out at the lobby desk; in others, guests check out through the TV. In still other hotels, checking out is done automatically and billed to the credit card you provided when you checked in. Be sure to indicate the preferred mode of checking out when you check in. When you are a guest of a certain hotel chain, you may be offered special services; therefore, staying at a few hotel chains may be preferable to staying at many different chains.

On the day you leave, leave a tip for the housekeepers who have cleaned your room during your stay. The correct amount to tip is $2–3 per person per day.[34]

Being sick is never pleasant; however, being sick when traveling alone on a business trip is even worse. One sick traveler was pleasantly surprised at the concern showed to her by the hotel bellman, who took her to her room in a wheelchair. In addition, he brought in her luggage and turned down her bed. He then gave her his business card and cell phone number and urged her to call him if she needed anything. The traveler, upon returning home, wrote a letter to the hotel manager praising the bellman and pointing out that his services were beyond the norm. The hotel manager replied, expressing appreciation for the letter. Hotels get numerous complaints but very few compliments. Many times the people who are complimented get special recognition for a job well done.

If you are in charge of room assignments for a conference, make a master list that shows the type of accommodation each person needs, extra meeting rooms, arrival and departure dates for all personnel, and the room numbers assigned to those attending the conference.[35]

In summary, traveling for business and pleasure can be very enjoyable if you take time to plan before you go. Take advantage of opportunities to travel in the United States and abroad. Travel will enrich your life and broaden your perspective. Knowledge gained during travel experiences simply cannot be found in books. Learning proper travel etiquette will give you confidence to face the challenges travelers often face.

14

Global Manners

Being able to negotiate your way through the etiquette patterns of another country when you are communicating can make or break a deal.[1]

Traveling and working globally involves learning what is acceptable and unacceptable in the different cultures in which we work. While global media has brought the different cultures of the world into our homes, many times we do not understand what we are actually seeing or reading. Lack of knowledge of the culturally accepted etiquette of a country contributes to misunderstandings when traveling abroad.

When traveling to other countries, you are an ambassador of your U.S. firm. As such, you should conduct yourself professionally twenty-four hours a day. Taking time to research the proper business manners of the country you are visiting is well worth the effort. This extra effort will pay dividends in the international business arena.

TRAVEL PREPARATION

The first thing you need for international travel is a passport since travel outside the borders of the United States is no longer possible without a passport. Visas are also required to travel to many countries and must be applied for through the country's embassy or consulate. Most embassies and consulates can be found by surfing the web. Be sure to allow plenty of time, as it takes several weeks to receive a passport, and the passport is needed to apply for a visa.

Using a travel checklist, such as the one that follows, when packing will help you remember to take everything you need.

____ Passport and visas	____ ATM card	____ Contact lists
____ Government-issued	____ Other lists for the	____ Hygiene products
picture ID	house and work	____ Alarm clock
____ Plane tickets	____ Medicines	____ Glasses or contacts
____ Lodging information	____ Credit cards	____ Electric current adaptor
____ Car rental information	____ Money	____ Raincoat
____ Insurance cards	____ Clothing	____ Camera
____ Business cards	____ Umbrella	
____ Presentation materials	____ Laundry bag	

Source: Jeanette S. Martin and Lillian H. Chaney, *Global Business Etiquette: A Guide to International Communication and Customs* (Westport, CT: Praeger, 2006), 3.

To reduce jet lag, exercise regularly before departure and get a full night's sleep the night before your flight. Change your watch to the destination time when you board the plane and switch to the new time zone routine. Taking a mild sedative to sleep on the plane can be very helpful in adjusting to the new time zone. Drink plenty of water on the plane and avoid caffeinated beverages, alcohol, and heavy meals. If you take any medications, be sure to adjust your dosage times. Once you have arrived, stay up until it is bedtime at your destination.

Include with your passport such information on your blood type, medications you take on a regular basis, medicines to which you are allergic, your doctor's address and telephone number, your insurance carrier, and an emergency contact.[2] While it is possible to purchase medical supplies in most modern cities in the world, taking an emergency first-aid kit is advisable.

If the area of the world to which you are traveling does not have medical care readily available or if there are diseases for which your immune system is not prepared, see a travel physician for immunizations that may be needed. Having a doctor's certificate listing medications you take regularly may make clearing customs easier. Leave medications in their original prescription bottles and pack them in your carry-on luggage, rather than putting them in your checked luggage.[3] Another recommendation is to have some currency of the destination country upon arrival for taxi fares from the airport to the hotel and for tipping. When making hotel reservations, it is wise to confirm that accommodations are Western style (such as having a bathroom in the room). If you decide to rent a car, be sure you know the local rules for operating a vehicle.

Your business itinerary should be planned before leaving home, taking into consideration differences in holidays and religious customs. Calling ahead permits your counterpart in the host country to schedule a meeting at a mutually convenient time and place. Remember to allow sufficient time to adjust to the time zone changes by arriving a day or two ahead so that your body and mind can make the necessary adjustments. Ask people who have traveled to the country for their recommendations on transportation, appropriate dress, and other tips for a successful intercultural encounter.

GUIDELINES FOR GLOBAL INTERACTIONS

Manners are often related to the customs of the country or region being visited. Many times these manners will be very different from what is experienced at home. A little reading before going will help you relax and enjoy the countries you are visiting without the apprehension that often accompanies visits abroad. If, for example, gift exchanges are common in the country, you will want to be prepared to reciprocate appropriately when gifts are exchanged.

One of the first impressions people make is when greeting others and when making introductions. Greetings and introductions vary from bowing with no touching to bear hugs and kisses. The U.S. greeting of "Good morning, how are you?" is very confusing to people from other cultures because we really do not want them to tell us how they are. If they do not understand our ritualistic greeting exchange, people of other cultures would think we are being rude by not listening to how they are doing. People in Latin American countries, for example, would ask about your family as part of the greeting and would expect you to talk at length about them; they would then talk about their families. In addition, many Latin Americans and people of the Russian Federation and Middle East will hug each other as part of the greeting (male to male or female to female). The French will give an air kiss next to your cheek; the people of China, India, and Japan would prefer to avoid touching when greeting others.[4]

Handshakes often accompany greetings and can vary with the culture. While the U.S. handshake is firm, about two or three seconds in length, and includes eye contact with a smile, handshakes in other countries deviate from the U.S. norm. The firm handshake would be impolite in England, France, and Asian and Middle Eastern countries where they use a gentle handshake. The German handshake is firm and brusque as are handshakes in many areas of the Russian Federation. While it is usual for the Chinese and Japanese to bow during their greetings, it is not unusual when dealing with people from the West that they will also shake hands. Many times it is appropriate to both bow and shake hands to show respect to both bowing and nonbowing cultures.[5]

International introductions are handled similarly to those in the United States. You introduce the less important person to the more important person; no consideration is given to gender or age. Since many countries are very formal, always use proper titles and surnames such as, "Dr. Armani, I would like to introduce Mrs. Smith, who has just been hired in our marketing department." Note that you include a little additional information to help the person remember the names of those to whom they have been introduced. While we use first names in the

A U.S. sales representative in England had a hard time convincing his U.S. employer to change his title to Director of European Sales rather than Sales Manager; he maintained that it would make it easier for him to see the decision makers in European companies. Finally, the company changed his title and sales escalated. Sometimes you have to make adjustments, especially in the use of job titles, when conducting business internationally.

United States fairly quickly, this is not the case in many other countries in the world. Most of the Asian countries, Germany, and Switzerland would not use given names. Also, it is important to remember that in Asian countries the surname is generally listed first followed by the given name, which is the reverse of the practice in the United States.[6]

Business cards can be a very important part of introductions in many countries. Before you travel to other countries, have your cards printed in English on one side and in the language of the country you are visiting on the reverse side. Stay with neutral colors—white or off-white card stock and black ink. Take a good supply of cards as in many countries cards are exchanged every time you meet someone new. Cards should be kept in a cardholder. Men would place the cardholder in a jacket pocket but never in a back trouser pocket. Women would place the cardholder in the jacket pocket, handbag, or attaché case.

Since the business card exchange is quite ritualized in many countries, it is best to do some research and know how to properly exchange cards before you visit. For example, in Japan you present the card with both hands, with the information facing the recipient, accompanied by a bow. In Saudi Arabia you present business cards only with the right hand.[7]

TIPS FOR WOMEN BUSINESS TRAVELERS

When traveling for business, women assume the same responsibilities as men. Women are responsible for their own luggage, lift their carry-on bags to the plane's overhead compartment, and share in transporting the joint business luggage. Women who are team leaders will take care of checking in and out of the hotel, paying bills, and tipping hotel and transportation personnel. When the group is primarily men, women should be included in activities the rest of the business group is planning, just as men would be included in activities when the group is predominately women. Men should not assume that all women want to shop when they have spare time on a trip.[8]

Both men and women should understand that sexual harassment has no place on a business trip. However, behavior that is considered sexual harassment in one country may be viewed in quite a different light in another country.

A U.S. firm, after acquiring a plant in Italy, brought some Italian employees to the United States for training. One Italian male, as is customary in Italy, squeezed a female's derriere to indicate that she was attractive. The young lady was not pleased. U.S. managers explained to the Italians that in this country squeezing females' derrieres was considered sexual harassment, which is not tolerated in the U.S. work environment. The Italians could not believe that this type of attention was unwelcome.[9]

To avoid any appearance of impropriety, men and women who travel together on business should not only have separate rooms but should request rooms on separate floors of the hotel as well. Business should be conducted in meeting rooms, not in hotel bedrooms. If someone has had too much to drink, this situation can generally be handled with a sense of humor rather than a charge of sexual harassment. The woman should leave the person making sexual overtones and go to her room by herself. A woman should never allow herself to be picked up by a man she knows nothing about. If you are attracted to someone, meet for lunch, or bring along someone in the group until you have time to find out about the other person. In some countries a woman is not allowed to be out by herself alone, so you may need to plan activities with others when visiting these countries. In all countries a woman would want to check with the concierge about transportation to events and transportation back to the hotel after the events, especially if she is going out alone.[10]

Because women are still not as active in the business world as men in many countries, they are sometimes a curiosity. This curiosity can hurt, but it can also gain women access to higher-level managers more easily than men.[11] While gender stereotyping is still prevalent in some countries, Western businesswomen are often seen as very competent. However, women should be prepared for stereotypes still held by men in many countries and for questions about their marital status.[12]

A married U.S. businesswoman was seated next to a South Korean man during a business meeting. She was surprised when he said to her, "I'm sorry about your husband." When she asked why he was sorry, he said, "I see you wear a wedding ring so I assume your husband is dead; otherwise, you would be at home caring for your family."[13]

Single women may particularly feel lonely and left out of social relationships that involve the family or spouses.[14] A woman may find having a social relationship with a male in another culture difficult whether she is married or not. Likewise, women in higher-status positions within the organization would not have social relationships with females or males of the host culture who are of a lower hierarchical status.[15] In some cultures women are successful, as they are seen as nurturing, compromising (rather than domineering), sensitive, compassionate, understanding, cooperative, and inclusive. Women are also successful because they are more indirect in their communications.[16] Above all, women must have confidence in themselves, just as men must have confidence in themselves, to be successful in intercultural encounters.

MANNERS FOR SELECTED REGIONS OF THE WORLD

The following section will provide information on proper behavior when visiting specific areas of the world. However, it is still necessary to do research on specific countries and visit with colleagues who have traveled to those countries to benefit from their experiences. All countries differ, and many times regions and people within the country will differ from the norms. Be sure to check the holiday schedule of the country being visited as many countries have more holidays than U.S. people celebrate.

Asia

In China and South Korea, passports must be good for at least six months beyond the expected exit date; visas are required. In Japan and Taiwan, passports are required, but visas are not required for short business trips. When booking hotel accommodations, remember that in many Asian countries Western accommodations may not be available; be sure to ask. Western-style hotel accommodations are available in larger cities, but accommodations in smaller towns may be different from those to which you are accustomed. Before you travel to any Asian country, it is advisable to check whether visas are required and to ask about hotel accommodations.

In most of the Asian countries, greet the most senior person first using the title and surname followed by the first name. People in many of the Asian countries will bow rather than shake hands. However, many Asians are beginning to both bow and shake hands. If you have never conducted business in an Asian country, using an agent to introduce you will help you do business and give you credibility. Business cards should be printed in English and the language of the country in black ink. Titles are very important in Asian countries; they show the importance of the person within the firm and should be included on business cards.[17]

In most of Asia, building a relationship is paramount to doing business with a company. Also because these are collectivistic cultures, direct questioning is generally viewed as rude.[18] Being on time for meetings in Asia is expected.

Throughout most of Asia, gift giving is an art. How the gift is wrapped and presented is almost as important as the gift itself. As there are many rules concerning the number and type of items to give, the color of the wrapping paper, and whether you should let them know in advance that you are bringing them a gift, checking the rules of gift giving for the particular country is wise. In many Asian countries, for example, it is considered rude to open a gift in the presence of the giver. (In the United States, on the contrary, it is viewed as rude when you do not open the gift in the presence of the giver.)

Gestures are not used as much in Asian countries as they are in the United States. Therefore, remember to keep gestures to a minimum when visiting Asia. Also realize that Asians do not use direct eye contact as much as do people of the United States. In addition, when they cannot do as you request, such as shipping an order by a certain date, they are more likely to look away and say that granting your request would be difficult. Because people of Asian cultures want to please and are very polite, it is difficult for them to say a direct "no." Another form of nonverbal communication that Asians use effectively against Westerners is silence. Asians value silence; Westerners are uncomfortable with silence. During negotiations, Westerners make unnecessary concessions when their offers are met with silence; Westerners incorrectly interpret this silence as rejection of the proposal and continue to make concessions. In most Asian cultures touching is not an appropriate form of communication to use in business settings. Asians also prefer at least an arm's length of space between themselves and people they do not know.

Europe

Passports are required for entry to European countries and return to the United States. Visas are not required for short-term stays. Hotel accommodations tend to be smaller by U.S. standards but will tend to be Western-style.

Greetings are different from U.S. greetings in some European countries but are quite similar in others. Handshakes, a part of greeting behavior, vary from the soft handshake of people in England, to the firm handshake of the Germans. The French handshake is light and quick and is accompanied by an air kiss in France. Europe tends to be very formal so people are called by their titles and surnames until they give someone permission to do otherwise. In some countries, such as France, being introduced by someone who knows both parties will give you more credibility. Business cards should be printed in English on one side and in the language of the host country on the other side. Status is important in most European countries so positions within the firm will be scrutinized.

Appointments should be made beforehand; in Europe, do not show up unannounced. Likewise, it is assumed that meetings will start on time. While employees tend to be more loyal to their employers in Europe than employees are in the United States, they are not workaholics and enjoy life. Europeans have more vacation time than any other geographic area in the world. In most of Europe, business gifts are not exchanged until a relationship has been established and negotiations have been completed. Gifts should be simple and tasteful. As there are some specific guidelines for gift giving in the various countries of Europe, check guidelines for the particular European country you plan to visit.

Since the hand gestures used in the United States have different meanings in much of Europe, it is best to refrain from any hand gestures when you are communicating with Europeans. Europeans do like direct eye contact; in fact, in many cultures not giving direct eye contact would be interpreted as hiding something. Attitudes toward touching are interesting in Europe. You will find that people in the colder climate countries touch less than those in the warmer climate countries or regions.

Africa

Passports and visas are required for almost all African nations. The African nations can be very different from one another not only because of their ethnic backgrounds but also because of their religious differences and the differences between the countries that colonized them.

The African handshake is different from the U.S. handshake; it is not as firm. Handshaking is done upon arrival and departure. Shake hands with women only if they offer their hand. In Kenya the longer you have known someone, the longer the handshake will be. Likewise, in Kenya, men shake hands only with men, and women shake hands only with other women. In addition, women may also hug or kiss each other on both cheeks if they are close friends. You may expect to be asked personal questions the first time you meet someone. While Africans, in general, have strong eye contact, women should not look men in the eye during greetings. It is also important to use a person's title such as Doctor or Teacher. In South Africa they use the African handshake, which involves shaking hands in typical U.S. fashion, then slipping your hand around the other person's thumb, and then returning to the traditional U.S. handshake. The African handshake is used whenever one of the parties in the greeting is black. Afrikaners shake hands between men and women, men and men, and women and women. In addition, Afrikaners may kiss a woman on the cheek or hug a close male friend. As most countries in Africa are formal, do not use first names until the African does.[19]

Business cards are very important and should be in English on one side and translated to the appropriate language on the other side. Personal references are very important, and connections should be made before the first meeting. Appointments should be made in advance. While you would be expected to be on time, do not be surprised if you have to wait. Decisions are normally made by a few people at the top, so answers to business questions may take some time.[20] South Africans are more reserved and will not ask as many personal questions nor should you ask personal questions of them.[21]

When visiting villages, you should not bring gifts, as they are not accustomed to the practice. However, when invited to a meal in the city, bring wine, flowers, chocolates, dinner mints, or hard candy. If the family has children, bring the children toys or books. Business people enjoy copies of the latest books or recent newspapers; they make nice gifts.[22]

Nonverbal communication is important to successful encounters with Africans. The U.S. habit of patting children on the head is inappropriate in Kenya; however, it is permissible to pat the child's back or shake hands with the child. When you are beckoning someone, be sure your palm is facing upward as the palm facing downward is a rude gesture. Kenyans will want to be asked before you photograph them, and they will expect to be paid. Also do not photograph a building with a Kenyan flag on it.[23] In South Africa it is a sign of disrespect for a black to look you directly in the eye. Swearing is also considered very disrespectful and should be avoided. A person should be complimented only in private, not in front of others. Gestures should be used with caution. For example, the positive "V" for victory sign used by people of the United States is obscene when used with the palm facing toward you.[24]

Latin America

Passports are required to travel to all Latin American countries and return to the United States. Visas are only required for long stays within the country.

Latin American countries vary in handshaking customs from a handshake that is a moderate grasp with repeated pumping action to an *abrazo* (hug), a brusque handshake, or kisses on the cheek. Status is very important in most of Latin America; dressing well is also very important when traveling to any of these countries. Also be sure to include titles and university degrees on your business cards to show your importance within your company. You will be treated as your age, social status, or position indicates you should be treated. Business cards should contain Spanish, Portuguese, or French translations on one side, depending on the country, and English on the other side. Being introduced by a third party is helpful to building trust and doing business in Latin America.

As Latin Americans tend to be very people oriented, meeting times are not generally strictly adhered to. While it is expected that you will be on time, being late will be excused. Likewise, if they have not finished with a prior meeting, they will expect you to understand and accept their apology for being late. Since relationships are very important, it will take some time to establish a business relationship and complete business negotiations. Gift giving is very common even for a first meeting. Be cautious in giving gifts of flowers as various types and colors of flowers have many meanings in Latin America. Checking with a florist or concierge first would be a good idea before choosing flowers.

Latin Americans use lots of gestures; however, be careful because many U.S. gestures are vulgar or inappropriate in a business setting in Latin America. Latin Americans also want everyone to be happy and will have trouble saying no or disappointing you which can make developing deadlines rather difficult. Most Latin Americans like to stand close and often touch the person with whom they are conversing.

Middle East

Passports and visas are required for travel to and from most Middle Eastern countries. Some countries, because of the U.S. diplomatic relationship, also require permission from the U.S. State Department before you may travel to the country. In some countries, such as Saudi Arabia, foreigners may only travel there on business. It is particularly difficult for a woman to do business there because of the separation of the genders and the laws that forbid a man and woman who are not married or related to socialize. In addition, women may not be served in a restaurant without a male relative, are not allowed to drive a vehicle, and must dress very modestly. A man should not look a woman in the eyes or shake hands with her. Not all Islamic countries are as strict as Saudi Arabia, however.

In the Middle Eastern countries, business revolves around their religion —Islam. Islam affects their culture, how women are perceived in business, what the proper clothing is for business, and many other business rules. The court system is ruled by religious law (*Shari'ah*) in most cases. Proselytizing about any other religion is illegal in most Islamic states.

Greetings will be handshakes and possibly embraces between men or between women but not between the genders. Middle Easterners may hold hands for a while, and you should wait until they release your hand rather than pulling it away. They may also want to hold hands while walking. While many businesspeople will speak English, business cards should be printed in English and Arabic. Titles are used with family names.

During Ramadan it will be difficult to have meetings, and it would be wise to avoid scheduling meetings during this time of year. Ramadan is a serious religious observance. Even visitors who are caught smoking, drinking, or eating in public during Ramadan will be sent to prison until Ramadan is over. Other times to avoid visits are during *El Fitr*, the pilgrimage to Mecca, and *al-Adha*.

Although it is not unusual to be kept waiting, it is expected that you will arrive on time. As they are polychronic, hosts will probably be doing multiple things, such as answering the telephone, while carrying on a business conversation. Since they do not like doing business with someone they do not know, getting to know your business associate is important to eventually doing business with them. Have someone introduce you to your Middle Eastern business associate.

Gestures are common, but be careful about using U.S. gestures until you learn what they may mean there. Middle Easterners are going to stand much closer when they talk and will have very strong eye contact. Use gestures with caution. Pointing at someone else is rude, as is showing the bottom of your foot to someone. The "thumbs up" gesture is rude.

Gift giving is acceptable; small gifts with a company logo or something that is made in the United States are appreciated. Gifts to avoid are alcohol and any item that represents a woman as these are illegal. Accept and give gifts and business cards with the right hand only. When giving compliments, be very general. If you admire something too much, a Middle Easterner will feel obliged to give it to you.

Cultural variations in dining etiquette are included in Chapter 8, "Dining Etiquette."

In summary, research the manners of the country you plan to visit before you go to avoid unintentionally offending people in the destination country. Behaving like "The Ugly American" is no way to make a positive impression when you travel abroad.

Notes

INTRODUCTION

1. Melissa Leonard, "Avoid the 'fatal' faux pas," *ABA Banking Journal* 96 (May 2004): 10.
2. June Hines Moore, *The Etiquette Advantage* (Nashville, TN: Broadman & Holman Publishers, 1998), 1.
3. Burton F. Schaffer, Craig A. Kelley, and Maryann Goette, "Education in Business Etiquette: Attitudes of Marketing Professionals," *Journal of Education for Business* 68 (July–August 1993): 331.
4. Mia Katz, "Examining the Etiquette Edge," *Women in Business* (July–August 2005): 32.
5. Karen Kelly, "New Concern that Politeness Is a Lost Art in the Office," *The New York Times,* 2004, 10.
6. Shirley A. Lazorchak, "Business Protocol and Etiquette: Preparing Students for the Global Business Environment," *Journal of Family and Consumer Sciences* 92 (2000): 100.
7. Leonard, "Avoid the 'fatal' faux pas," 14.
8. Ibid., 10.

CHAPTER 1

1. Susan Morem, *How to Gain the Professional Edge: Achieve the Personal and Professional Image You Want,* 2nd ed. (New York: Ferguson, 2005), 35.
2. Dana May Casperson, *Power Etiquette: What You Don't Know Can Kill Your Career* (New York: AMACOM, 1999), 127–29.
3. "Top Job Boards," *OfficePRO* 66 (November–December 2006): 5; Clifford W. Eischen and Lynn A. Eischen, *Résumés, Cover Letters, Networking, and Interviewing,* 2nd ed. (Mason, OH: Thomson, 2007), 74–79.

4. Caryl Krannich and Ron Krannich, *Interview for Success,* 8th ed. (Manassas Park, VA: Impact Publications, 2003), 112.

5. Moren, *How to Gain the Professional Edge,* 36.

6. Ibid., 12.

7. William H. Bonner and Lillian H. Chaney, *Communicating Effectively in an Information Age,* 2nd ed. (Mason, OH: Thomson, 2004), 286–90.

8. Ibid., 290–91; Eischen and Eischen, *Résumés, Cover Letters, Networking, and Interviewing,* 44–45.

9. Eischen and Eischen, *Résumés, Cover Letters, Networking, and Interviewing,* 62.

10. Roger E. Axtell, *Do's and Taboos of Humor Around the World* (New York: John Wiley & Sons Inc., 1999), 186.

11. Susan Bixler and Nancy Nix-Rice, *The New Professional Image,* 2nd ed. (Avon, MA: Adams Media, 2005), 5.

12. Teri Agins and Laurie Vickery, "Heads Up—The Suits Are Coming," *Wall Street Journal* (April 6, 2001): B1.

13. Eischen and Eischen, *Résumés, Cover Letters, Networking, and Interviewing,* 83.

14. Bonner and Chaney, *Communicating Effectively in an Information Age,* 324–25; Lillian H. Chaney and Catherine G. Green, "Business Students' Perceptions of Job Interview Etiquette," *NABTE Review* 58 (April 2004): 18.

15. Bonner and Chaney, *Communicating Effectively in an Information Age,* 322–24.

16. Chaney and Green, "Business Students' Perceptions of Job Interview Etiquette," 18; Mary Mitchell, *The Complete Idiot's Guide to Business Etiquette,* 3rd ed. (Indianapolis, IN: Alpha Books, 2000), 41.

17. Chaney and Green, "Business Students' Perceptions of Job Interview Etiquette," 19–20.

18. Ibid., 20.

19. Barbara Pachter and Marjorie Brody, *Complete Business Etiquette Handbook* (Paramus, NJ: Prentice Hall, 1995), 191.

20. Chaney and Green, "Business Students' Perceptions of Job Interview Etiquette," 19.

21. Krannich and Krannich, *Interview for Success,* 59–60.

22. Ibid., 60.

23. Bonner and Chaney, *Communicating Effectively in an Information Age,* 343.

24. Pachter and Brody, *Complete Business Etiquette Handbook,* 191; Beverly Langford, *The Etiquette Edge: The Unspoken Rules for Business Success* (New York: AMACOM, 2005), 67; "The Art of Following Up After an Interview," *OfficePRO* 66 (November–December 2006): 5.

25. Langford, *The Etiquette Edge,* 66–67.

26. William W. Larson, *Conducting a Job Interview* (Indianapolis, IN: Macmillan USA, 2001), 85–86.

27. Larson, *Conducting a Job Interview,* 90.

28. Langford, *The Etiquette Edge,* 68.

29. Ibid.

30. Ibid., 68; Larson, *Conducting a Job Interview,* 80.

31. Langford, *The Etiquette Edge,* 69.

32. Ibid.

CHAPTER 2

1. Victoria A. Seitz, *Your Executive Image,* 2nd ed. (Holbrook, MA: Adams Media, 2000), 36.

2. Ibid.

3. Bixler and Nix-Rice, *The New Professional Image,* 7.

4. Ibid., 6–7.

5. John T. Molloy, *New Women's Dress for Success* (New York: Warner Books, 1996), xii, xiii.

6. Morem, *How to Gain the Professional Edge,* 98.

7. Jeanette S. Martin and Lillian H. Chaney, *Global Business Etiquette: A Guide to International Communication and Customs* (Westport, CT: Praeger, 2006), 74.

8. Karyn Repinski, *The Complete Idiot's Guide to Successful Dressing* (New York: Alpha Books, 1999), 263.

9. Martin and Chaney, *Global Business Etiquette,* 77; Repinski, *The Complete Idiot's Guide to Successful Dressing,* 28–29.

10. Peggy Post and Peter Post, *Emily Post's the Etiquette Advantage in Business,* 2nd ed. (New York: HarperResource, 2005), 28.

11. Joe Sharkey, "Avoiding Tan Suits and Other Travel Gaffes," *The New York Times* (May 2, 2006): C8.

12. Pachter and Brody, *Complete Business Etiquette Handbook,* 316.

13. Fred E. Jandt, *An Introduction to Intercultural Communication,* 4th ed. (Thousand Oaks, CA: Sage, 2004), 140.

14. Molloy, *New Women's Dress for Success,* 129.

15. Martin and Chaney, *Global Business Etiquette,* 79.

16. Molloy, *New Women's Dress for Success,* 139–42.

17. Bixler and Nix-Rice, *The New Professional Image,* 14.

18. Morem, *How to Gain the Professional Edge,* 61–64.

19. Bixler and Nix-Rice, *The New Professional Image,* 55; Martin and Chaney, *Global Business Etiquette,* 76.

20. Bixler and Nix-Rice, *The New Professional Image,* 58; Martin and Chaney, *Global Business Etiquette,* 76–77; Molloy, *New Women's Dress for Success,* 61–61; Seitz, *Your Executive Image,* 55.

21. Repinski, *The Complete Idiot's Guide to Successful Dressing,* 67–69; Seitz, *Your Executive Image,* 49–50.

22. Bonner and Chaney, *Communicating Effectively in an Information Age,* 337.

23. Caryl Rae Krannich, *101 Secrets of Highly Effective Speakers,* 3rd ed. (Manassas Park, VA: Impact Publications, 1998), 114.

24. Bonner and Chaney, *Communicating Effectively in an Information Age,* 338.

25. Ibid.

26. Letitia Baldrige, *Letitia Baldrige's New Manners for New Times: A Complete Guide to Etiquette* (New York: Scribner, 2003), 165–68.

27. Repinski, *The Complete Idiot's Guide to Successful Dressing,* 114–18.

28. Molloy, *New Women's Dress for Success,* 99.

29. Bixler and Nix-Rice, *The New Professional Image,* 81.

30. Repinski, *The Complete Idiot's Guide to Successful Dressing,* 118–19.

31. Molloy, *New Women's Dress for Success,* 109.

32. Seitz, *Your Executive Image,* 45.

33. Molloy, *New Women's Dress for Success,* 193–203.

34. Bixler and Nix-Rice, *The New Professional Image,* 120.

35. Wati Alvarez-Correa, "Relax, It's Friday," *The Washingtonian* (October 1996): 134–37.

36. Lillian H. Chaney and Julie R. Lyden, "Putting the 'Business' in Business Casual," *OfficePRO* (April 1999): 17–18.

37. Sherry Maysonave, *Casual Power* (Austin, TX: Bright Books, 1999), 4–5.

38. Ibid., 16–17.

39. Molloy, *New Women's Dress for Success,* 213, 249.

40. Baldrige, *Letitia Baldrige's New Manners for New Times,* 166; Martin and Chaney, *Global Business Etiquette,* 81–82.

41. Ibid., 166.

42. Martin and Chaney, *Global Business Etiquette,* 81–82; Repinski, *The Complete Idiot's Guide to Successful Dressing,* 167.

43. Repinski, *The Complete Idiot's Guide to Successful Dressing,* 166.

44. Casperson, *Power Etiquette,* 35–36.

45. Ibid., 37–38.

46. Patricia A. Thompson and Brian H. Kleiner, "How to Read Nonverbal Communication," *The Bulletin* (September 1992): 82.

CHAPTER 3

1. Mark Holden, *Positive Politics: Overcome Office Politics and Fast-Track Your Career* (Warriewood, NSW, Australia: Business & Professional Publishing, 1998), 3.

2. Casey Hawley, *100+ Tactics for Office Politics* (Hauppauge, NY: Barron's, 2001), vi.

3. Andrew DuBrin, *Winning Office Politics* (Paramus, N J: 1990), 1.

4. Mark Holden, *The Use and Abuse of Office Politics* (Crows Nest, NSW, Australia: Allen & Unwin, 2003), 1.

5. Michael S. Dobson and Deborah S. Dobson, *Enlightened Office Politics* (New York: AMACOM, 2001), xii; Catherine G. Green and Lillian H. Chaney, "The Game of Office Politics," *Supervision* 67 (August 2006): 3.

6. Terry Bragg, "Nine Strategies for Successfully Playing Office Politics," *Occupational Hazards* 66 (2004 February): 49; Green and Chaney, "The Game of Office Politics," 3; Laurie Rozakis and Bob Rozakis, *The Complete Idiot's Guide to Office Politics* (Indianapolis, IN: Alpha Books, 1998), 172.

7. "FastCompany's Five Rules of Office Politics," *Administrator* 22 (January 2003): 5.

8. Green and Chaney, "The Game of Office Politics," 3.

9. DuBrin, *Winning Office Politics,* 168.

10. Hawley, *100+ Tactics for Office Politics,* 126.

11. Susan Bixler and Lisa Scherrer Dugan, *5 Steps to Professional Presence* (Avon, MA: Adams Media, 2001), 22–23.

12. Bixler and Dugan, *5 Steps to Professional Presence,* 25.

13. Lillian H. Chaney, "Curb Appeal," *OfficePRO* 65 (August–September 2004), 28–29.

14. Bixler and Dugan , *5 Steps to Professional Presence,* 26.

15. Chaney, "Curb Appeal," 29.

16. Post and Post, *Emily Post's the Etiquette Advantage in Business,* 202–3.

17. Jan Yager, *Business Protocol: How to Survive and Succeed in Business,* 2nd ed. (Stamford, CT.: Hannacroix Creek Books, 2001), 201.

18. Harriette Cole, *How to be* (New York: Simon & Schuster, 1999), 28; Green and Chaney, "The Game of Office Politics," 4.

19. Sue Fox and Perrin Cunningham, *Business Etiquette for Dummies* (Foster City, CA: IDG Books Worldwide, 2001), 168.

20. Ibid., 169.

21. Marjabelle Young Stewart, *The New Etiquette* (New York: St. Martin's Griffin, 1997), 278.

22. Hawley, *100+ Tactics for Office Politics,* 57.

23. Baldrige, *Letitia Baldrige's New Manners for New Times,* 606.

24. Ibid., 606–7.

25. Ibid., 607–8.

26. Judith Martin, *Miss Manners' Basic Training: The Right Thing to Say* (New York: Crown Publishers, 1998), 50.

27. Rozakis and Rozakis, *The Complete Idiot's Guide to Office Politics,* 171.

28. Green and Chaney, "The Game of Office Politics," 4; Rozakis and Rozakis, *The Complete Idiot's Guide to Office Politics,* 172.

29. Green and Chaney, "The Game of Office Politics," 4.

30. DuBrin, *Winning Office Politics,* 96.

31. Ibid., 97.

32. Langford, *The Etiquette Edge,* 39; Rozakis and Rozakis, *The Complete Idiot's Guide to Office Politics ,* 98.

33. Rozakis and Rozakis, *The Complete Idiot's Guide to Office Politics ,* 98–99.

34. Green and Chaney, "The Game of Office Politics," 5.

35. Cole, *How To Be,* 484–85.

36. Ibid., 485; Mitchell, *The Complete Idiot's Guide to Etiquette,* 209.

37. Rozakis and Rozakis, *The Complete Idiot's Guide to Office Politics,* 173; Cole, *How To Be,* 485–86.

38. Holden, *Positive Politics,* 70.

39. DuBrin, *Winning Office Politics,* 161–62.

40. Rozakis and Rozakis, *The Complete Idiot's Guide to Office Politics,* 209–10.

41. Holden, *Positive Politics,* 71.

42. DuBrin, *Winning Office Politics,* 23.

43. Hawley, *100+ Tactics for Office Politics,* 6.

44. DuBrin, *Winning Office Politics,* 79.

45. Ibid., 81; Rozakis and Rozakis, *The Complete Idiot's Guide to Office Politics,* 213.

46. Rozakis and Rozakis, *The Complete Idiot's Guide to Office Politics,* 211.

47. DuBrin, *Winning Office Politics,* 163.

48. Ibid., 162–63.

CHAPTER 4

1. Linda Kaplan Thaler and Robin Koval, *The Power of Nice* (New York: Doubleday, 2006), 3.

2. Ibid., 10.

3. Sue Fox, *Etiquette for Dummies* (Foster City, CA: IDG Books Worldwide, 1999), 100.

4. Bonner and Chaney, *Communicating Effectively in an Information Age,* 334.

5. Ibid., 335.

6. Post and Post, *Emily Post's the Etiquette Advantage in Business,* 221.

7. Ibid., 222.

8. Bonner and Chaney, *Communicating Effectively in an Information Age,* 346–47.

9. Stewart, *The New Etiquette,* 73.

10. Bonner and Chaney, *Communicating Effectively in an Information Age,* 347.

11. Ibid.

12. Post and Post, *Emily Post's the Etiquette Advantage in Business,* 79.

13. Bonner and Chaney, *Communicating Effectively in an Information Age,* 348.

14. Post and Post, *Emily Post's the Etiquette Advantage in Business,* 74–76.

15. Elizabeth Craig, *Don't Slurp Your Soup* (St. Paul, MN: Brighton Publications, Inc., 1996), 152–53; Fox, *Etiquette for Dummies,* 311–13;Mitchell, *The Complete Idiot's Guide to Etiquette,* 235–39.

16. Fox, *Etiquette for Dummies,* 319.

17. Jacqueline Whitmore, *Business Class: Etiquette Essentials for Success at Work* (New York: St. Martin's Press, 2005), 26–27; Bonner and Chaney, *Communicating Effectively in an Information Age,* 37.

18. Bonner and Chaney, *Communicating Effectively in an Information Age,* 353.

19. Fox and Cunningham, *Business Etiquette for Dummies,* 149–51.

20. Mitchell, *The Complete Idiot's Guide to Etiquette,* 199–200; Pachter and Brody, *Complete Business Etiquette Handbook,* 88–89.

21. Ibid., 204.

22. The U.S. Equal Employment Opportunity Commission, *Title VII of the Civil Rights Act of 1964,* Retrieved February 12, 2007, http://www.eeoc.gov/policy/vii.html.

23. Ibid.

24. Nancy Tuckerman and Nancy Dunnan, *The Amy Vanderbilt Complete Book of Etiquette* (New York: Doubleday, 1995), 485.

25. Letitia Baldrige, *Letitia Baldrige's New Complete Guide to Executive Manners,* 2nd ed. (New York: Rawson Associates, 1993), 72.

26. Rozakis and Rozakis, *The Complete Idiot's Guide to Office Politics,* 224.

27. Ibid., 230.

28. Tuckerman and Dunnan, *The Amy Vanderbilt Complete Book of Etiquette,* 485–86.

29. Fox, *Etiquette for Dummies,* 45.

30. Grace Fox, *Office Etiquette and Protocol* (New York: Learning Express, 1998), 96.

31. Ibid., 95.

32. Ibid., 228.

33. Hal Urban, *Life's Greatest Lessons: 20 Things That Matter,* 5th ed. (New York: Fireside, 2005), 65.

CHAPTER 5

1. Mary Mitchell, *The First Five Minutes* (New York: John Wiley & Sons Inc., 1998), 132.

2. Sonya Hamlin, *How to Talk So People Listen: Connecting in Today's Workplace* (New York: HarperCollins Publishers, 2006), 3.

3. Mitchell, *The Complete Idiot's Guide to Etiquette*, 165.

4. Mitchell, *The First Five Minutes*, 133.

5. Bonner and Chaney, *Communicating Effectively in an Information Age*, 350–51.

6. Ibid.

7. Nancy J. Friedman, *Telephone Skills from A to Z* (Menlo Park, CA: Crisp Publications, 1995), 33.

8. Ibid., 18.

9. Bonner and Chaney, *Communicating Effectively in an Information Age*, 351.

10. Friedman, *Telephone Skills from A to Z*, 44.

11. Ibid., 17.

12. Craig, *Don't Slurp Your Soup*, 47; Judith Martin, *Miss Manners' Basic Training: Communication* (New York: Crown Publishers, 1997), 15; Whitmore, *Business Class*, 108–9.

13. Audrey Glassman, *Can I FAX a Thank-You Note?* (New York: Berkley Books, 1998), 52–54; Post and Post, *Emily Post's the Etiquette Advantage in Business*, 297.

14. Mitchell, *The Complete Idiot's Guide to Etiquette*, 167.

15. Lillian H. Chaney, Catherine G. Green, and Barbara D. Davis, "Netwits and Cell Fools," *OfficePRO* (August–September 2000): 14; Glassman, *Can I FAX a Thank-You Note?* 54.

16. Post and Post, *Emily Post's the Etiquette Advantage in Business*, 300.

17. Glassman, *Can I FAX a Thank-You Note?* 54.

18. Mitchell, *The Complete Idiot's Guide to Etiquette*, 167.

19. Whitmore, *Business Class*, 119.

20. Ibid., 121–22.

21. Craig, *Don't Slurp Your Soup*, 56.

22. Chaney, Green, and Davis, "Netwits and Cell Fools," 14.

23. Post and Post, *Emily Post's the Etiquette Advantage in Business*, 301.

24. Mitchell, *The First Five Minutes*, 131.

25. Ibid.

26. Chaney, Green, and Davis, "Netwits and Cell Fools," 14.

27. Diane Brady, "*!#?@the E-mail. Can We Talk?" *BusinessWeek* (December 4, 2006): 109.

28. Chaney, Green, and Davis, "Netwits and Cell Fools," 15.

29. Samantha Miller, *E-Mail Etiquette* (New York: Warner Books, 2001), 3.

30. Ibid., 88.

31. Ibid., 18.

32. Ibid., 20.

33. Bonner and Chaney, *Communicating Effectively in an Information Age*, 352; Chaney, Green, and Davis, "Netwits and Cell Fools," 15; Moore, *The Etiquette Advantage*, 200–202.

34. Leah Ingram, *The Everything Etiquette Book*, 2nd ed. (Avon, MA: Adams Media, 2005), 116.

35. Whitmore, *Business Class*, 114–16.

36. Miller, *E-Mail Etiquette*, 105, 19, 16, 13, 4.

37. Whitmore, *Business Class*, 117–18.

38. Craig, *Don't Slurp Your Soup*, 48–50.

39. Chaney, Green, and Davis, "Netwits and Cell Fools," 15.

40. Glassman, *Can I FAX a Thank-You Note?* 71.

41. Chaney, Green, and Davis, "Netwits and Cell Fools," 14.

CHAPTER 6

1. Martha McCarty, "Office Parties: 'Tis the Season To Be Savvy," *Office PRO* 66, 8 (2006): 12.

2. Ibid.

3. Ibid., 11.

4. Ann Marie Sabath, *Business Etiquette: 101 Ways to Conduct Business with Charm and Savvy*, 2nd ed. (Franklin Lakes, NJ: Career Press, 2002), 125.

5. Mitchell, *The Complete Idiot's Guide to Etiquette*, 230.

6. Post and Post, *Emily Post's the Etiquette Advantage in Business*, 148.

7. Karen Grigsby Bates and Karen Elyse Hudson, *Basic Black: Home Training for Modern Times* (New York: Doubleday, 1996), 415.

8. Post and Post, *Emily Post's the Etiquette Advantage in Business*, 50.

9. Charlotte Ford, *21st-Century Etiquette* (New York: Penguin Books, 2001), 194.

10. Baldrige, *Letitia Baldrige's New Complete Guide to Executive Manners*, 185.

11. Tuckerman and Dunnan, *The Amy Vanderbilt Complete Book of Etiquette*, 118.

12. Ibid.

13. Baldrige, *Letitia Baldrige's New Complete Guide to Executive Manners*, 194–95.

14. McCarty, "Office Parties," 12; James E. Challenger, "Office Parties: Benefit from Celebrations Without Going Overboard," *The Commercial Appeal*, December 17, 2006: F1.

15. Fox and Cunningham, *Business Etiquette for Dummies*, 245.

16. Ibid., 12.

17. Baldrige, *Letitia Baldrige's New Complete Guide to Executive Manners*, 440–41.

18. Post and Post, *Emily Post's the Etiquette Advantage in Business*, 149.

19. Fox, *Business Etiquette for Dummies*, 246.

20. Mitchell, *The Complete Idiot's Guide to Etiquette*, 232–33.

21. Fox and Cunningham, *Business Etiquette for Dummies*, 273–74.

22. Ibid., 126–28.

23. Post and Post, *Emily Post's the Etiquette Advantage in Business*, 280–81.

24. Fox, *Business Etiquette for Dummies*, 270–71.

25. Ibid., 148.

26. Post and Post, *Emily Post's the Etiquette Advantage in Business*, 280–81.

27. Sabath, *Business Etiquette*, 129–30.

28. Post and Post, *Emily Post's the Etiquette Advantage in Business*, 280.

29. Ibid., 247.

30. Ibid., 247–48; Mitchell, *The Complete Idiot's Guide to Etiquette*, 233–34.

31. Baldrige, *Letitia Baldrige's New Complete Guide to Executive Manners*, 199, 208.

32. Ibid., 548.

33. Fox, *Business Etiquette for Dummies*, 247–48.

34. Post and Post, *Emily Post's the Etiquette Advantage in Business*, 148–49; Fox, *Business Etiquette for Dummies*, 248.

35. Ford, *21st-Century Etiquette*, 197–98.

36. Ibid., 149.

37. Fox, *Business Etiquette for Dummies*, 248.

38. Baldrige, *Letitia Baldrige's New Complete Guide to Executive Manners*, 551.

39. Ibid., 559.

CHAPTER 7

1. Post and Post, *Emily Post's the Etiquette Advantage in Business*, 304.

2. David Peers, "Writing Wrongs," *Director* 60, 2 (2006): 39.

3. Bonner and Chaney, *Communicating Effectively in an Information Age*, 237, 307.

4. James L. Clark and Lyn R. Clark, *How 10: A Handbook for Office Professionals*, 10th ed. (Mason, OH: Thomson, 2004), 88–89.

5. Bonner and Chaney, *Communicating Effectively in an Information Age*, 236.

6. Baldrige, *Letitia Baldrige's New Complete Guide to Executive Manners*, 189–94.

7. Ibid., 187; Bonner and Chaney, *Communicating Effectively in an Information Age*, 422–23.

8. Steven L. Feinberg, ed., *Crane's Blue Book of Stationery* (New York: Doubleday, 1994), 179–81.

9. Post and Post, *Emily Post's the Etiquette Advantage in Business*, 251.

10. Baldrige, *Letitia Baldrige's New Complete Guide to Executive Manners*, 189.

11. Bonner and Chaney, *Communicating Effectively in an Information Age*, 58–75, 230–34; Pachter and Brody, *Complete Business Etiquette Handbook*, 143–49; Post and Post, *Emily Post's the Etiquette Advantage in Business*, 321–23.

12. Whitmore, *Business Class*, 142.

13. Baldrige, *Letitia Baldrige's New Complete Guide to Executive Manners*, 177–79; Mitchell, *The Complete Idiot's Guide to Etiquette*, 261.

14. Whitmore, *Business Class*, 141.

15. Ford, *21st-Century Etiquette*, 110–11.

16. Post and Post, *Emily Post's the Etiquette Advantage in Business*, 120.

17. Sabath, *Business Etiquette*, 59.

18. Mitchell, *The Complete Idiot's Guide to Etiquette*, 261.

19. Ibid., 262; Bonner and Chaney, *Communicating Effectively in an Information Age*, 254; Moore, *The Etiquette Advantage*, 210.

20. Mitchell, *The Complete Idiot's Guide to Etiquette*, 262.

21. Moore, *The Etiquette Advantage*, 211.

22. Ibid., 212.

23. Bonner and Chaney, *Communicating Effectively in an Information Age*, 253.

24. Baldrige, *Letitia Baldrige's New Complete Guide to Executive Manners*, 505–511.

25. Post and Post, *Emily Post's the Etiquette Advantage in Business*, 110–11.

26. Baldrige, *Letitia Baldrige's New Complete Guide to Executive Manners*, 512–13; Ford, *21st-Century Etiquette*, 113.

27. Baldrige, *Letitia Baldrige's New Complete Guide to Executive Manners*, 174–75; Bonner and Chaney, *Communicating Effectively in an Information Age*, 273–76.

28. Mitchell, *The Complete Idiot's Guide to Etiquette*, 314.

29. Ibid., 281.

30. Post and Post, *Emily Post's the Etiquette Advantage in Business*, 249.

31. Sue Fox, *Business Etiquette for Dummies* (New York: Wiley Publishing, 2001), 119.

32. Ibid., 119.

33. Mitchell, *The Complete Idiot's Guide to Etiquette*, 266.

34. Baldrige, *Letitia Baldrige's New Complete Guide to Executive Manners*, 175–77.

35. Ford, *21st-Century Etiquette*, 114.

36. Lesley Mitchell, "Complaints: Give Them Your Very Best Shot," *Knight Ridder Tribune Business News* (Washington, DC: 2005): 1.

37. Ibid., 1.

38. Post and Post, *Emily Post's the Etiquette Advantage in Business*, 83–84.

39. Ibid., 85–86.

40. Baldrige, *Letitia Baldrige's New Complete Guide to Executive Manners*, 183–85; Bonner and Chaney, *Communicating Effectively in an Information Age*, 247.

41. Ford, *21st-Century Etiquette*, 116.

CHAPTER 8

1. Lillian H. Chaney and Catherine G. Green, "Working Like a Dog Will Get You Promoted; Eating Like a Pig Will Not," *OfficePRO 62* (June–July 2002): 16.

2. Ibid., 17.

3. John T. Molloy, *Molloy's Live for Success* (New York: William Morrow & Company, 1981), 201.

4. Bixler and Nix-Rice, *The New Professional Image*, 208–9; Bonner and Chaney, *Communicating Effectively in an Information Age*, 341–42; Pachter and Brody, *Complete Business Etiquette Handbook*, 203.

5. Ibid.

6. Molloy, *Molloy's Live for Success*, 198.

7. Marjabelle Young Stewart, *Commonsense Etiquette* (New York: St. Martin's Griffin, 1999), 56–57.

8. Bixler and Dugan, *5 Steps to Professional Presence*, 215.

9. Ibid.

10. Bixler and Nix-Rice, *The New Professional Image*, 208–9; Bonner and Chaney, *Communicating Effectively in an Information Age*, 339–44; Chaney and Green, "Working Like a Dog will Get You Promoted," 18–19; Fox, *Etiquette for Dummies*, 223–24.

11. Ingram, *The Everything Etiquette Book*, 83.

12. Stewart, *The New Etiquette*, 352–53.

13. Bonner and Chaney, *Communicating Effectively in an Information Age*, 343; Craig, *Don't Slurp Your Soup*, 93–95.

14. Stewart, *The New Etiquette*, 202–3.

15. Fox, *Etiquette for Dummies*, 219–21.

16. Ibid., 222.

17. Ibid., 222–23.

18. Norine Dresser, *Multicultural Manners* (New York: John Wiley & Sons Inc., 1996), 70.

19. Jandt, *An Introduction to Intercultural Communication*, 59.

20. P. Christopher Earley and Elaine Mosakowski, "Cultural Intelligence," *Harvard Business Review* 82, 10 (2004): 139.

21. Jandt, *An Introduction to Intercultural Communication*, 58.

22. Bonner and Chaney, *Communicating Effectively in an Information Age*, 340; Chaney and Green, "Working Like a Dog Will Get You Promoted," 18; Judith Martin, *Miss Manners' Guide to Excruciatingly Correct Behavior* (New York: W.W. Norton & Company, 2005), 163.

23. Martin and Chaney, *Global Business Etiquette*, 107–8.

24. Ibid., 108–9.

25. Ibid., 112.

26. Roger E. Axtell, *Do's and Taboos of Hosting International Visitors* (New York: John Wiley & Sons Inc., 1990), 58.

27. Dresser, *Multicultural Manners*, 70.

28. Axtell, *Do's and Taboos of Hosting International Visitors*, 60.

29. Dresser, *Multicultural Manners*, 70–71, 112–14.

30. Ibid., 68.

31. Chaney and Green, "Working Like a Dog Will Get You Promoted," 19.

CHAPTER 9

1. Post and Post, *Emily Post's the Etiquette Advantage in Business*, 390.

2. Fox and Cunningham, *Business Etiquette for Dummies*, 191–92.

3. Ford, *21st-Century Etiquette*, 71.

4. Craig, *Don't Slurp Your Soup*, 109.

5. Fox, *Etiquette for Dummies*, 228–31; Pachter and Brody, *Complete Business Etiquette Handbook*, 200.

6. Morem, *How to Gain the Professional Edge*, 173.

7. Martin and Chaney, *Global Business Etiquette*, 114–15.

8. Mitchell, *The Complete Idiot's Guide to Business Etiquette*, 199.

9. Fox, *Etiquette for Dummies*, 233; Martin and Chaney, *Global Business Etiquette*, 115.

10. Mitchell, *The Complete Idiot's Guide to Business Etiquette*, 215–16; Post and Post, *Emily Post's the Etiquette Advantage in Business*, 419–20.

11. Post and Post, *Emily Post's the Etiquette Advantage in Business*, 420.

12. Ibid., 424.

13. Ibid., 424–25.

14. Ibid., 438–39.

15. Bixler and Dugan, *5 Steps to Professional Presence*, 208.

16. Ibid., 220.

17. Fox and Cunningham, *Business Etiquette for Dummies*, 194–95.

18. Ibid., 196.

19. Bixler and Dugan, *5 Steps to Professional Presence*, 224.

20. Mitchell, *The Complete Idiot's Guide to Business Etiquette*, 214.

21. Ibid., 195–96, 202–3.

22. Ibid., 218.

23. Ingram, *The Everything Etiquette Book*, 183–85.

24. Martin and Chaney, *Global Business Etiquette*, 116.

25. Axtell, *Do's and Taboos of Hosting International Visitors*, 56–57.

26. Ibid., 56.

27. Ibid., 57.

28. Ibid., 66–67.

29. Ibid., 68.

30. Dresser, *Multicultural Manners*, 73.

31. Moore, *The Etiquette Advantage*, 229.

CHAPTER 10

1. Pachter and Brody, *Complete Business Etiquette Handbook*, 158.

2. Mitchell, *The First Five Minutes*, 79.

3. Lillian H. Chaney and Catherine G. Green, "Meeting Manners," *OfficePRO*, November–December, 2003, 19.

4. Bixler and Dugan, *5 Steps to Professional Presence*, 129.

5. Post and Post, *Emily Post's the Etiquette Advantage in Business*, 366.

6. Chaney and Green, "Meeting Manners," 19.

7. Bonner and Chaney, *Communicating Effectively in an Information Age*, 99, 354–55.

8. Pachter and Brody, *Complete Business Etiquette Handbook*, 159.

9. Bonner and Chaney, *Communicating Effectively in an Information Age*, 354.

10. Tuckerman and Dunnan, *The Amy Vanderbilt Complete Book of Etiquette*, 522–23.

11. Pachter and Brody, *Complete Business Etiquette Handbook*, 152–63; Post and Post, *Emily Post's the Etiquette Advantage in Business*, 371.

12. Post and Post, *Emily Post's the Etiquette Advantage in Business*, 373.

13. Craig, *Don't Slurp Your Soup*, 18.

14. Bixler and Nix-Rice, *The New Professional Image*, 197; M. Kay duPont, *Business Etiquette and Professionalism* (Menlo Park, CA: Crisp Publications Inc., 1998), 63.

15. Craig, *Don't Slurp your Soup*, 18.

16. Chaney and Green, "Meeting Manners," 20; Fox, *Business Etiquette for Dummies*, 261.

17. Eli Mina, *The Complete Handbook of Business Meetings* (New York: AMACOM, 2000), 80.

18. Bixler and Dugan, *5 Steps to Professional Presence*, 127.

19. Taggart E. Smith, *Meeting Management* (Upper Saddle River, NJ: Prentice Hall, 2001), 25.

20. Pachter and Brody, *Complete Business Etiquette Handbook*, 174.

21. Chaney and Green, "Meeting Manners," 20.

22. Hamlin, *How to Talk So People Listen*, 268–69.

23. Post and Post, *Emily Post's the Etiquette Advantage in Business*, 370.

24. David Robinson, *Business Protocol: Contemporary American Practice* (Cincinnati, OH: Atomic Dog Publishing, 2003), 86–87.

25. Fox and Cunningham, *Business Etiquette for Dummies*, 262–63.

26. Post and Post, *Emily Post's the Etiquette Advantage in Business*, 373–74.

27. Mitchell, *The Complete Idiot's Guide to Etiquette*, 176.

28. Sabath, *Business Etiquette*, 108.

29. Morem, *How to Gain the Professional Edge*, 157–58.

30. Mitchell, *The Complete Idiot's Guide to Etiquette*, 176–77.

31. Pachter and Brody, *Complete Business Etiquette Handbook*, 166–67; Tuckerman and Dunnan, *The Amy Vanderbilt Complete Book of Etiquette*, 524.

32. Pachter and Brody, *Complete Business Etiquette Handbook*, 167.

33. Ibid.; Post and Post, *Emily Post's the Etiquette Advantage in Business*, 379.

34. Chaney and Green, "Meeting Manners," 21; Fox, *Etiquette for Dummies*, 103.

35. Post and Post, *Emily Post's the Etiquette Advantage in Business*, 378–79.

36. Pachter and Brody, *Complete Business Etiquette Handbook*, 184–85.

37. Post and Post, *Emily Post's the Etiquette Advantage in Business*, 379.

38. Ibid., 391.

39. duPont, *Business Etiquette and Professionalism*, 76.

40. Ibid.

41. Post and Post, *Emily Post's the Etiquette Advantage in Business*, 391–93.

42. Tuckerman and Dunnan, *The Amy Vanderbilt Complete Book of Etiquette*, 525.

43. Post and Post, *Emily Post's the Etiquette Advantage in Business*, 257–58; Tuckerman and Dunnan, *The Amy Vanderbilt Complete Book of Etiquette*, 525–26.

44. Mina, *The Complete Handbook of Business Meetings*, 275.

45. Bonner and Chaney, *Communicating Effectively in an Information Age*, 99.

46. Mina, *The Complete Handbook of Business Meetings*, 275–76.

47. Ibid., 279.

48. Axtell, *Do's and Taboos of Humor Around the World*, 7–8.

49. Lillian H. Chaney and Jeanette S. Martin, *Intercultural Business Communication*, 4th ed. (Upper Saddle River, NJ: Prentice Hall, 2007), 208–9.

50. Farid Elashmawi and Philip R. Harris, *Multicultural Management 2000* (Houston, TX: Gulf Publishing Company, 1998), 127, 130–31.

51. Bixler and Dugan, *5 Steps to Professional Presence*, 128.

CHAPTER 11

1. Krannich, *101 Secrets of Highly Effective Speakers*, 23.

2. Lillian H. Chaney and Catherine G. Green, "Presenter Behaviors: Actions Often Speak Louder than Words," *Supervision* 63 (2002): 17.

3. Roger E. Axtell, *Do's and Taboos of Public Speaking* (New York: John Wiley & Sons Inc., 1992), 67.

4. Bixler and Nix-Rice, *The New Professional Image*, 222; Krannich, *101 Secrets of Highly Effective Speakers*, 132.

5. Seitz, *Your Executive Image*, 11.

6. Steve Mandel, *Effective Presentation Skills*, 3rd ed. (Menlo Park, CA: Crisp Learning, 2000), 79.

7. Malcom Kushner, *Public Speaking for Dummies* (Foster City, CA: IDG Books Worldwide, 1999), 247; Jackie Jankovich Hartman and Elaine A. Lemay, *Presentation Success* (Cincinnati, OH: South-Western, 2001), 95–97.

8. Krannich, *101 Secrets of Highly Effective Speakers*, 119.

9. Chaney and Green, "Presenter Behaviors," 17.

10. Pachter and Brody, *Complete Business Etiquette Handbook*, 188.

11. Hartman and Lemay, *Presentation Success*, 98.

12. Chaney and Green, "Presenter Behaviors," 18.

13. Tuckerman and Dunnan, *The Amy Vanderbilt Complete Book of Etiquette*, 709.

14. Mandel, *Effective Presentation Skills*, 15–16.

15. Kushner, *Public Speaking for Dummies*, 252.

16. Chaney and Green, "Presenter Behaviors," 18.

17. Ibid.

18. Krannich, *101 Secrets of Highly Effective Speakers*, 121.

19. Hartman and Lemay, *Presentation Success*, 90–92.

20. Kushner, *Public Speaking for Dummies*, 263; Robinson, *Business Protocol*, 99–100.

21. Chaney and Green, "Presenter Behaviors," 18.

22. Pachter and Brody, *Complete Business Etiquette Handbook*, 188.

23. Bonner and Chaney, *Communicating Effectively in an Information Age*, 95.

24. Ibid.; Hartman and Lemay, *Presentation Success*, 26–32.

25. Hartman and Lemay, *Presentation Success*, 28–31.

26. Ibid., 35–37.

27. Tuckerman and Dunnan, *The Amy Vanderbilt Complete Book of Etiquette*, 711.

28. Hartman and Lemay, *Presentation Success*, 43.

29. Axtell, *Do's and Taboos of Public Speaking,* 84.

30. Krannich, *101 Secrets of Highly Effective Speakers,* 63–64.

31. Hartman and Lemay, *Presentation Success,* 101–2.

32. Axtell, *Do's and Taboos of Public Speaking,* 106–7.

33. Kushner, *Public Speaking for Dummies,* 177.

34. Axtell, *Do's and Taboos of Public Speaking,* 113; Mandel, *Effective Presentation Skills,* 56–57.

35. Chaney and Green, "Presenter Behaviors," 19.

36. Axtell, *Do's and Taboos of Public Speaking,* 106.

37. Kushner, *Public Speaking for Dummies,* 208.

38. Ibid., 210–11.

39. Hartman and Lemay, *Presentation Success,* 103.

40. Tuckerman and Dunnan, *The Amy Vanderbilt Complete Book of Etiquette,* 710; Robinson, *Business Protocol,* 91.

41. Chaney and Green, "Presenter Behaviors," 19.

42. Ibid.

43. Lillian H. Chaney, Catherine G. Green, and Janet T. Cherry, "Trainees' Perceptions of Distracting or Annoying Behaviors of Corporate Trainers," *Association for Business Communication Southwestern United States Refereed Proceedings,* 2005, 38–39.

44. Ibid., 39.

45. Hartman and Lemay, *Presentation Success,* 59–75.

46. Ibid., 96–97.

47. Kushner, *Public Speaking for Dummies,* 248–49.

48. Mitchell, *The Complete Idiot's Guide to Business Etiquette,* 136.

49. Bonner and Chaney, *Communicating Effectively in an Information Age,* 92.

50. Bonner and Chaney, *Communicating Effectively in an Information Age,* 93.

51. Mitchell, *The Complete Idiot's Guide to Business Etiquette,* 136–37.

52. Kushner, *Public Speaking for Dummies,* 17–23.

53. Krannich, *101 Secrets of Highly Effective Speakers,* 147.

CHAPTER 12

1. Mitchell, *The Complete Idiot's Guide to Etiquette,* 11.

2. Baldrige, *Letitia Baldrige's New Manners for New Times,* 90.

3. June Hines Moore, *Social Skills Survival Guide* (Nashville, TN: Broadman & Holman Publishers, 2003), 84.

4. Mitchell, *The Complete Idiot's Guide to Etiquette,* 11.

5. Ibid., 84–85.

6. Ibid., 86–87.

7. Will Keim, *Fan Etiquette* (Mason, OH: Viaticum Press, 2003), xvii–xviii, xxi.

8. Ibid., 3.

9. Ibid., 6–7.

10. Ibid., 16.

11. Craig, *Don't Slurp Your Soup,* 162–64.

12. Ibid., 165.

13. Fox, *Business Etiquette for Dummies,* 238.

14. Ibid., 235.

15. Ibid., 236.

16. Moore, *Social Skills Survival Guide*, 88.

17. Daniel Henninger, "Wonder Land: Golf as Antidote to Bonds, Enron and Abramoff," *The Wall Street Journal*, June 23, 2006, A.10, (accessed from Proquest December 13, 2006).

18. Thomas Wailgum, "Mastering the Secret Etiquette of Golf; Tiger Woods May Have Nothing to Fear from You, but You Still Have to Know the (Unwritten) Rules of the Game," *CIO*, April 1, 2005, 1, (accessed from Proquest December 13, 2006).

19. Craig, *Don't Slurp Your Soup*, 162.

20. Ibid., 167.

21. Fox, *Business Etiquette for Dummies*, 237.

22. Mitchell, *The Complete Idiot's Guide to Etiquette*, 12.

23. Ford, *21st-Century Etiquette*, 271–72.

24. Craig, *Don't Slurp Your Soup*, 168.

25. Mitchell, *The Complete Idiot's Guide to Etiquette*, 13.

26. Ibid., 12.

27. Ford, *21st-Century Etiquette*, 272.

28. Mitchell, *The Complete Idiot's Guide to Etiquette*, 14.

29. Ibid., 19.

30. Craig, *Don't Slurp Your Soup*, 170.

31. Richard Carter, "Clueless Cell Phone Clods Annoy the Hell Out of Many People," *The New York Amsterdam News*, March 23–29, 2006, 10, 28.

32. Moore, *The Etiquette Advantage*, 252.

33. "Suspensions Without Pay, Won't be Staggered," November 22, 2006, http://sports.espn.go.com/espn/print?id=1928540&type=story (accessed December 13, 2006).

34. Erin Sullivan, "Bring the Noise: Athletes Realize Sound Plays Pivotal Part in the Games We Enjoy," *Knight Ridder Tribune Business News*, June 25, 2006, 1, (accessed from Proquest December 13, 2006).

35. Sasha Talcott, "A Sporting Chance," *Boston Globe*, February 13, 2005, 44, (accessed from Proquest December 13, 2006).

36. Steve Hummer, "Etiquette for the Unruly,"*The Atlanta Journal-Constitution*, February 21, 2004, C.2, (accessed from Proquest December 13, 2006).

37. Dick Heller, "Woody Hayes KO'd Himself in 1978 Gator Bowl," *The Washington Times*, December 27, 2004 (accessed December 16, 2006 http://www.washtimes.com/sports/20041227-124047-2522r.htm).

38. Wayne Drehs, On the Trail of the Most Reclusive Man in Sports, July 9–10, 2005, (accessed December 16, 2006, http://sports.espn.gocom/espn/eticket/story?page=bartman).

39. Jukka Suutari, "Al Secord-Points'n Punches," *After the Whistle*, 2003, (accessed December 16, 2006 www.afterthewhistle.com).

40. Keim, *Fan Etiquette*, 23–25.

CHAPTER 13

1. Welcome to the Quote Garden, "Quotations About Travel," (2006, December 11), http://www.quotegarden.com/travel.html

2. Fox, *Etiquette for Dummies*, 287.

3. Wayne Dosick, *The Business Bible* (Woodstock, UT: Jewish Lights Publishing, 2000), 50.

4. Casperson, *Power Etiquette*, 161.

5. Pachter and Brody, *Complete Business Etiquette Handbook*, 256.

6. Mitchell, *The Complete Idiot's Guide to Etiquette*, 313.

7. Baldrige, *Letitia Baldrige's New Complete Guide to Executive Manners*, 58–59.

8. Baldrige, *Letitia Baldrige's New Manners for New Times*, 133.

9. Stewart, *The New Etiquette*, 6.

10. Casperson, *Power Etiquette*, 163; Bonner and Chaney, *Communicating Effectively in an Information Age*, 357.

11. Repinski, *The Complete Idiot's Guide to Successful Dressing*, 194.

12. Casperson, *Power Etiquette*, 163; Baldrige, *Letitia Baldrige's New Complete Guide to Executive Manners*, 59.

13. Mitchell, *The Complete Idiot's Guide to Etiquette*, 145–47.

14. Tuckerman and Dunnan, *The Amy Vanderbilt Complete Book of Etiquette*, 577.

15. Ingram, *The Everything Etiquette Book*, 146.

16. Mitchell, *The Complete Idiot's Guide to Etiquette*, 322.

17. Ingram, *The Everything Etiquette Book*, 141–42.

18. Mitchell, *The Complete Idiot's Guide to Etiquette*, 319.

19. Baldrige, *Letitia Baldrige's New Complete Guide to Executive Manners*, 61.

20. Baldrige, *Letitia Baldrige's New Manners for New Times*, 133.

21. Casperson, *Power Etiquette*, 162; Ingram, *The Everything Etiquette Book*, 132.

22. Ingram, *The Everything Etiquette Book*, 148.

23. Pachter and Brody, *Complete Business Etiquette Handbook*, 258.

24. Tuckerman and Dunnan, *The Amy Vanderbilt Complete Book of Etiquette*, 562.

25. Ingram, *The Everything Etiquette Book*, 148.

26. Ibid., 127–28.

27. Mitchell, *The Complete Idiot's Guide to Etiquette*, 316.

28. Tuckerman and Dunnan, *The Amy Vanderbilt Complete Book of Etiquette*, 564–65.

29. Ingram, *The Everything Etiquette Book*, 132.

30. Tuckerman and Dunnan, *The Amy Vanderbilt Complete Book of Etiquette*, 577–78.

31. Ingram, *The Everything Etiquette Book*, 133.

32. Ibid., 133.

33. Casperson, *Power Etiquette*, 165.

34. Ingram, *The Everything Etiquette Book*, 134.

35. Baldrige, *Letitia Baldrige's New Complete Guide to Executive Manners*, 371.

CHAPTER 14

1. Jim Barksdale, cited in Martin and Chaney, *Global Business Etiquette: A Guide to International Communication and Customs*, back cover.

2. Roger E. Axtell and John P. Healy, *Do's and Taboos of Preparing for Your Trip Abroad* (New York: John Wiley& Sons Inc., 1994), 66.

3. Ibid., 70.

4. Bonner and Chaney, *Communicating Effectively in an Information Age,*, 367.

5. Ibid., 367–68.

6. Ibid., 367.

7. Ibid., 368.

8. Baldrige, *Letitia Baldrige's New Manners for New Times*, 143–44.

9. Martin and Chaney, *Global Business Etiquette*, 62.

10. Cynthia G. Emrich, Florence L. Denmark, and Deanne N. Den Hartog, "Cross-Cultural Differences in Gender Egalitarianism," in *Culture, Leadership, and Organizations: The GLOBE Study of 62 Societies,* ed. Robert J. House, Paul J. Hanages, Mansour Javidan, Peter W. Dorfman, and Vipin Gupta (Thousand Oaks, CA: Sage, 2004), 145–46.

11. Nancy K. Napier and Sully Taylor, "Experiences of Women Professionals Abroad: Comparisons Across Japan, China, and Turkey," *The International Journal of Human Resource Management* 13 (2002): 843.

12. Paula Caligiuri and Mila Lazarova, "A Model for the Influence of Social Interaction and Social Support on Female Expatriates' Cross-Cultural Adjustment," *The International Journal of Human Resource Management* 13 (2002): 764.

13. Roger E. Axtell, Tami Briggs, Margaret Corcoran, and Mary Beth Lamb, *Do's and Taboos Around the World for Women in Business* (New York: John Wiley & Sons Inc., 1997), 28.

14. Caligiuri and Lazarova, *A Model for the Influence of Social Interaction and Social Support on Female Expatriates' Cross-Cultural Adjustment,* 764.

15. Ibid., 765.

16. Rosalie L. Tung, "American Expatriates Abroad: From Neophytes to Cosmopolitans," *Journal of World Business* 33 (1998): 136.

17. Ann Marie Sabath, *International Business Etiquette: Asia and the Pacific Rim* (New York: ASJA Press, 2002), 34; Larry A. Samovar and Richard E. Porter, *Communication Between Cultures,* 5th ed. (Belmont, CA: Wadsworth/Thomson Learning, 2004), 295.

18. Dennis A. Pitta, Hung-Gay Fung, and Steven Isberg, "Ethical Issues Across Cultures: Managing the Differing Perspectives of China and the USA," *Journal of Consumer Marketing* 16 (1999): 248.

19. Elizabeth Devine and Nancy L. Braganti, *The Travelers' Guide to African Customs and Manners* (New York: St. Martin's Griffin, 1995), 1, 82, 165.

20. Ibid., 93.

21. Ibid., 166.

22. Ibid., 91.

23. Ibid., 84–85.

24. Ibid., 167–168.

Index

Africa, 16, 93, 162–63, 183
Announcements, 57, 82
Answering machines, 54
Applicant interview etiquette, 2–8; interview preparation, 2–5; interview termination, 7; follow-up activities, 7–8; participation, 5–6
Asia, 15, 93–94, 105, 117, 157–58, 160–61, 183
Automobile etiquette, 69, 79, 143, 148–49

Births and birthdays, 61–63, 71, 84
BlackBerry devices, 57–58, 68, 129
Bus travel, 147
Business dress and grooming, 1, 4–6, 13–24; age, 14; attributes of dress, 17–18; business casual attire, 21–22; business professional attire, 18–21; color, 17; culture, 15; dress for special events and occasions, 22–23; fabric and quality, 17–18; gender, 14; geography, 15; industry, 16; research, 18
Business cards, 1–2, 27, 34, 67, 158, 160, 165

Business entertaining, 97–106, 115
Business socializing, 33–35

CareerBuilder, 2
Cellular telephones, 49, 52–53
CollegeRecruiter, 2
Complaint letters, 83–84
Compliments, 26, 29–30, 44, 149, 153, 165
Condolences, 59, 69–70, 75, 79
Congratulatory letters, 80
Continental eating style, 92–93
Conventions, 67–68, 115–16
Correspondence cards, 75
Cruise ship etiquette, 143, 150–51

Dining etiquette, 34, 85–95; business dining, 86–89; cultural variations in dining, 86, 92–95; difficult-to-eat foods, 91–92; problem dining situations, 89–91
Disabled persons, 42–43

Eating styles, 86
Electronic communication etiquette, 49–58
Electronic mail (e-mail), 55–56

Enclosure cards, 66, 81
Entertaining, 26, 34, 37, 87, 97–106,
   115; cocktail parties, 23, 102–3;
   home entertaining, 103;
   international visitors, 104–6;
   private clubs, 32, 101; receptions,
   67, 102; restaurant entertaining, 7,
   16, 23, 34, 52–53, 62, 68, 86–90, 92,
   94, 97–98, 103–5, 146–47, 151–52,
   164; sporting events, 101–2; theater,
   97, 101–2; toasting, 99–101
Equal Employment Opportunity
   Commission (EEOC), 5, 45, 172
Europe, 15–16, 92–93, 105, 117, 158,
   161–62
Events, 1–2, 17, 22–24, 33–34, 37, 53,
   139, 141, 150, 159
Eye contact, 6, 39, 68, 110, 112, 119–20,
   157, 161–62, 165

Facsimiles (fax), 49, 58–59
Favors and hidden motives, 32
Flattery, 26, 29–30
Funerals, 16, 53, 69–71

Gasoline cards, 69
Gestures, 2, 45, 112, 118–20, 127,
   161–65
Global interactions, 157–58
Gossip, 26, 30–32, 47
Greeting cards, 63, 70, 84
Greetings, 38–39, 56, 84, 118, 157,
   161–64

Holiday and office parties, 23, 64–66,
   174
Honesty and truth-telling, 26, 28–29,
   32–33, 129
Hospital etiquette, 63–64, 77
Hotel etiquette, 137, 143, 151–53, 156,
   158–64
Humor, 45, 54, 56, 69, 76–77, 116–17,
   122–25, 128, 159, 168

Illnesses and injuries, 63
Interviewer etiquette, 8–11; behavior
   during the interview, 9–10;
   interview termination and follow-
   up activities, 10–11; preparation, 9
Introductions, 38–40

Invitations, 33, 66, 80–81, 103, 132;
   acceptance or regrets, 81–82

Job interview etiquette, 1–11
Jones' Parliamentary Procedure at a
   Glance, 111

Latin America, 92, 105, 117, 157,
   163–64
Letter and memorandum formats,
   73–75
Letters of appreciation, 8, 27, 59
Limousine etiquette, 149–50

Mass transit etiquette, 147–48
Meeting etiquette, 29, 41, 107–17, 117,
   152–53; chairing, 110–11, 118; face-
   to-face meetings, 84; follow-up
   activities, 78, 113–14; introductions,
   109–10; Jones' Parliamentary Procedure at a Glance, 111; meals, 97–98,
   105, 114–15; multicultural meetings, 105, 116–17, 156–57, 159–65;
   online meetings, 5; participant
   responsibilities, 112–13; planning
   and preparation, 108–9; refreshments, 113; Robert's Rules of Order,
   111; seating arrangements, 109–
   110; virtual meetings, 5, 116
Middle East, 93, 117, 157, 164–65
Monster, 2

Nonverbal courtesies, 40–41
Nonverbal impressions, 2
Note cards, 75, 125, 128

Office conflict, 43–44
Office courtesies, 38
Office politics, 25–35, 170
Office romance, 31, 38, 46–47

Pagers, 52–54
Place settings, 86, 93
Posture, 2, 88, 112, 119–20, 128–29
Presentations, 67, 108, 110–11, 14,
   119–28; attire, 120–21; audience
   etiquette, 128–29; distracting or
   annoying presenter behaviors,
   126–27; eye contact, posture, and
   gestures, 119–20; humor, 123–24;

etiquette, 125–26; presenter introductions, 127–28; visual aids, 124–25;vocal characteristics, 121–22
Promotions, 5, 14, 25–26, 31, 35, 68–69

Receptions, 67–68, 102–3
Reply cards, 82
Retirement announcement cards, 69
Retirements, 68–69
Robert's Rules of Order, 111

Salutations, 74
Self-promotion, 26–28
Sexual harassment, 38, 44–46, 83, 158–59
Socializing, 26, 33, 66, 150
Social sensitivity, 37–47, 66
Speakerphones, 52
Special occasions, 23, 61–71, 97
Sports etiquette, 131–41; golf, 134–36; gym or health club, 136–38; handball, 133–34; hunting and fishing, 138; racquet sports, 133–34; running, biking, and rollerblading, 138; spectator etiquette, 138–41;

sport rules, 131–33; water sports, 136
Stationery, 63, 75–76, 81

Taxicab etiquette, 149–50
Telephone etiquette, 49–51
Thank-you notes, 32, 77–79, 104, 115, 132
Trade shows, 67–68
Train etiquette, 53, 143, 147–48
Travel etiquette, 5–6, 16, 20, 29, 37, 81, 93, 115–16, 143–56, 158–59; air travel, 144–46; preparation, 143, 155

Voice mail, 54

Weddings and wedding anniversaries, 21, 66–67, 82, 100, 159
Wine and toasting etiquette, 99–101
Women business travelers, 158–60
Writing guidelines, 76–77

Zigzag eating style, 86

About the Authors

LILLIAN HUNT CHANEY is Professor of Management Emeritus at The University of Memphis. She is the author of over 100 articles and presentations, with a specialty in intercultural business communication, and has received many teaching and research awards in the field. She has conducted training programs on communication, international and U.S. corporate etiquette, and business ethics for international corporations, educational institutions, and government agencies. She is coauthor, with William H. Bonner, of *Communicating Effectively in an Information Age* (2004) and, with Jeanette St. Clair Martin, of the textbook *Intercultural Business Communication* (2007) and the best-selling *Global Business Etiquette* (Praeger, 2006).

JEANETTE ST. CLAIR MARTIN is Professor at The University of Mississippi, School of Business. She has served as associate editor of the *Journal of Business Communication* and is the recipient of several national awards and the author of dozens of articles, book chapters, and conference presentations on intercultural business communication, education, emotional and cultural intelligence, and management information systems. She is coauthor, with Lillian H. Chaney, of the textbook *Intercultural Business Communication* (2007) and the best-selling *Global Business Etiquette* (Praeger, 2006).